Technical Automation in
Classical Antiquity

Also available from Bloomsbury

Costume in Greek Tragedy, Rosie Wyles
The Materialities of Greek Tragedy: Objects and Affect in Aeschylus, Sophocles, and Euripides, edited by Mario Telò and Melissa Mueller
Theorising Performance: Greek Drama, Cultural History and Critical Practice, edited by Edith Hall and Stephe Harrop

Technical Automation in Classical Antiquity

Maria Gerolemou

BLOOMSBURY ACADEMIC
LONDON • NEW YORK • OXFORD • NEW DELHI • SYDNEY

BLOOMSBURY ACADEMIC
Bloomsbury Publishing Plc
50 Bedford Square, London, WC1B 3DP, UK
1385 Broadway, New York, NY 10018, USA
29 Earlsfort Terrace, Dublin 2, Ireland

BLOOMSBURY, BLOOMSBURY ACADEMIC and the Diana logo are trademarks
of Bloomsbury Publishing Plc

First published in Great Britain 2023
Paperback edition published 2024

Copyright © Maria Gerolemou, 2023

Maria Gerolemou has asserted her right under the Copyright, Designs and Patents Act,
1988, to be identified as Author of this work.

For legal purposes the Acknowledgements on p. vi constitute an
extension of this copyright page.

Cover design: Terry Woodley
Cover image: Ancient Greek steam engine as designed by Hero of Alexandria. Hand-
coloured woodcut. © North Wind Picture Archives/Alamy Stock Photo

All rights reserved. No part of this publication may be reproduced or transmitted
in any form or by any means, electronic or mechanical, including photocopying,
recording, or any information storage or retrieval system, without prior permission
in writing from the publishers.

Bloomsbury Publishing Plc does not have any control over, or responsibility for, any
third-party websites referred to or in this book. All internet addresses given
in this book were correct at the time of going to press. The author and publisher
regret any inconvenience caused if addresses have changed or sites have
ceased to exist, but can accept no responsibility for any such changes.

A catalogue record for this book is available from the British Library.

Library of Congress Cataloging-in-Publication Data
Names: Gerolemou, Maria, author.
Title: Technical automation in classical antiquity / Maria Gerolemou.
Description: London ; New York : Bloomsbury Academic, 2023. | Includes
bibliographical references and index.
Identifiers: LCCN 2022021810 | ISBN 9781350077591 (hardback) | ISBN 9781350303843
(paperback) | ISBN 9781350077607 (ebook) | ISBN 9781350077614
(epub) | ISBN 9781350077621
Subjects: LCSH: Greek literature–History and criticism. | Technology in
literature. | Machinery in literature. | Robots in literature. | Automatic machinery–Greece–
History–To 1500. | Technology–Greece–History–To 1500.
Classification: LCC PA3015.T4 G47 2023 | DDC 880.9/356–dc23/eng/20220809
LC record available at https://lccn.loc.gov/2022021810

ISBN: HB: 978-1-3500-7759-1
PB: 978-1-3503-0384-3
ePDF: 978-1-3500-7760-7
eBook: 978-1-3500-7761-4

Typeset by RefineCatch Limited, Bungay, Suffolk

To find out more about our authors and books visit www.bloomsbury.com
and sign up for our newsletters.

Contents

Acknowledgements — vi

Introduction — 1

1 Natural Automation — 11
2 Dramatic Automation — 31
3 Mechanical Automation — 67

Conclusions — 93

Notes — 97
Bibliography — 141
Index — 187

Acknowledgements

I thank all who in one way or another contributed to the completion of this book. I am most grateful to the A. G. Leventis Foundation and the Classics and Ancient History Department at the University of Exeter which supported financially this project.

I would like to thank my colleagues in the Centre for Knowledge in Culture in Antiquity and Beyond, especially Gabriele Galluzzo, Daniel King, Rebecca Langlands, David Leith, as well as Tatiana Bur, Giulia Maria Chesi and Isabel Ruffell who shared their ideas and work on ancient science and technology with me.

For their advice, support in difficult times and inspiration I would like to thank Lilia Diamantopoulou, George Kazantzidis, Karen ní Mheallaigh, Lynette Mitchell, Richard Seaford, Matthew Wright and my editor, Lily Mac Mahon.

Last but not least, I would like to thank my family whose love and guidance are with me in whatever I pursue. I dedicate this book to my late parents, Gerolemos Gerolemou and Georgia Tsaggari.

Introduction

Scope of the book

In Plato's *Statesman* 269c, we read that when the Demiurge lets go of the universe, this turns backward 'of its own accord [*automaton*]', since it is 'a living creature' (ζῷον ὄν). Whatever the force behind the motion of the universe might be, the term *automatos* here suggests that self-powered motion is related to a living force.[1] On the other hand, Hellenistic engineers inform us that automation requires technologies which seem to operate ἄνευ πόνου, without human labour. Modern scholars in the past and recently Adrienne Mayor's book *Gods and Robots: Myths, Machines, and Ancient Dreams of Technology* have studied this latter type of automation.[2] My work here has been influenced by the careful assessments of these scholars but my purpose is to try to expand the meaning of technical automation by exploring the connection between automation as the product of a natural force and automation as the result of technological force. In this context, I employ the notion of automatism which is reflected in nature and could be copied and supplemented, as I argue, through *technê*.

Automatisms appear in a variety of fields and take on different functions depending on the context. According to the Cartesian understanding of bodily automatisms and automatisms of animals, automatisms do not depend on human consciousness: they describe reflex responses, habitual behaviors and emotional responses to environmental stimuli.[3] This perspective is also mirrored in Aristotle's *Physics* 197b23–33, where he explains that the term αὐτόματος, while its first part, i.e. αὐτός clearly indicates the creature or object in question, the second is associated with the adverb μάτην, which means acting with 'no purpose'.[4] The automaton here describes a kind of accidental generation or action (by brute animals and inanimate things), which is considered the result of a non-teleological process of causation. As such it differs from things happening by *tychê*, luck, which is often associated with choice, προαίρεσις, and mind (διάνοια) and thus with human beings (Aristotle *Physics* 197a36–197b19).[5]

When automatisms are related to the human body, they describe everything from the digestion of food, respiration, walking and blinking to other similar actions which occur with regularity. Brooke Holmes in her book *The Symptom and the Subject* detects the notion of the 'automatic human body' in the Hippocratic corpus,[6] and explains that the term 'automaton' here refers to everything that could happen in or by the cavity without medical technical intervention, hence naturally and accidentally (*automata*).[7] In this context, bodily automatisms stand in direct contrast to *technê* which results from the ἀνάγκη, necessity, ἀμηχανία, want of means, ἀτεχνία, want of skills, and ἀπορία, general lack of solutions of human beings. Natural automatisms, in general, are often accompanied by the adjective ἄγριος, wild, uncultivated, and challenge everything that is χειρόκμητον, χειροποίητον, wrought by human hand (see e.g. Herodotus 2.94; Theophrastus, *Historia Plantarum* 2.1.1). By characterizing natural patterns, i.e. by being part of nature's plan, they are also succinctly captured by the motif of the *automatos bios* in the age of Cronus, where 'all the fruits of the earth sprang up automata for men' (see e.g. Plato's *Statesman* 271d–e, 272a; *Laws* 713c), without agriculture or human toil, and could be associated with what is described as spontaneous generation or action.[8]

Hellenistic mechanics attempts to reconcile *technê* with nature, i.e. to reproduce the natural automatisms that define the age of Cronus but without abandoning the effective results of technology. What the mechanical art detects is the following: while automatisms operate by their nature spontaneously, they exhibit a certain regularity in terms of repetitiveness which may render them simple to describe, manipulate or reproduce. Within this framework, automation is comprehended not as the result of a spontaneous process but as the product of technological processes which are designed to take place spontaneously. The activity of living organisms, on the other hand, is characterized both by its relative autonomy from external forces and dependence on unpredictable inner automatisms. Thus, the mechanical automaton refers to a material entity which functions as a living being – a being positioned between *technê* and nature or at their borders. As such, it could be described as a hybrid, similar to Haraway's 1991 cyborg which blurs the line between human and machine and sets human life on a continuum with non-human and non-living processes.[9]

These three types of automation, the natural, the one which is being defined through its juxtaposition to *technê* and the mechanical, which reunites, even if artificially, the natural and the technical, are all associated – each one of them in its own unique way – with a certain type of *technê*. One should bear in mind that *technê*, which comprises technology, art and the artificial, is determined by the respective historical period, its users or consumers and it does not have a unified definition.[10] In this light, what we mean by technical automation, for example in the fifth century BCE Athenian stage, differs from what the Hellenistic engineers understood as *technê*. In the archaic period, *technê* neither controls nor challenges nature and natural automatisms; rather, it reflects their materiality and technicity while the craftsman's work is meant to reveal any kind of hidden natural forces in materials, tools and artefacts.[11] In the classical era, on the other hand, *technê* works in the service of a *nomos*, custom and law; it thus transforms to the instrument through which the disorder which could be created by natural forces, such as the automaton, is examined, controlled or limited.[12] This is what we learn, for example, from the Hippocratic treatise *The Art* where it is argued that patients who recover without the help of a physician should not attribute their recovery to the automaton. Medical art, on the other hand and in contrast to the *automaton*, which, according to the author of the treatise, under scrutiny proves to be a mere name (since everything seems to have a cause for happening), presents a reality (6.14–7.3): it is based both on the skills and knowledge of the physician, can be taught and thus distributed.[13] Serafina Cuomo, who investigates the characteristics of *technê* in classical Athens through the example of ancient medicine, adds a further point: *technê* in the fifth century, as a symbol of change and movement, is potentially dangerous to the aristocratic social order.[14] Technology is thus seen as a threat to the natural rights of aristocracy founded on nobility of birth since it offers the opportunity to non-aristocrats to acquire power through the advancement of their skills and natural endowment.

Later on, the art–nature distinction is challenged by the introduction of the notion of the mechanical, which is used as a process showcasing natural phenomena and explaining the function of living organisms. This development makes fluid the boundaries between *technê* and nature. But already for Aristotle at *Physics* 199a15–17, '*technê* either completes what nature is incapable of completing or imitates nature'.[15] Or, as Hans Blumenberg remarks in relation to Aristotle's dictum in his *Imitation of Nature*: 'Nature and "art" are structurally identical: The immanent characteristics of one sphere can be transposed into the other.'[16]

What underlies the mechanical process is the tangible *mêchanê*. Vitruvius describes machines as continuous material systems (*On Architecture* 10.1.3) or, as Sylvia Berryman puts it, machines are 'the sum of their parts'.[17] Jean De Groot suggests too that the term *mêchanê* in Greek philosophical texts is better translated as 'device' rather than 'machine', and she explains that a device depends on a 'construal or arrangement of existing things in a way that makes them instrumental to an otherwise unrealisable end'.[18] Machines or devices are thus defined by the nature of their components, tools and materials, and the purpose or design they fulfil during their operation. The mechanical product is the result of these components and techniques and does not in opposition to its natural original or parallel; on the contrary, it either reveals it in full (even with details hidden from the naked eye), or it expands its potential: pneumatic mechanical birds, for instance, instead of singing under the blue sky, they are placed inside a hall and sing during a banquet.[19] This is associated with the fact that the mechanical procedure, in general, is not merely mimetic but it depends on the potential of the machine to produce things that can go beyond physical reality.[20]

In this respect, the *thauma*, wonder, which often accompanies mechanical automation, rather than defining only the mechanical effect, is particularly related to the way mechanical workings are explained.[21] This type of technological wonder, as Alfred Gell puts it,[22] reflects on the character of visibility or familiarity with technological artefacts, an idea which is close to what Gilbert Simondon in a brief letter to Jacques Derrida in 1982, describes as *phanero*-technics. Simondon, gives two examples, that of the Eiffel Tower and the architectural practice of Le Corbusier. Referring to the latter, he emphasizes that Le Corbusier's *technê* renders visible what is normally hidden,

Le Corbusier's Saint-Pierre in the commune of Firminy, France (Wikimedia/Lapin).

for instance, pipes and cables – the elements which are responsible for the functional design of an artefact (see image above).

The exposure of the techniques of manufacture, which could be either embedded in the design, as in the case of Le Corbusier, or presented in an accompanying narrative, creates what Simondon calls 'techno-aesthetic': the latter, I argue, is construed in the Greek and Roman world as the result of the mechanical art and is evident particularly in engineering texts describing the manufacture of automata and in ekphrastic texts of the late antiquity and early Byzantium.[23]

Outline of the chapters

The book consists of three chapters, unequal in length, yet organically connected. Their main purpose is to provide and discuss the sociological, scientific and philosophical frameworks through which the notion of technical automation emerges at various stages and periods in classical antiquity. Concepts of technical automation are discussed here in several ways: materials and artefacts express nature's principles; devices threaten to replace human intentions and perceptions; machines imitate and widen the overall potential of natural automatisms and, by magnifying the complementary aspect of the artificial dissolve the very boundaries between the animate and inanimate.

In the archaic period the technical automaton resembles nature's functionality and, thus, displays the continuities between nature and technology. *Technê* is identified here as an originating force, similar to nature. This is what the first chapter of this book, 'Natural Automation' – dealing with Homer's *Iliad* 18 and Hesiod's Pandora – suggests. In the first part, I examine the way the Homeric automata are placed between the natural and the artificial. This discussion is placed alongside the discussions of modern scholars who explore the self-powered motion of the Homeric automata through the lens of the mechanical, the magical, the ekphrastic or notions such as material vibrancy.[24] The second part of the chapter turns to Hesiod's story of Pandora and shows how she is different from the Hephaestean automata in the sense that Pandora represents an attempt of *technê* to distinguish itself from nature with the purpose of overpowering it. The behaviour of the manufactured – non-born – Pandora, in contrast to Hephaestus' Iliadic automata, goes beyond a reflection of natural automatisms, since it is both automatic, i.e. technical and natural, as well as human and autonomous. To put it differently: technical and natural automatisms are depicted as a counterpart to intentional acting in Pandora's story, since Pandora's unconscious gesture to take off the lid of the jar proves to be a representation of how her human identity – not her technical or material identity – can be conceived. Her description as a source of evil, demonizes, eventually, *technê* in favour of the automatic, paradisiac age of Cronus.[25]

'Dramatic Automation', my second chapter, is the first work of scholarship to discuss the notion of automation in the Greek drama of classical Athens. The discussion focuses on the relationship between natural automatisms, as processes of unplanned structure, and theatrical techniques of human and divine representation as a result of a type of *technê* which is self-conscious and declares itself autonomous from nature, as Sophocles' emphatically claims in the famous ode in *Antigone* at vv. 332–83. Construction of characters, their body and mind, is associated, moreover, with a set of issues regarding the limits and the potential of *technê*. In the Athenian drama, I argue, a character's representation could be absolute, limited or enhanced through a procedure which I call *technomimesis* and which depends on the potential or limitation of the instruments of mimesis and on how these could improve, replace or abolish an original. The results of *technomimesis* include augmented body parts, e.g. through weapons, or living human-like eidola and statues which can interact with people. By skilfully mimicking biological and cognitive functions and automatisms, animated statues and eidola question the role of physical speech and motion as key features of liveness. On the other hand, various instruments are conceived as animated extensions which threaten human intentionality and agency. As far as the technical reproduction of the mental activities is concerned, education plays here an active role: mental abilities, by being reduced to a series of instructions and perceptual and cognitive abilities acquired through learning, are open to improvement, 'augmentation' and manipulation. But when malicious powers interfere, mental and bodily automatisms can be twisted: this is the case of the mad characters in Greek tragedy transformed into automata by a divine power which controls them. Underlining these possibilities, Athenian drama both parodies and bemoans the artificial reproduction of body and mind automatisms. At the same time, however, the technical automaton in tragedy by reinforcing art's unique potential is an astounding forerunner of the Hellenistic automaton which is equally depended on technological ingenuity. Hence, despite modern scholars' objection to including ancient figures from myth and fiction into mechanical narratives, the automaton both in archaic epic and theatrical context can be seen to function as a locus for contemplating the differences and similarities between living beings and machineries which we witness later on, from the Hellenistic period onwards.[26]

With the systematic introduction of machinery (such as, for instance, weightlifting technologies, ballistic devices) during the Hellenistic period, techniques which produce automatic motion benefit from the mechanical advantage of various new tools and forces, such as for instance, the 'power of the lever' or the 'power of the void'. The third chapter, 'Mechanical Automation', deals specifically with the mechanical reproduction of automatisms and, furthermore, with how it is explained by the engineers and is perceived by their audience. The latter is informed that behind the mechanical automaton's representation of bodily actions or automatisms lie the engineer's tools, materials, techniques and design or engineering plan and not a θαυματοποιός, wonder-maker, who by hiding behind/inside the process of automation or the device wishes to deceive his audience through spectacular and inexplicable shows.

This chapter also investigates the importance of the mechanical automaton in depictions of artworks.[27] This last section, by no means exhaustive, explores the way in which orators who describe works of art, highlight the ways in which perception of motion is influenced by mechanical procedures and production and life-like motion. It appears that in the light of technological advancements in 'motion techniques' and under the influence of Neoplatonic aesthetics and re-evaluation of matter, a new general reading of motion and material was produced especially in late antiquity; this, in effect, formed the audience's expectations. An audience experienced in engineered artefacts was expected to decode via a type of *phantasia*, imagination, which could penetrate the machine and artefact, the technical details or conditions that were implied, or sometimes explicitly articulated, in relation to a moving artefact; the latter could be an automaton or an allegedly moving sculpture. The book ends with a brief discussion of cases of what I call 'automatic art' at the intersection between nature, science and engineering in early Byzantium.[28]

Despite the historical and ideological divergence of the texts under discussion in this book, we can trace a lineage among them because of the connecting link provided by the discourse of natural, artificial and mechanical representation of automation. Having said that, one needs also to accept that technical automata as figures owe much of their presence to textual and cultural traditions that has little to do with techological actuality; that is to say, we should not always attempt to draw one-to-one correlations between pre-Hellenistic, Hellenistic and post-Hellenistic stories of automata.[29]

Notes on the text

I avoid title abbreviations. Single words or short phrases of Greek (such as *thauma* or *automatos bios*) are transliterated in italics while for phrases or passages I use Greek script. I use the editions of Greek texts from the Thesaurus Linguae Graecae (TLG), exceptions are stated in the notes. Unless otherwise noted, the translations of Greek and Roman sources are my own.

The first part of Chapter 1 benefitted from the feedback of audiences at two conferences: the 'Technological Animation in Classical Antiquity Conference' which took place in Exeter, December 2019 and the 'Greek Epic and Artificial Intelligence Conference', organized by Silvio Bär and Andriana Domouzi, in Oslo, September 2020. A version of the second part of Chapter 1 was first presented at the 'Classical Association Conference', in Leicester, April 2018, and at the 'Technosômata, Transhistorical and Intersectional Perspectives', in Berlin, July 2021.

The second chapter draws on material from Gerolemou (2018, 2019c and 2020b). Parts of this were also presented at the '3rd Technosômata Workshop', organized by Giulia-Maria Chesi and Francesca Spiegel, in Berlin, October 2019, and at the 'Medical Knowledge and its '*Sitz im Leben*': Body and Horror in Antiquity', organized by George Kazantzidis and Chiara Thuminger, in Kiel, November 2021. I thank the audiences of these conferences for their constructive criticism.

Earlier versions of the third chapter were presented at the 'Classical Marvels Conference' at the University of St Andrews, organized by Alexia Petsalis-Diomedes, May 2019, and at the 'Prosthetic Embodiment Webinar Series', organized by Giulia Maria Chesi and Sophia Varino, in Berlin, February 2021.

1

Natural Automation

1.1 Introduction

To produce a mechanical automaton, we need the intervention of an artist, manufacturer and of a non-living agent, the machine. In the archaic period, however, the self-powered motion of technical automata is depicted and conceived as a phenomenon in nature, like the growth of a flower or the fall of a snowflake. This first chapter will discuss the ways in which technical automation reflects natural automatisms specifically in the archaic Greek epic. In the first part, I examine the relationship between natural automatisms and the technically fashioned automatic motion of the *Hephaestoteukta* in Book 18 of the *Iliad*. I draw the conclusion that the automatic motion of the Hephaestean devices does not require any magical forces, but also it cannot be explained by technology or their material credentials alone: the automatic motion of an artificial entity in Homer differs from that of, e.g., a chariot, in which the cause of motion is the driver and the horses. Rather, technical automatic motion in Homer depends on and emerges from the organizational structure and forces of nature and living beings.

The second part of this chapter invites us to think, through the story of the Hesiodic Pandora, especially about the differences between autonomous and technical automatic activity. Was Pandora designed and constructed to act autonomously as a human being or is her activity the result of her artificial body, hence she behaves like a technical automaton? The archaic fusion of the natural and the artificial opens the door to post-human understandings of the living body. In the story of Pandora, it suggests the possibility that nature can be designed in accordance with the principles of *technê* – after all, all women descend from Pandora. Pandora's material female body blurs the boundaries between natural and artificial and obscures the concept of physicality. However, after Pandora has been transformed into a woman through various technologies (clothes, jewelleries, female skills), and, at the moment Epimetheus welcomes her as a full-blown living being, we learn that she opens a jar containing ἐλπίς, hope, but also sickness, death and innumerable other evils. At this specific moment, her act, which is the result of her reaction as a human agent to a novel sensory stimulus,[1] i.e., the jar – and not the gesture of a technical automaton – implies the failure of *technê's* dream to create the perfect, obedient automaton.[2] In other words, Pandora's activity is disconnected from her artificial body whereas the opening of the jar (πίθος) and the eventual escape of the evils suggest a human self-directed act on her part, and as such they result in the condemnation of women.

1.2 The Iliadic *Hephaestoteukta*

In Book 18 of the *Iliad*, Thetis, upon entering Hephaestus' workshop, finds the god sweating as he is moving to and fro working with his bellows, adding handles to a set of twenty tripods on wheels; these objects can move back and forth, without any assistance, αὐτόματοι, during the Olympian assemblies (373–9). Later on, in the same book, at 417–20, golden handmaids, also products of Hephaestus' forge, identical in sight to living girls, hurry to support the lame Hephaestus as he moves towards Achilles' mother. Finally, twenty bellows, blowing on melting pots and sending forth a strong blast, support Hephaestus in any way he may find them to be handy (18.469–73). Although the term αὐτόματος is not used for directly defining the activity of the bellows and the golden handmaids, we could assume that the girl-like metal maidens' and behaviour of the bellows is perceived by the intended audience as automated.[3] Much later, Procopius, in the sixth century CE, in his *Horologion of Gaza* 1.9f.[4] makes explicit reference to the αὐτόματος φορά, the 'automatic motion' of the handmaids – whom he calls εἴδωλα – presumably establishing in this way an analogy with the automatic movement of the wheeled tripods in the *Iliad*.[5]

Ancient and modern commentators are puzzled over the 'automatic' way in which these self-powered devices were supposed to be functioning. The epic poet's description of instances during which inanimate matter appears to become animate causes confusion, first between the phenomenal world and the real essence of things, and second, between *technê* and *physis*, internal and external causes. Several interpretations have been advanced for the reasons why automatic motion is particularly attributed to the tripods and the handmaids: they were considered by some to be cases of a narrative enactment of the subtlety of art,[6] or they were read as products of divine and magical power.[7] In recent years, the animated character of these crafted objects has been explained as the result of a kind of material agency or as part of a cognitive process: more specifically, some scholars proposed that they function as extensions of Hephaestus' mind.[8] Finally, they have also been identified as a kind of proto-mechanical automata.[9]

The argument that the automatic tripods, along with Hephaestus' twenty bellows and the humanlike servants, are products of the god's magical faculties (as Christopher A. Faraone mentions briefly in relation to Alcinous' animated dogs and their prophylactic service in *Odyssey* 7.92)[10] might indeed help to explain how tripods and handmaids move at Hephaestus' commands. Magic could be described as being closely related to technology in general. Fritz Graf is right to observe that both magic and technology involve an autonomous agent who, when being faced with natural and divine powers, tries to modify the weak human condition.[11] Still, to consider the *Hephaestoteukta*'s self-motion and overall activity merely as evidence for a magical framework for interpreting animate matter has its limitations. Such an interpretation, while acknowledging the importance of the animating capacities of Hephaestus, overlooks, in the end, the significance of automatic motion as such. The same is true for those who propose that automation in this scene reflects the mental workings of Hephaestus, as has been recently argued mainly by Amy Lather.[12]

Another explanation for the self-moving Iliadic *Hephaestoteukta* is that they are merely an example of what could be labelled 'ekphrastic or descriptive animation', i.e. a narrative trick that leads to ἐνάργεια or ἐνέργεια and which describes an immersion into the narrative through what Aristotle in his *Rhetoric* calls a metaphor (1411b–12a).[13] Already in antiquity, it appears that it was not clear whether automation in the scene under discussion implies that the *Hephaestoteukta* are animated by a divine or magical force and, consequently, if they really move, or if their motion is just a literary trope indicative of the artist's (in this case, Homer's) skill or excellence. According to a story cited by some ancient scholars, Dionysius of Thrace, a Greek grammarian of the second century BCE, argued that Achilles' shield is alive in the same way, i.e., through magic or the divine (τερατωδῶς), as the tripods of Hephaestus (*Iliad* 18. 478–608). On the other hand, Aristonicus, an Alexandrian grammarian (1st century BCE), and his followers objected that the shield is an animated artwork; according to that interpretation, it was not Hephaestus but the Homeric narrator who was responsible for the animation of the shield.[14] Some modern scholars, too, take the Homeric animated artefacts to be the result of the illusory nature of art and they, accordingly, discuss the tripods and the golden maidens, the moving young men, dancers, warriors and workers depicted on Achilles' shield as though they belong to the same context, without differentiating, that is, ekphrastic from magical or any other kinds of animation.[15] It is indeed difficult to decide whether, for example, Hephaestus' dogs at *Odyssey* 7.91–4 are regarded as animated simply because they 'look real' or whether this has something to do with Hephaestus' magical, animating powers. Be that as it may, the dogs show no signs of motion in the *Odyssey*, in contrast to what some scholars have argued.[16] However, Hephaestus, as we know, who is in this instance emphatically identified as their maker-artist, could manufacture artefacts that can move.

Moreover, similar to magical animation, in cases of illusory, descriptive motion, what is presumed to be at play is a force which acts independently of the moving, animate object; that force, conceived in both cases as the manufacturer, is always identified as being directly responsible for the artefact's motion. This is what Stephen Halliwell argues in his book *The Aesthetics of Mimesis* when differentiating between the products of mimetic art from those produced by mechanical crafts; the former, unlike the latter, embodies its maker's identity and expression whereas in a mechanical procedure the engineer or manufacturer is only partly responsible for the final product: materials, tools and mechanisms also influence the results.[17] In order to illustrate better this last point, let me use Daedalus' moving statues as an example.[18] Various sources praise Daedalus' magical skills by highlighting the animated nature of his creations which can move and sometimes even talk.[19] This is why, for instance, Palaephatus (late 4th century BCE) decided to inform his readers that the impossible scenario of statues moving of their own accord is the product of a misconception. As he puts it, Daedalus was simply the first to make statues striding with one foot forward (*Unbelievable Stories* 21).[20] Whether they result from his activity as a magician or a simple innovative artist, his artefacts are directly associated with his skills. Among the stories about Daedalus' animated statues, however, one appears to be associated with self-motion and automation, that is, with a kind of motion that claims independence from its creator (and as such it is similar to mechanical motion). Specifically, in a fragment by the comedian Plato (fr. 188), Hermes' wooden statue made by Daedalus is portrayed as entering the stage of its own accord. Here, the *automatic* statue, presented as a non-manipulated stage prop, appears to serve as a meta-theatrical comment on the importance of a 'lively' performance.[21]

This leads to the main point that I wish to make in this chapter on Homeric automation. As I have briefly mentioned in the 'Introduction' of this book, three kinds of automation exist in antiquity: the most obvious refers to technical automation. In its most elaborate form, technical automation is described as mechanical automation which has to do with an automation process that occurs because of the collaboration of mechanisms, i.e., of various tools, and specific materials (see, e.g., Hero, *On Automata Making* 27.4). The engineer is only a part of this mechanical process.[22] A second type of automation could be called 'natural automation', and it mainly describes natural, spontaneous and often recurring processes. In the archaic period, natural automation applies to nature, for instance, the cry of the Delphic bee in Pindar (*Pythian* 4. 60), the death of a cat or the flourishing of a rose.[23] Natural automation is also associated with what is nostalgically evoked later on as an αὐτόματος βίος, 'an effortless life' or the phenomenon of spontaneous generation.[24] This kind of automation – which does not involve any real mechanism that produces self-motion – could help to explain the behaviour of the *Hephaestoteukta*. This interpretation is close to what the Materialists, especially Ruth Bielfeldt, claim with regard to the agency of the *Hephaestoteukta* in the *Iliad*. They are right to observe that what is striking in that case is that the activity of those objects is not the direct result of the god's use of his divine or magical powers.[25] One could not, however, completely disregard Hephaestus' impact over their action. What is more, while matter appears to be self-moving in this scene – in a manner similar, for instance, to the way iron moves towards magnetic stones as though it were, according to Thales, 'ensouled'[26] – it is important to bear in mind that in Homer, when *things*, for instance, literally go wrong, it is the gods who are blamed and not the objects' inner élan. For example, when Teucer's newly made arrows snap in the air while he is aiming at Hector, the hero believes that the gods have intervened (*Iliad* 15.458–70).[27] In that sense, the *Hephaestoteukta*'s automatic motion could not depend entirely on their own material conditions; just as the flowers in Delos automatically sprout the moment that Apollo steps his foot on the island (*Hymn to Apollo* 135–9) – which would seem to suggest some sort of connection between the two events[28] – so is Hephaestus' presence in *Iliad* 18 linked in a way to the spontaneous motion of his constructions.

The natural type of automation that characterizes the Iliadic automata is associated with the idea of mechanical automation, which develops later in the Hellenistic period. That is to say, as in the case of mechanical automation, this type of automation is also suggestive of a 'technique' or a 'design, plan' that could explain the vivacity of matter – and this, in a context in which the manufacturer's labour and intentions remain hidden, thus allowing wonder to be aroused at the *moving* result.[29] Indeed, the Iliadic *Hephaestoteukta* point towards a disconnection between the creator's labour on the one hand, and the moving artefact on the other: in the scene that I am discussing here, the image of Hephaestus who is sweating over his tripods is contrasted with the latter's effortless, automatic movement in space once they have been created (*Iliad* 18.372, see also 380, ἐπονεῖτο).[30]

Could it then be argued that Homeric automatic motion anticipates the mechanical automation described in the texts of the Hellenistic engineers, especially Hero's of Alexandria? Sylvia Berryman, in her book *The Mechanical Hypothesis in Ancient Greek Natural Philosophy*, claims that there is no strong evidence for a mechanical concept before the fourth century BCE, hence, for mechanical motion before the Hellenistic period. She argues that the self-moving *Hephaestoteukta* are simply meant as a 'hyperbolic representation of the practical power and social status of craftsmen'. She concludes by noting that: 'These stories are not about the capacities of ordinary technological devices, but about the mysterious and unanalysable ability of the gods to convey life.'[31] Indeed, these Iliadic devices do not appear to involve and be controlled by real mechanisms that generate self-motion. Genevieve Liveley and Samantha Thomas argue that the reference, for instance, to the tripods' κύκλα, 'wheels', is not a sufficient indication.³² These κύκλα, are not different in form or function from the κύκλα which Hebe, for instance, affixes to a carriage in *Iliad* 5.722, or from those mentioned in the simile at *Iliad* 18.600f., where the motion of the dancers engraved in Achilles' shield is compared to the movement of a potter's wheel; finally, they are not different from the wheels placed underneath Helen's basket, in *Odyssey* 4.131.

But the tripods' κύκλα are distinctive insofar as they have been manufactured with the capacity to move in analogy to self-regulating natural forces – which is something that modern scholarship does not take into account. This point is, however, of great importance; for, by recognizing, in general, how natural activity shapes ideas about technological processes, we can subsequently appreciate better the degree to which later technological concepts reflect natural phenomena and their functionality. References to natural forces are attested in several Homeric passages as describing various types of motion: At *Iliad* 19.357–61, for instance, the 'thick and fast', ταρφειός, motion of the helmets, shields, the corselets and the spears is compared to the 'thick and fast' movement of the snowflakes which 'flutter down from Zeus'. In that sense, the Iliadic *Hephaestoteukta* anticipate the mechanical automata of later periods, however not in association with the existence of real mechanism but in their shared connection with nature. This reading is not meant to entirely disregard the divine, magical craftsmanship of Hephaestus; rather, it invites us to re-evaluate the nature of the god's role and, instead of seeing him as the direct operator of those devices, to afford him a 'supervising' role.

In order to investigate the nature of this type of technical automation further, we should now turn to other occurrences of the term αὐτόματος in Homer. Apart from describing the motion of the tripods in Book 18, the word αὐτόματος occurs also at *Iliad* 2. 408 and 5.749 (= 8.393); in the latter case, the heavenly doors open of their own accord (αὐτόμαται δὲ πύλαι) in order to allow the enraged Hera to exit the skies. In a way, Hera's κότος, 'wrath', has an impact on the doors' technical automation (5.747).³³ At *Iliad* 2.408, Menelaus travels αὐτόματος, of his own accord, to meet his brother because he knows deep in his heart that he is in trouble. In both passages, the automatic motion is activated by forces that operate internally or in an opaque fashion, and it is conducted according to a plan which is being executed in a way that is not random. This is Eustathius' point (12th century CE), when he says that the αὐτόματος Menelaus corresponds to αὐτόκλητος, 'self-invited', but not κατὰ τύχην, 'randomly', since Menelaus knew somehow that his brother was in trouble and he would have visited him anyway (at 408, vol 1, p. 376f.). The use of αὐτόματος instead of αὐτόκλητος suggests an even stronger relationship between the two brothers: in contrast to the other warriors who are invited by Agamemnon (402–7), Menelaus belongs next to him in a natural, automatic way (ᾔδεε γὰρ κατὰ θυμὸν, 'for he knew in his heart').[34] The tripods on wheels automatically move where and when needed, in the same way that Menelaus automatically walks towards his brother. Hence, if man-made objects often move of their own accord, this is no artistic exaggeration or the result of magic; what is conveyed here instead is the essence of technical automation in its purest, most natural form.

The natural character of the Homeric self-moving devices survives in later times: automatic tripods resembling Ganymede and Pelops serve Apollonius of Tyana at a banquet during his travels to India in Philostratus' *Apollonius of Tyana* 3.27; at 6.10.6 and 6.11.18, in a conversation between Thespesion, the leader of the Gymnosophist community in Ethiopia and Apollonius, the tripods' automatic quality is highlighted with the use of a parallel: the tripods and golden handmaidens placed in the idyllic milieu of the *automatos bios* are compared to the earth that feeds the Cyclops in *Odyssey* 9. 106–11 without cultivation.

Aristotle's way of using the example of the Homeric tripods, reflects only to some extent the Homeric concept of technical automation.[35] In his *Politics* 1.1253b, the philosopher defines slavery by arguing that, in an ideal society, tools (ὄργανα) – a category which also includes slaves – should be capable of carrying out their work on their own, without any external assistance, like Daedalus' statues or Hephaestus' tripods.[36] The argument here seems to be that if slaves could be automatic, then there would be no need for a master to give them orders – something that is considered by some to be παρὰ φύσιν, 'against nature' (τοῖς δὲ παρὰ φύσιν τὸ δεσπόζειν, 1253b 21–3). What is also important here is the fact that Aristotle appears to differentiate between two kinds of technically produced, unforced motion which might reflect the motion of the Iliadic automata: on the one hand, we have artefacts that move when they receive an order (κελευσθέντα) to do so; on the other hand, we have artefacts which 'sense' what they must do 'in advance' (προαισθανόμενα) (1253b 34f.).[37]

The former category could be referring to the Homeric tripods which follow Hephaestus' orders but roll into the assembly of the gods on their own accord; the second category could be describing the golden maids which seem to be able to act without being ordered to do so by Hephaestus. However technically produced automatic motion in Homer, by reflecting natural automatisms, does not directly associate with their manufacturer's plan.

Similar to Aristotle, Hellenistic reports on the various other moving *Hephaestoteukta* are only halfway consistent with the Homeric description of how technical automation works, presumably because Hellenistic thinkers take the technology of their own day to offer an analogy for Hephaestus' artefacts. The Hellenistic Talos, who is often described by modern scholars as a mechanical *automaton*,[38] is neither a product of Hephaestus nor an *automaton*. Apollonius Rhodius' text makes it clear that Talos descends from the last bronze race of men, and that he is born from ash trees (4.1639–93). It is only in later sources that Talos is depicted as a bronze giant made by Hephaestus and given as a present to Minos. In ps.-Apollodorus 1.140, Talos appears to have some pneumatic features, presumably under the influence of Hellenistic pneumatic engineering: specifically, a pipe carrying ἰχώρ is called φλέβα, 'vein', and is described as going through his body (in Apollonius Rhodius, this is called σύριγξ and carries blood); it is also said to be sealed with an ἧλος, a 'nail'; this is reminiscent of the construction of large statues whose sheets of metal are joined together with bronze nails,[39] thus pointing both to Talos' statuary and mechanical identity.[40] This is the nail which, when unsealed by Medea, causes the giant's death.

In Galen, too, comparisons between human bodily functions and automata are inspired by the mechanical operation of actual self-regulated, moving objects. In this context, Galen compares the function of bodily organs to the self-moving (αὐτοκίνητα) constructions of Hephaestus, the bellows and the serving golden maidens.[41] What is important in this case, as Sylvia Berryman notes,[42] is the role of the god-designer, Hephaestus, who, like nature, causes the artefacts to start moving and ensures that they will operate on their own, without any further intervention. This reading brings us fairly close to the natural character of the Iliadic *Hephaestoteukta*. However, Galen overemphasizes the divine designer's intentions and, thus, the prearranged condition of the self-moving artefact, in a way that has no parallel in Homer.[43]

Eustathius, on the other hand, argues that mechanical automata are similar to the automatic Iliadic tripods since they both function on the basis of unforced motion; both of them stand in juxtaposition to pneumatic devices which operate by means of running water (at *Iliad* 18.376, vol. 4, p. 195).[44]

The differences in use and meaning of the *Hephaestoteukta* in later authors depends, moreover, on the way they understand the relationship between *physis* and *technê*. In Homer, *physis* and *technê* do not stand as opposing concepts.[45] The term φύσις occurs twice in Homer: at *Odyssey* 10.302–6, Hermes gives Odysseus the plant μῶλυ to protect him from Circe's spell. The *physis* of the herb is described by Hermes as follows: its root is black, but its flower is like milk; it has been domesticated by the gods to meet their needs – they call it μῶλυ and it cannot be located without their intervention.[46] The interrelationship between *technê* and *physis* is also attested in Book 1 of the *Iliad*, where Achilles swears his great oath by the sceptre, which is again identified as a product of Hephaestus' art (*Iliad* 2.100f.). This wooden staff is said to be adorned with bronze, which removes its leaves and covers its bark (*Iliad* 1.234–9). Natural and technical forces co-evolve here too, to suit the needs of their users. Similar to *physis*, Homeric *technê*, according to Jörg Kube and others, often refers to the natural capacity of a hand-worker or his tools and materials (e.g. in *Iliad* 3.60–2; *Odyssey* 3.433); it is not mean to suggest something that is taught, and it does not point in the direction of a broader, distinctive discipline or subject.[47] In the case of the Iliadic *Hephaestoteukta*, the φῦσαι, the bellows, are the devices which mediate Hephaestus' *technê* by blowing into the melting vats, 'sending out' a forceful blast, εὔπρηστος ἀϋτμή, to shape each one of the artefacts (e.g. tripods, handmaidens), providing them with the ability to move of their own accord (18.470f.).

Further insight can be gained if we compare Homeric αὐτόματος to the word αὐτοδίδακτος, which also reflects the notion of *technê* acting as a natural force from within. In Book 22 of the *Odyssey*, Phemius, hoping that Odysseus will feel sorry for him and pleading for his life, says: 'I am αὐτοδίδακτος and the Muses have implanted all kinds of songs in my mind' (347f.). The prefix αὐτός is the agent of διδάσκω, in a way similar, for instance, to αὐτάγρετος ('self-chosen', *Odyssey* 16. 148f.). As a further parallel, we can adduce the vers ἀλλ' αὐταὶ ἴσασι νοήματα καὶ φρένας ἀνδρῶν (8.559), here it defines the Phaeacians' ships which know the thoughts and minds of men and can travel to their destination without pilots or steering-oars.⁴⁸ Although the notion of αὐτόματος excludes any agential choice, both αὐτάγρετος, αὐτοδίδακτος and αὐτὸς οἶδα could be seen as valid contextual parallels to αὐτόματος; in all three cases, self-managed activity is not described as the result of an obvious procedure that is laborious and time-consuming, but it is paralleled – even if not directly – to actions which are designed to happen automatically, i.e. effortlessly and naturally.

Margalit Finkelberg, in her book *The Birth of Literary Fiction in Ancient Greece*, treats αὐτόματος as equal in meaning to αὐτοδίδακτος, and goes on to differentiate between that which is offered, i.e. the gift of the Muses, on the one hand and the spontaneous knowledge which the bard himself could possess naturally (αὐτοδίδακτος) on the other hand.⁴⁹ The commonly accepted reading of χ 347 appears to confirm this as it explains αὐτοδίδακτος as someone who is taught by nature (ἐκ φύσεως δεδιδαγμένος).⁵⁰ Hence, the meaning of the term cannot be autodidact, that is, literally self-taught. Moreover, the term διδάσκω in Homer does not have the meaning of 'providing a set of instructions'. Rather, it denotes a process of conveying certain skills to others (see e.g. *Odyssey* 1.384; *Iliad* 5.51, 11. 831, 16.811; see also *Hymn to Hermes* 556).⁵¹ In the case of Phemius, his father Terpes was a professional singer, too,⁵² and probably he was the one who taught the bard how to sing. The hypothesis that αὐτοδίδακτος can refer to inherited knowledge is confirmed through the use of the same verse by Maximus Tyrius in his *Dissertationes* 10.5, 38.1, where it is stated that αὐτοδίδακτος art is like αὐτογενής fortune, since both are inherited.⁵³ Thus, Phemius, by using the term αὐτοδίδακτος, aims to convince Odysseus that he can be of good use; he can sing Odysseus' song without any specific prior knowledge, therefore spreading his rumour more quickly. If this is what Phemius means by αὐτοδίδακτος, then he would be implying something like the following: 'I have poetic skills (coming from my father), but no one can see where this comes from, hence, I am a natural or divine wonder to see';⁵⁴ this should impress Odysseus enough not to kill Phemius.

As in the case of the Homeric self-moving devices, Phemius' αὐτοδίδακτος knowledge is construed in analogy to nature's workings, and is conceived as being complementary to the poetic gift of the gods, which is also naturally implanted in his mind, ἐμφύειν (*Odyssey* 22.347). The verb ἐμφύω here finds its linguistic analogue in Hephaestus' φῦσαι: as already mentioned, the bellows help producing the Iliadic *Hephaestoteukta* by blowing on them.⁵⁵

Aeschylus' *Agamemnon* provides us with firm evidence showing that a shift has taken place in the relationship between αὐτοδίδακτος and the concept of *technê* during the fifth century BCE and consequently between *technê* and *physis*. The chorus is singing that its θυμός is αὐτοδίδακτος while intoning the lyreless lament of the Erinys (992f.). The αὐτοδίδακτος singing of the Erinys, however, is associated with the ἀκέλευστος and ἄμισθος, uncalled and unpaid song of the chorus, at 979, for which Eduard Fraenkel has claimed that it 'clearly points to the origin and nature of the knowledge of the moral law which occupies the central position in this chorus';⁵⁶ this law is unwritten, and thus natural, which means that it is not the result of a *technê* based, for instance, on learned techniques such observations and deductions, or writing. This αὐτοδίδακτος song is even contrasted to the solid information on the army's return, which the chorus has acquired through its own eyes (πεύθομαι ... αὐτόμαρτυς). The meaning of αὐτοδίδακτος in *Agamemnon* could thus be construed as follows: 'although I have secure knowledge, my θυμός goes on to produce a song which is not based on investigation and knowledge, but on experience'; this means a song which is not the result of *technê* and specific regulations, but whose cause is inexplicable, and, therefore, natural.⁵⁷

In the Hippocratic corpus, the *automaton* along with τύχη are recognized as posing limitations on the efficiency of the physician's *technê*, since they serve as constant reminders of a natural world which is determined by chance, spontaneity or necessity.⁵⁸ In this context, the author of the Hippocratic *On Diseases* 1.7 explains that automatic bodily forces can eschew the physician's knowledge and observation, and they can act of their own accord, in some cases harming and in others helping the patient to recover. Hippocratic treatises like the *Art*, which support the idea that there actually is a *technê* of medicine, reject the *automaton* as a force that could lead to a patient's recovery; such assumptions are believed to result from the physician's defective ἔλεγχος, testing (ch. 6). In *Epidemics* 6.5. *physis* is ἐοῦσα καὶ οὐ μαθοῦσα, *physis* is beyond learning (ἀπαίδευτος ἡ φύσις ἐοῦσα καὶ οὐ μαθοῦσα τὰ δέοντα ποιέει) and in *On Diet* 1.15 *physis*, in contrast to the art of the physicians, can understand everything αὐτομάτη, in an immediate, spontaneous way.⁵⁹ In the same manner, Democritus at fr. 182, opposes the *automaton* to *technê*, and claims that the latter originates from πόνος, 'effort' and μάθησις, 'learning'.[60] In Homer, on the other hand, natural automatisms merge with *technê*: the latter assumes the automaticity of a natural cause.

*

Let us now turn to a different type of *Hephaestoteukton*, which, due to its female and material form, appears to stand close to Homer's golden handmaidens: the Hesiodic Pandora.[61] The stories of the golden handmaidens and that of Pandora share some common ground with aetiological myths about the origin of humans.[62] Homer's narrative appears to modify what was originally a Mesopotamian myth of creation. Specifically Hephaestus' creation of the metal handmaidens revise what was by far the most important element in these stories, namely the fact that in this case the humankind was said to have been created in order to serve the gods and to set them free from any tedious labour.[63] The Iliadic handmaidens do not function as mere servants of the god: the lame Hephaestus, whom they help to walk.[64] Hephaestus is scorned by the other gods because of his deformity – hence, it could be said that his reliance on the handmaidens, who in addition are self-powered, is substantial (see *Iliad* 1.584–600; 18. 394–6).[65] The Hesiodic Pandora is created, too, in order to facilitate Zeus' revenge plan against humanity. Nonetheless, after acquiring human skills and artefacts, Pandora engages in disastrous activity: she opens a πίθος and unleashes innumerable evils to the world; this is an act which was not presumably included in Zeus' original plan and ends in condemnation of the female race. Thus, although Hesiod's Pandora acts as a servant of the gods, her activity serves in the end as a means of contesting hegemonic masculinity and, in general, indicates a questioning of female subordination.

1.3 The case of Hesiod's Pandora

Adrienne Mayor has recently argued that Pandora, like other Hephaestean creations, is an early example of a mechanical automaton: she is manufactured and designed by Hephaestus, and she is capable of automatic movement.[66] How far can this assumption get us? First, the notion of the mechanical is not a given. It is, as already mentioned and as Sylvia Berryman argues, a historical category which first emerges during the Hellenistic period.[67] Could we then say that Pandora resembles the Iliadic automata which in their turn reflect natural automatisms and motion, anticipating in this way the actual mechanical automata of the Hellenistic era? The clay-bodied Pandora is, indeed, manufactured and moves of her own accord. At some point in Hesiod's *Works and Days* she opens and closes a jar, performing an act that releases evils into the world. At first sight, this action seems spontaneous and automatic, and, in this respect, it is opposed to the forced motion witnessed at *Theogony* 585f. where Hephaestus, once he has completed his work and has produced Pandora's body, brings her out to the gods as a marvel; or at *Works and Days* 83–5, where she is brought to Epimetheus by Hermes as a gift. Nevertheless, unlike the Iliadic tripods and the handmaidens, Pandora's act of opening the jar, while it seems to be conducted automatically in accordance with nature's unconscious, unrevealed mechanisms, appears to be further defined by socially constructed models of gender, thus raising various interpretive possibilities as to the actual force that lies behind her action.[68] To put it differently, although the Iliadic automata are described as possessing some kind of agency, it would be hard to argue that they manifest the intentionality attested in Pandora's story.[69] For this reason, Pandora is, at least conceptually, closer to Homeric crafted *eidola* which are also the result of divine manufacturing; these *eidola* enjoy the human privilege of speech and motion and, most important, they possess a social identity (cf. *Odyssey* 4.797–838, cf. *Iliad* 22.227).[70]

But the material part and technicity in Pandora's story cannot be left unacknowledged. Some feminist readings, although they accept the artificiality of her body, that is, the fact that she is constructed and not naturally born (*Theogony* 571; *Works and Days* 60f., 70), do not take her material status into consideration, putting the emphasis instead on the gendering process and her actions after she has been manufactured.[71] Scholars argue that Pandora's story, especially in the *Works and Days* where she is explicitly accused of infesting mankind, is a reflection of a male anxiety: men are suspicious of women's reproductive and procreative powers.[72] According to Froma Zeitlin, the story associates Pandora's constructed body and her jar with a hungry belly and a uterus that are a threat to men, whereas the ἐλπίς that is left inside the jar corresponds to the hopes and anticipations related to the birth of a child.[73]

On the other hand, Nicole Loraux argues that Pandora does not portray a gendered body nor is she meant to represent fertility; she is simply part of the male dream of autochthony, which denies reproduction through the womb; women are presented, on the other hand, as exploiting the fruits of men's labour.[74] Emannuela Bianchi, while following Loraux's interpretation, considers technology and materiality in the story of Pandora as key issues and discusses her as a technological puppet which celebrates 'masculine autogenesis, the pure manifestation of *logos* through *technê* without the detour of bodily materiality: reproduction without women'.[75] Overall, the story of the Hesiodic Pandora, by refusing the direct relationship between women and reproduction, reveals the origin of Greek misogyny – as the latter is encapsulated in the Hesiodic maxim: 'women are most lascivious', or they are 'a calamity for mortal men' (*Works and Days* 586, μαχλότaται δὲ γυναῖκες), companions only in wealth as they feed like drones on the labour of men (*Works and Days* 373f., 703–5).[76]

Other readings, which have been influenced by feminist approaches, add that Pandora is not a figure of otherness only because she is a woman; her otherness is mainly reinforced by her artificial status. Jean-Pierre Vernant argues that Pandora is not a mere imitation; her prowess lies in her artificial *resemblance* to an ideal, mortal woman, and in her female sexuality:[77] thus she is not a *faux-semblant*.[78] Elissa Marder develops this idea further and highlights the prominence of Pandora's manufactured body by referring to her jar as a '*mechanical reproduction* of the womb rather than as a *representation* of it'.[79] The result of a mechanical reproduction, as Walter Benjamin puts it in his *The Work of Art in the Age of Mechanical Reproduction*, could be independent of the original by revealing different aspects of the latter or by changing its core features, and, as such, it is recognized as an addition to the original rather than a *mimêma*, i.e. a copy.[80]

Discussing Pandora along with issues of *technê* raises, as I have implied above, an important question: who or what 'forces' Pandora to open the jar?[81] Is her activity the result of a kind of an automation which reflects natural automatisms, as is the case with the Iliadic automata? If we dissociate her act from her acquired humanness, skills and gender identity, Pandora's action could be approached as operating within the dynamics of her technicity, that is, as automatic – in a way similar to the automatic operation of the tripods, the hand maidens and the bellows in Homer. Just as Hephaestus has not been described in that case as being the direct source of her action, so cannot he or even Zeus be held directly responsible for Pandora's opening of the jar in Hesiod. Moreover, could Pandora's activity be occurring according to her own 'vital material' self – to use an appropriate phrase employed by Jane Bennett?[82] The fact that matter seems capable of deliberate action was addressed by early philosophers who explained the creation of the universe by investigating its material principle and cause. This material *archê* is characterized – by Empedocles and others[83] – as being 'alive', signifying a creative force. Differences, of course are noted among the early materialists, particularly with regard to the cause behind material activity: certain materialists, like Democritus, acknowledge the automatic as the cause of natural formations (Aristotle *Physics* 196a 25-9). Others, however, such as Anaxagoras, believe that it is not sufficient to attribute change of matter to spontaneity and chance, arguing instead for the existence of a central mind that regulates everything (see Aristotle, *Metaphysics* 984b14–21).[84] Hesiod is counted among the thinkers who belong to the latter category, as Aristotle informs us in *Metaphysics* 984b24–7: he introduces Eros, i.e. desire or love, as the cause behind the creation of the world (see Eros in *Theogony* 116–20, 203–6).[85] Hence, in theory, Pandora could be described as a kind of vibrant matter and as such it could have functioned as a great relief for the hardworking man, just like the artificial servants offer relief to the sweating and toiling god, Hephaestus. More specifically, Pandora's artificial body could have further helped to contest and redefine the link between sexual and maternal with economic concerns, which is such a persistent cause of worries in Hesiod: women, according to the poet, pose a threat to the production of wealth, poking around in granaries (*Works and Days* 373–5). Pandora's constructed body could have helped to eliminate this unfair division of labour, which wearies the lives of men and benefits the women who stay at home, spending their idle days doing practically nothing.

Alas, however, Pandora is designed as a mere punishment to men. By introducing marriage and birth – Hesiod states it clearly in the *Theogony* that all women descend from her (590) – she unleashes evils on mankind.[86] Moreover, with just one gesture, she wastes all the goods of hardworking men stored in the jar – although in reality the jar was full of evils; these evils bring additional troubles to humans and increase the need for physical labour which eventually wears down the human body. Thus, by opening the jar, Pandora marks the end of the un-laborious, natural and spontaneous production of goods, which, according to Hesiod, characterizes the Golden Era, when men lived together with gods (*Works and Days* 118).[87] Ironically, after the opening of the jar, it is sickness which is now enjoying such advantage, since it is described to be wandering αὐτόματος, 'of its own accord', and silently among men.

But does Pandora just scatter by mistake the evils contained in the jar? Her action seems to involve some degree of deliberation. The verb μήδομαι in *Works and Days* 95 (ἀνθρώποισι δ' ἐμήσατο κήδεα λυγρά) could bear the meaning of 'to plan' or 'to think'.[88] However, it can also mean 'to bring something upon someone or something', with or without following a particular plan.[89] This interpretation opens the possibility of a non intentional as well as of an intentional act on her behalf. But if we assume that Pandora is not acting as an automatic device, does this mean that she should be held responsible for the opening of the jar which, as Immanuel Musäus puts it,[90] just happened to be in Epimetheus' house? This is close to what Martin West argues when he says that Pandora could have been motivated by her own drives, for instance, by her curiosity or because she thought that by opening the jar she could acquire something precious.[91] The presence of Aphrodite in the adornment scene, who pours desire on Pandora's head, could perhaps be taken as evidence of a πόθος, desire being the moving force behind Pandora's act (*Works and Days* 67).[92]

This brings us to the next question: does the fact that Pandora instantly tries to close the lid imply an initiative based on the awareness that she did something wrong? Ps.-Plutarch, in his *Consolation to Apollonius* 105 d–e, omits line 99 of *Works and Days*.[93] This could be because the line reads: 'by the plans of the aegis-holder, the cloud-gatherer Zeus', which completes the thought expressed in lines 96–8, where it is stated that 'only Anticipation remained there in its unbreakable home under the mouth of the storage jar, and did not fly out; for before that could happen she closed the lid of the storage jar', and it is confusing in relation to lines 104f.: 'since the counsellor Zeus took their – sc. sicknesses – voice away. Thus it is not possible in any way to evade the mind of Zeus'.[94] West argues against the omission of line 99, stating that 'it is rather important that the relief from misery that Hope brings should be part of Zeus' intention and not an accidental sabotage of it.'[95] However this may have been, even if we accept that Pandora was prevented by Zeus from letting all the evils out of the jar while keeping hope inside it, we cannot but acknowledge that she opens the jar of her own accord, making 'Zeus's project for mankind her own', as Jenny Clay puts it.[96] This kind of behaviour is inherent in her ἐπίκλοπος ἦθος (*Works and Days* 67, 78), which makes Zeus merely a partner, ξυνήων, in her evil planning (600–2). What is more, the emphasis laid on her hands at the moment she is opening the jar speaks in favour of Pandora's agency (v. 94).[97] Hands, according to Aristotle, differentiate intelligent humans from the rest of the animals (*Parts of Animals* 687a 23–6).[98] They stand as symbols of human deliberation and planning. This is how we should read, for instance, Clytemnestra's claim in Aeschylus when she says: 'This is Agamemnon, my husband, a corpse, the work of my right hand' (... τῆσδε δεξιᾶς χερὸς / ἔργον, at *Agamemnon* 1404–6).[99]

What plays an important role in Pandora's transformation from material entity into human agent is a humanizing process emerging as the result of an adornment scene. In the *Theogony*, Athena adorns Pandora with silvery raiment and covers her head with a long-embroidered veil. She places on the maiden's head a beautiful golden crown, also wrought by Hephaestus who obeys Zeus' commands (573–84). In the *Works and Days*, Peithô and the Charites adorn Pandora with golden necklaces, and the Hours crown her head with spring flowers (73–5). She is taught by Athena the feminine arts such as needlework and weaving (63f.). Most importantly, as we have already seen, Pandora is endowed with female characteristics such as grace, desire, and limb-devouring cares (66); Hermes adds to her a shameless mind and a wily character and gives her speech (77–80). Pandora's humanity and gendered characteristics are, again as in the case of her body, the outcome of technological tools (in this case clothes and jewelleries) and skills.

Pandora's manufactured, female and adorned body causes the wonderment of the gods (*Theogony* 588); however, her gendered body is what deceives Epimetheus into accepting her as his wife. She is, thus, misconceived not with regard to her outer appearance but with regard to her female *êthos* and activity.[100] This is different from what Admetus, for instance, experiences in Euripides' *Alcestis*. Admetus appears to be reluctant to accept the silent woman, who has been brought to him by Heracles and who looks just like his dead wife, because he is afraid that she might be a replica sent by the gods as a deception (1061–3).¹⁰¹ Artificiality could indeed be hidden under female garments or other female insignia. The story of the iron Apega, as told by Polybius, is even more suggestive in this respect. Apega replicates Nabis' wife, who uses her to get more tax money from the unwilling Spartan citizens. Her breasts are covered with iron nails, concealed under her fancy dress. Nabis, who stands behind the false Apega, manipulates her into using her arms to crush the victim (13.7).¹⁰²

The development of Pandora's techno-body into a human agent is a crucial step in her story. The activity of the Iliadic handmaidens, by contrast, who also look like living young women – they are intelligent, they can speak, they have strength and gods have taught them how to do things – is presented as a mere automatic action which is meant as a help for Hephaestus. The female form of their bodies does not seem to play any significant role in the kind of activity they eventually undertake. Manly servants or other animated artefacts could have served the same function. By contrast, Pandora's act of removing and closing the lid of the jar is defined by a series of cultural and social norms.¹⁰³ Moreover, her behaviour challenges, in a way, societal rules (she acts against the benefit of men and of her creators, Zeus and Hephaestus), which leads Hesiod to condemn the whole female race as hateful (*Works and Days* 586).¹⁰⁴

1.4 Conclusions

In this chapter, I tried to rethink the technical character of the moving *Hephaestoteukta* in Homer and Hesiod. The former were explained by scholars as examples of a literary trope for artistic effect, as products of divine and magical animation, as results emerging from a kind of material agency inherent in matter itself and, most recently, as mechanical automata; the latter of these interpretations applies specifically to Hephaestus' metal maidens and Pandora. This chapter rereads the story of the Hephaestean automatic artefacts by focusing on the meaning of αὐτόματος, a term which describes natural automatisms that are incorporated into technological processes. However, while the Iliadic *Hephaestoteukta* appear to present natural automatisms in exactly this way, Pandora's material body moves a step further, foregrounding not simply the power of technology to manufacture natural, automatic action. In Pandora's case, *technê* does not replicate nature's automatic moments; it is further shaped by social conditioning and, therefore, it proves to be potentially κακή, δόλια, or κακοδαίμων, 'deceptive and pernicious' (*Theogony* 302, 540, 770).

2

Dramatic Automation

2.1. Introduction

While the previous chapter discussed how technical automation in the archaic period reflects natural processes, this chapter argues that technical automation in classical Athens is premised on a conceptual rift between natural and human resources: by the latter, I refer to human work effort, both physical and mental, and its results. What is more, this new notion of automation is intrinsically linked to man-made devices, which have the capacity to expand the potential of both the natural and the human. Although this development takes its full form from the Hellenistic period onwards, as a result of scientific and technological advances, it is already envisioned, as I will show, at the end of the fifth century, mainly in Euripidean and Aristophanic drama. In contrast to Aeschylus and Sophocles where *technê* reflects the human capacity to control nature, in Euripides and Aristophanes *technê* promises to enhance and improve human skills by effectively replacing bodily and mental function.

As I have already discussed in the Introduction of this book and briefly in the first chapter in relation to Hephaestus' Iliadic automata, what defines activity and liveness both in nature in general and in human bodies are, among other things, the unintentional, spontaneous and automatic actions through and around which life is organized. Such actions could indicate instinctive bodily activities, such as blinking, breathing or walking. In the Hippocratic texts, bodily automatisms or the automaton, in contrast to *tychê* which is often associated with the physician's successful or unsuccessful intervention in the body, are conceptualized as an innate force which signifies how things in the body occur spontaneously, such as, for instance, sickness or health (see, e.g., *Humours* 5 and *On Art* 6. 6–15).[1] Nevertheless, and although bodily automatisms resist explanation, they are detected and described by Hippocratic physicians. That is to say, even if they do not occur intentionally and/or are not being governed by an external force or developed according to a prearranged design, they still have a discernible pattern. On this basis, it is possible for a bodily automatic process to be artificially reproduced.[2] The author of the Hippocratic treatise *Ancient Medicine*, for instance, explains that organs such as the bladder, the head and the womb are shaped like medical 'cupping glasses' (σικύαι) which allows them to draw and attract blood from the flesh (22). Similarly, Empedocles explains the physiology of breathing through an analogy with a *klepsydra* (100) and claims that the ear functions after the manner of a bell (93 A). Visualizing how automatisms, such as breathing, are operating and how an organ is functioning through analogies with tangible technological artefacts might be taken to imply that at least theoretically organs and their functions can be artificially reproduced.[3] Moreover, the technical manipulation of the body, suggested by various body modification techniques such as, for instance, healthy diets or athletics, paves the way towards fulfilling the dream of a *restitutio ad optimum* of the human body, that is, of 'body enhancement'. Such cases are further related to the idea of prosthetics, which refers to the artificial reproduction of body parts for health or cosmetic reasons.[4] But not only parts of the body are being reproduced and/or enhanced through *technê*. Technology promises the production and/or upgrade of mental automatisms and faculties as well as, for instance, learning skills or memory.[5]

The artificial reproduction and moreover enhancement of the human body and mind, along with their automatisms, is achieved through a process which I call *technomimesis*. I understand this concept as being similar to what Plato describes as 'phantastic imitation' in *Sophist* 267a.[6] Both *technomimesis* and phantastic imitation pay less attention to what is being imitatively reproduced (*Sophist* 236c3), that is, they are not so much concerned with the faithful reproduction of the original. In this respect, they are different, e.g., to Plato's *eikastic* imitation which is a likeness-making procedure (*Sophist* 236b2), that keeps a close eye on the original as it produces an imitation by 'reproducing to the proportions of length, breadth, and depth of his model, and also by retaining the appropriate colors of its parts' (*Sophist* 235d7–e1).[7] However, whereas the phantastic art of imitation depends on various instruments in producing something that will appear beautiful and appealing to its viewers (*Sophist*

236b4–5),⁸ *technomimesis* depends specifically on the potential or limitation of the instruments and how these could improve or substitute the original.⁹ This type of mimesis is later identified as providing the basis of mechanical art which acts both παρὰ φύσιν, i.e. supplementary and/or contrary to nature, and κατὰ φύσιν, i.e. according to nature (see e.g. ps.-Aristotle, *Mechanics* 849a14–16).¹⁰

Along with the technical advancements in the classical period especially in the field of medicine,¹¹ what must have facilitated the development of what I describe as *technomimesis* is, on the one hand, the challenge of nobility in birth as a criterion for political and social power and esteem posed by the Sophists. This resulted in the formation of a new class founded on individual skill that could be further improved through technical interventions, training and instructions. At the same time, various socioeconomic factors associated with the democratic city allowed the emergence of an elite that could afford to 'buy', for instance, all these new-fangled techniques.

The possibility of reproduction and modification of the human body and mind through technological means and instructions which manipulate the body's exterior form and control its internal and mental forces, gives rise, during the classical period, to a debate concerning the limits of *technê*, and, by association, the limits of mimesis. The results of *technomimesis* are, on the one hand, 'rejected' in Greek drama either as being products of deception or as directly threatening human skills, agency and consequently social core values such as, for instance, courage. On the other hand, the discussion around *technomimesis* displays a certain optimism about the promise of technological advancement in general. The Euripidean drama, in particular, appears to explore its beneficial potential by welcoming the products of this type of fashioning of bodily and mental automatisms as alternatives to their natural, limited condition. By precisely treating bodies and minds which go beyond natural limits as, in a way, equal to biological ones, technological mimesis, here, offers different experiences of embodiment.

*

This chapter falls into three sections: the first section explores the ways in which the actors' body interacts with theatrical devices such as masks, costumes and theatrical machines in order to imitate the actions of other characters or things. At the same time, it discusses the ethical dilemmas that arise with the use of this kind of technology in theatre. This leads to a discussion in the second section of this chapter about the ways in which *technê* is depicted, in classical drama as a means of reproducing or expanding bodily and mental activity through the creation of self-moving, animate material entities which can respond automatically to changes in their environment. In this section, I focus on three categories of artificially designed bodies or minds. The first concerns animated statues and images which generate through motion and sometimes speech the illusion of liveness, and thus of physical presence. Some of the cases which I will be discussing in this part have been explored in Deborah T. Steiner's study on images and statues,[12] and by Jean-Pierre Vernant, specifically with regard to his idea of the 'double', according to which images exhibit a kind of mimetic animus which promotes its own technicity, substituting effectively the real or the original.[13] By building on their conclusions, I take the idea of a technical automaton that appears to act spontaneously, and place it side by side with the idea of animate statues and eidola: such pairing allows me to draw the conclusion that statues and eidola, in a way similar to technical automata, challenge both human motion and speech as the key features of liveness. I, then, proceed to pose the following question: who or what motivates these material beings so that they can act? Instrumentality is a key concept in this discussion. This applies also to the second category of automated bodies, which includes the reproduction of automatisms in terms of body and mind enhancement. This category applies to human bodies which are the outcome of prosthetic technologies, specifically weaponry. Moreover, this section discusses education and training in prosthetic terms, that is, as the result of ideas of the malleability of the human mind.

The third category applies to bodies in relation to what may be termed the 'divine automaton'. In this case, I choose not to explore the obvious cases of divine epiphanies as assisted by technological means since these are briefly discussed in the first section of this chapter, where I examine the notion of *technomimesis* with regards to actors, drama techniques and technologies.[14] Instead, in this last section, I discuss the impact of divine forces which master bodily and mental automatisms: attacks of divine madness to human bodies and minds will be my focus here. Under the influence of divine madness, characters tend to become almost artificial and act in a way similar to technical automata, which only seem to behave in an automatic, spontaneous way. However, and in contrast to the loss of their autonomy, the bodies of *mad* characters are conceptualized as being superior to the bodies of the *sane*: the latter have a limited power which is further restricted by moral restraints.

All three categories of technical automata suggest that there is no such thing as a single and uniform version of a human body and mind in Greek drama of the classical period. The artificially reproduced body and mind in Athenian drama, by stretching the limits of the conventional body and mind, essentially manage to expand their potential.[15] At the same time, the plays emphasize, however, that technologies and techniques also work to the effect of methods of control and manipulation of the individual.

2.2 *Technomimesis* on stage

Masks, costumes, theatrical machines, styles of delivery, gestures and scripts provide actors with opportunities to achieve a beyond-the-real-body effect which maintains a different, dramatic reality by exactly helping them to accurately reproduce mental and bodily automatisms of others; these modify and thus conceal their own bodies and thoughts.[16] As Agathon puts it in Aristophanes' *Thesmophoriazusae*, full enactment of a plot often requires a 'correction' of the imitator's body through various devices: this would seem to suggest that what an actor does not possess by nature, he can acquire through mimesis (155f., ἃ δ'οὐ κεκτήμεθα/μίμησις ἤδη ταῦτα συνθηρεύεται) – relatedly, there is no point in imitating something that one already possesses.[17] With proper preparation and the right equipment, an actor could imitate anything. The art which represents everything is, however, vulgar, φορτική, according to Aristotle (*Poetics* 1461b): he, for example, notes, some crude flute-players could even imitate a discus by rolling around on the stage (οἷον οἱ φαῦλοι αὐληταὶ κυλιόμενοι ἂν δίσκον δέῃ μιμεῖσθαι).[18] Likewise in his *Poetics* I461b 34–5 it is reported that Mynniskos, a senior actor, calls a younger fellow actor, Kallippides, an ape because of his exaggerated mimesis (ὡς λίαν [...] ὑπερβάλλοντα).[19] In a discussion of this passage, Eric Csapo provides a different – rather platonic – interpretation (cf. e.g. in *Republic* 393c 5f., 395d

1f., 397a 3–397b2, 398a 1–3). As he puts it, 'Kallippides is not an ape because he immoderately reproduced gestures which might have been acceptable in moderation, but because, like an ape that imitates everything and will produce any gesture, Kallippides produced gestures that non-vulgar sensibilities would rather not see in tragedy, specifically the gestures of the non-elite'.[20] Later sources, however, invite us to consider the possibility of Kallipides being described as an ape because of his exaggerated mimesis: Plutarch, for instance in his *Agesilaus*, in a context discussing Kallippides' encounter with the king of Sparta, describes Kallippides the actor as δεικηλίστης, i.e. as someone who is able to extravagantly imitate everything. For this reason, the king chooses not to listen to his imitation of the nightingale adding that: 'I have [already] heard the bird herself' (21.4f.).

At the same time, however, mimetic excess is embraced by the public. Theodorus, a famous tragic actor of the fourth century BCE, was enjoying great success exactly because he could imitate even the sound of a windlass, τροχιλία (Plutatch, *How the Young Man Should Study Poetry* 18b–c).[21] What lies behind Kallippides' and Theodorus' achievements is the divide between physical vs artificial style and delivery (cf. Aristotle *Rhetorics* 1404a 15f.). In the *Rhetoric*, Aristotle observes that Theodorus' voice 'seemed to be the voice of the speaker, while that of the others the voice of someone else'; Theodorus has learned to cleverly conceal his art behind ordinary language (1404b 20–4).[22] Notably, according to Aristotle at 1404b 24f., Euripides was the first to acknowledge the rift between a physical and an artificial style and delivery and cultivated a natural, direct contact with the audience by having his characters using colloquial diction. This type of mimesis that depends on various techniques complements an actor's natural skills which can only be detected in the αὐτοσχεδιαστική, the spontaneous, early form of poetry, as Aristotle explains in *Poetics* 1448b and 1449a (1149a γενομένη δ' οὖν ἀπ' ἀρχῆς αὐτοσχεδιαστικῆς).[23]

A focus on the technical excessiveness in the process of mimesis and on its undesirable outcomes is not exclusively related, of course, to the style and delivery of speech, i.e. to what Aristotle describes in his *Rhetoric* as *entechnos lexis* (1404a). Discussions on the limits of *technê* in orators' deliveries highlight, for instance, the need to restrict the technicity reflected in the repetition of already written words.[24] To mention just one case: Philostratus, in the *Lives of the Sophists* 482f., reports how Gorgias became the founder of the art of extempore oratory. According to Philostratus' account, it appears that, fearing that he would become like Prodicus of Ceos, who wrote down a fable and then toured around Greece reciting the written story in public, which would eventually become obsolete and outdate, Gorgias decided to leave himself to the inspiration of the moment (ἐπαφῆκεν ἑαυτὸν τῷ καιρῷ). Orators are mentioned in this context as counter-examples to performers in general (see, e.g., Quintilian, *Institutes of Oratory* 11.3.91 on comic actors).[25] What must have created such analogies, and eventually concerns, was the fact that poets no longer delivered their works in public (Aristotle, *Rhetoric* 1403b 23f.),[26] which is why actors were taken to merely reproducing words written by a different person, the poet (see, e.g., Cicero, *On the Orator* 2.194).[27] That said, because of the fact that performers were the ones seen and heard, they were, effectively, given more attention compared to the poets themselves (cf. Aristotle, *Rhetoric* 1403b 32f.).[28]

Theatrical devices in general and theatrical machines in particular appear to challenge the limits of an actor's and character's given skills in the same way that masks, costumes, the *entechnos lexis* and a script do. The crane, for instance, used by the tragedians as a closure pointer and helps to overcome a theatrical *aporia* (cf., e.g., Plato, *Cratylus* 425d 5f.),[29] compensates for the performer's and, more broadly, for a tragic character's natural inability to rise up in the air.[30] In comparison with the crane or *mêchanê* which expands human movement, the *ekkyklema* or 'out-roller', probably a shallow platform on wheels (sometimes also called ἐξώστρα, Pollux 4.128), is more complicated since it simulates human presence. Tragedy, for instance, uses the *ekkyklema* in order to bring out an interior tableaux, usually corpses, through the central doors of the *skene*.[31] In doing so, it helps to provide additional information or confirmation for a preceding report. This re-enactment of oral reports, by means of bodies which can be now visually perceived by the audience, functions, according to Peter von Möllendorff, 'as an inverted ekphrasis of sorts by providing the picture for the text. As a result, the picture has to be more than a mere documentation of past actions. On the contrary, it obeys different, pictorial rules of presentation (in the same way that the verbal description has to superimpose a narrative character on the picture described).'[32] To support his argument, Möllendorff discusses the use of the *ekkyklema* in Euripides'

Heracles. In that case, it is argued, what is displayed on the tableaux incurs a changed perspective on what actually happened. That is, what we witness is Heracles lying among the bodies of his dead children (1032f.), whereas the messenger had reported that their bodies were scattered all over the palace (977–1015). Using physical evidence via a technical apparatus to supplement an already horrifying report at a climactic moment contributes, according to Möllendorff, to the emotional enhancement of the spectator's memory of the event.

A certain anxiety regarding the need to impose certain limits on technological mimesis in drama, nevertheless, can be detected in Aristophanes' metatheatre. Aristophanes essentially asks for a return to a kind of drama that relies on less technical devices or other technical media; a drama that is capitalizing instead on an unpredictable story (cf. *Wasps* 1044f., *Clouds* 545–8).[33] This type of theatre requires a more interactive kind of spectator, one that should be in the position to complement, by means of his imagination, any missing or non-visible evidence (see, for example, Aeschylus at *Frogs* 1053f. *contra Frogs* 1109–14). On the other hand, full enactment of a story reflects an audience that does 'not notice anything unless the performer stresses it', as described by Aristotle in his *Poetics* (1461b 27–32).

Aristophanes understands theatrical machines as something inherently tragic, and specifically as a Euripidean apparatus.[34] From *ekkyklemata* that are being used to climax the action, suspending gods intervening to solve tragic dilemmas and amaze the spectators,[35] to animate statues, letters and other props, the Euripidean drama appears indeed to display a dependence on various technical media. Aristophanes reacts against this technology-oriented drama: by introducing, for example, the device of a living machine, such as the noisome beetle in *Peace* 79–176, he aims to ridicule the use of man-made *mêchanê*. But there is also a further inversion: for in his plays, the machine does not serve to facilitate gods' entrances to the stage but helps humans, instead, to rise to the skies (see the indicative example of his *Peace*, Trygaeus, and his dung beetle).[36] At the same time, Aristophanes mocks machine users who employ technological effects with the sole purpose of impressing the public with their supposed technological ingenuity. Aristophanes makes use of the crane's technological effects but significantly he also presents the device for what it really is: a technological artefact monitored through a labourer's work.[37]

In a scene of the *Peace*, which serves as a parody of the flying Pegasus in Euripides' *Bellerophon* (see the ancient scholia *ad* 76 and 136),³⁸ Trygaeus is using a giant dung beetle with outstretched wings in order to reach the Olympus (154); the operator of the monstrous beetle is called a *mêchanopoios*, 'crane-maker', and Trygaeus warns him to pay attention so that he protects him from falling down (173-6). In *Thesmophoriazusae* 1098-1102 Aristophanes parodies Euripides' frequent use of the crane by bringing the poet onstage by way of a flying machine, having dressed him as Perseus. However, the most striking example of this type of mocking is found in the *Clouds*. Socrates makes his appearance on a *mêchanê*, from which he looks down on Strepsiades and asks: 'Why do you summon me, ephemeral creature?' (τί με καλεῖς, ὦ 'φήμερε, v. 223). He then explains his tone by adding: 'I am walking on air, investigating the sun' (ἀεροβατῶ καὶ περιφρονῶ τὸν ἥλιον', v. 225). Aristophanes does not make fun of the mechanical devices as such (the crane is not explicitly mentioned, see vv. 218, 225, 237); still, by associating machines with philosophical elites, he mocks the distinction suggested by Socrates between those who have access to new technologies, and thus look down on others, even on gods themselves (226, ἔπειτ' ἀπὸ ταρροῦ τοὺς θεοὺς ὑπερφρονεῖς, says Strepsiades), and those uninformed people who have no knowledge of the potential of technical devices.³⁹

The comic *ekkyklema* likewise serves to make fun of tragedy's over-dependence on technical media. In Aristophanic comedy, the *ekkyklema* makes its appearance unexpectedly, whereas in tragedy, as noted above, it complements reports with visual evidence. In *Acharnians* 407-9, for example, Euripides uses the *ekkyklema* to speed up his entrance into the stage and thus save precious time for his poetic composition. Again, what is being mocked here is not so much the *ekkyklema* itself but the way in which it is being used in tragedy, that is, as a scene-shifting device.⁴⁰ Moreover, what the use of this machine implies here is that Euripides' poetic mastery is determined through stage props (448, 453, 458f., 462-4, 469) and clothes (418f., 432-4, 438) presented on a rolling platform.⁴¹ In *Lysistrata* 430-2, Aristophanes, once more, parodies the tragic use of this particular device: this is how we should understand Lysistrata's proud claim that she is coming out of the Acropolis on her own, *automatê*, without needing any crowbars, but using only her brain and intellect (μηδὲν ἐκμοχλεύετε·/ἐξέρχομαι γὰρ αὐτομάτη τί δεῖ μοχλῶν;/οὐ γὰρ μοχλῶν δεῖ μᾶλλον ἢ νοῦ καὶ φρενῶν, 'Don't force the gates with crowbars; I'm coming out on my own. Why do you need crowbars? It's not crowbars you need, but rather brains and sense'). The μοχλοί in the play, iron bolts (i.e. defensive means), are, up to this point, in the hands of the women who have shut themselves in the Acropolis (246, 263f., 310, 487). But when the μοχλοί fall into the hands of men and transform into 'levers' or 'crowbars' (424–8), Lysistrata decides to come out without the assistance of a technical equipment, defensive or offensive, relying only on her intellect.[42] In this case, the use of 'automatic' imagery is reclaimed by the female character's body and mind (*nous* and *phrenes*) rendering human intelligence and agency superior to any technical devices.

However, Aristophanes' mocking of theatrical technology and of its overstretched dramatic effects is one thing. This comic ridicule should not lead us to ignore that in their plays dramatic authors, especially Euripides, explore the potential of technological mimesis and technological or mediated agency, so much so that they establish *technê* as a distinctive force which, though 'accused' of reducing human agency and of highlighting the activity of inanimate devices, it, nonetheless, allows the development of a relationship between technical artefacts and their 'users', which can prove immensely useful for human agents in general and dramatic art in particular.[43]

2.3 Automatic images

God-statues and various other images presented in Greek drama as possessing human behavioural flexibility and adaptability, hence, social skills,[44] allow us to observe the intermingling of the human characters and bodies with the artificial setting of their environment and, as Milette Gaifman and Verity Platt recently argued, the human body as itself a material object.[45] In Euripides' *Andromache*, for instance, the protagonist holds that the statue of Thetis exhibits an affective behaviour: the statue gazes with a fearful expression at her rival Hermione, who intends to harm Andromache (246, 311, cf. 1226f.).[46] Andromache's understanding of Thetis' statue as though it were an autonomous social actor brings her comfort, as she links her emotional state with the expressiveness of the statue.[47] This raises further important questions not just about the significance of statues in Greek drama but also about the ways in which human emotions and actions could be materially projected and reflected in artefacts.[48] Andromache's body in the same play is juxtaposed to a statue's (267f.; cf. 261 and 533f.); this, according to Nancy Worman, points to 'a vivid exteriorization of Andromache's "hardness"'.[49]

Heraclitus maintains that some people do indeed believe that they interact with statues; however, he considers them to be ill-advised because they know nothing about gods or heroes (fr. 5).[50] These people, according to Heraclitus, literally identify the statue with the deity and thus fail to understand the true nature of the divine.[51] The matter raised by Heraclitus touches upon issues of acknowledging divine agency in a material context whereby materiality shapes and is shaped by its producer's and users' intentions. In *Iphigenia in Tauris*, the miraculous solution to Iphigenia's and Orestes' *aporia*, conceived by Iphigenia, is designed according to this principle: by making Artemis' statue move automatically, Iphigenia appears to know how a specific bodily behaviour displayed by the artifact can be taken advantage of, triggering certain reactions to those who are not aware of her trick.[52] The statue of the goddess Artemis is made to move from its place and to close its eyes automatically (1165–7).[53] The audience is of course aware that this is an invention (ἐξεύρημα), a trick by Iphigenia, aiming to convince Thoas of the heroine's cunning (1180, σοφία), so that she and her brother escape from the land of the Taurians. Thoas is indeed convinced by the false miracle. A line is drawn here between a σοφός, a wise person, who can see behind the curtains of the manufacturing process of representation, and an ἀμαθής, ignorant viewer, in this case Thoas, who is incapable of discerning the 'mechanisms' that determine *technê* and consequently a false automatic miracle which relies both on certain technicity on behalf of the designer of the miracle and the amazement of an audience.[54]

In the case of Artemis' statue, an increased degree of verisimilitude is guaranteed by that statue's automatic action, its reproduction of spontaneous bodily movement and the blinking of its eyes. The goal of animated agents is to act 'believably' according to the representation they serve. Helen's eidolon in Euripides, for example, which is also a product of a treacherous *mêchanê*, in this case designed by Hera (*Helen* 610), is indistinguishable from the true Helen. In the play, emphasis is indeed given to the ontological confusion between the living and the non-living, which is caused by the eidolon's physical presence; moreover, although it has been manufactured from ether (32–6,

584), it is a living breathing body (34, ἔμπνους).⁵⁵ As such, it enjoys a certain degree of self-sufficiency. It has the capacity to interact directly with humans, and hence, to experience an emotional reality in which the eidolon ends up being held responsible for the suffering of the Greeks in the Trojan War (72–4, 608–15). Eventually, the eidolon leaves at the right moment (612f.), of its own accord, and declares true Helen free from all charges (57–9). The intelligent behaviour displayed by the eidolon, significantly, a behaviour that is not constantly monitored by any external divine intervention and guidance, is what renders it more believable and lifelike.

Related to this case, the immobility of Andromeda in Euripides' *Andromeda* (fr. 125), who lies bound and transfixed on a rock, confuses Perseus as to whether she is alive or not. In discussing this scene, Matthew E. Wright poses the following question: 'Does this mean that the real Andromeda somehow lacks the lifelike quality which a real human being would possess?'⁵⁶ The same issue, according to Wright, applies also to Helen and her eidolon. In a way similar to Perseus, Teucer is impressed by the replica that is identical to real Helena (71–7, 160–3).⁵⁷ Menelaus also appears to be puzzled with the spectacle of this second Helen and doubts she is actually real (as the true Helena was with him in Troy); hence, his *aporia* carries great weight:⁵⁸ 'What kind of craftsman can fashion a body that can see, that is, a living body?' he asks (583, καὶ τίς βλέποντα σώματ' ἐξεργάζεται;). A dead body could be replaced by a material entity, like the urn in the Sophoclean *Electra* (1113f., cf. *Ag.* 435f.),⁵⁹ or the cenotaph in Euripides' *Helen* or a σῆμα, tomb (1240–3).⁶⁰ However, the substitution of a living body with a humanlike counterpart or replica could raise certain questions again with regard to the limits of *technê* and the authority that the latter is exerting on living human bodies.⁶¹ For this reason, the Right Argument in Aristophanes' *Clouds* 975f. advises young men not to leave imprints of their penises in the sand because they could irritate prospective lovers who will make them suffer under their domination. The μιμήματα could fall victims of manipulation, both by their producers and their consumers.

According to the Hippocratic treatise *Regimen*, arts should imitate natural processes and organic structures (1. 10–24, here 24.14f., οὕτω μὲν αἱ τέχναι πᾶσαι τῇ ἀνθρωπίνῃ φύσει ἐπικοινωνέουσιν).⁶² The skilful balance between liveness and artificiality seen above in Euripides' plays convinces the viewers that the two realms can hardly be distinguished, offering ultimately a new amalgam of the living body and mind.[63] On a different level, the messenger in *Helen*, who had previously witnessed the departure of the eidolon into the sky, says in a flat tone, since he is not aware of the second Helen's existence: 'Ah here you are, I did not know that your body had wings' (618f., 1515f.).[64] Hence, the discussion in Euripides' *Helen* revolves both around the capacity to create copies but also around that copy's automatic animus, how it is demonstrated and how it is perceived by others.[65]

Animated statues render themselves even more believable if they effectively display mental and rhetorical rather than merely physical skills. In the Aeschylean satyr play *Theoroi* or *Isthmiastai* (fr. 78a–82), the eidola re-enact the satyrs' features so perfectly that, as the satyrs claim, even their own mothers would not have recognized them (fr. 78c).[66] Nevertheless, in contrast to Daedalus' automatic statues which walk and talk,[67] they still lack voice (fr. 78a 7).[68] Since they are unable to speak, these eidola remain a mere imitation, μίμημα, of the satyrs, which compromises their liveness. In a comedy by Plato (fr. 204), by contrast, the wooden statue of the god Hermes declares that not only can it enter the stage of its own accord, but it also possesses a voice that was given to it by Daedalus (Ἑρμῆς ἔγωγε Δαιδάλου φωνὴν ἔχων / βαδίζων αὐτόματος ἐλήλυθα). Likewise, Hecuba visualizes Agamemnon as a painter and herself as a creation by Daedalus or some other god: an artefact whose arms, hands, hair and feet have 'grown' a voice (Euripides, *Hecuba* 807–40).[69]

The conceptualization of women as statues[70] underlines, on the other hand, the objectification of women and their commodification by a male dominant Athenian society.[71] The statuary body of women envisioned in these analogies could provide a lens through which one can see a reverse procedure, through which a body's condition monitored as it is by male members of the society, causes it to lose any automatic, spontaneous response to external stimuli. An example of this kind of artificialization missing any lifelike, automatic features is provided by Euripides' *Alcestis*, when the protagonist reappears onstage in a taciturn and (literally) lifeless state (1143–6) as a young woman (1049-50, νέα γυνή, 1059, νέα 1052 ἀκραιφνής) and becomes a commodity in Heracles' hands.[72]

Alcestis' artificialization is apparent already at the beginning of the play, where she is depicted as dying in the place of her spouse, barely breathing, σμικρόν εμπνέουσαν (205). Her death creeps in when her hands and eyes stop moving (398f., βλέφαρον καὶ/παρατόνους χέρας): she cannot hear or see (404). After she dies, Admetus orders the construction of a statue 'by the wise hands of sculptors' (348) which will resemble his wife, with the purpose of keeping it and embracing it as a substitute for Alcestis (348–54, cf. 996–1005).[73] But Alcestis' real body, recovered from Hades by Heracles, fails to repossess its social role as Admetus' dear wife, since it remains speechless like a lifeless statue; for this reason, and although it has the same face and body as the deceased Alcestis, it cannot be recognized and thus accepted by Admetus as his wife (1061–3). Even after Heracles reveals to Admetus the identity of the woman, the bereaved husband is troubled by the 'unexpected duration of her silence'[74] and being aware that a manufacturer could produce an exact replica, he is reasonably afraid that the woman standing in front of him is merely a *phasma*, an image sent by the gods to trick him (1126f.).[75] The non-speaking image of Alcestis underlines the importance of speech in the perception of liveness and, moreover, thought or γνώμη, in both living and manufactured bodies.[76]

The issue of speech vs non-speech and their relationship to liveness and artificiality, becomes even more complicated once we turn our attention to artificial speech, i.e. to speech mediated by technological means and not coming from a living body.[77] Artificial speech challenges the importance of physical presence as a necessary requirement for liveness; it also contests the value of live theatre which depends on bodily presence (artificial or live), pointing instead in the direction of a mediated type of theatre.[78]

We can recall also here cases of artificial speech in Euripides' plays in the form of letters whose contents are integrated into the plot. In Euripides' *Iphigenia in Tauris*, for instance, the challenge posed to face-to-face performance is evident since it becomes associated with the uncertainty concerning Iphigenia's bodily existence, that is, with the veracity of her sacrifice in Aulis. Orestes, at v. 772, poses an illuminative question: 'But where is she? Did she come back from the dead?' (ποῦ δ' ἔστ' ἐκείνη; κατθανοῦσ' ἥκει πάλιν;). When Iphigenia meets Pylades and Orestes, who believe her to be dead, reads a letter to them in which she explains to her brother that she is alive in Tauris and needs to be rescued. The letter is a silent representation of Iphigenia's words (σιγῶσα τἀγγεγραμμένα), i.e., it functions precisely as a substitute for living speech (763–5).[79] As Iphigenia adds in an address to Pylades: 'But if something happens to the ship and the letter is lost, by saving your body you are saving my words' (764f.). The survival of Iphigenia's words in the memory of others, by any means possible, bears tremendous importance on this occasion.[80] Written, i.e. artificial speech, and live speech operate interchangeably in the play: Iphigenia often interrupts her own reading to answer Orestes' questions, who is listening to her (769–87).[81] The intriguing association between speech and liveness, both with regard to artificial and live bodies, is presented in cases of backstage speeches as well. In *Hecuba*, Polydorus' prologue speech is identified as a back-stage speech, as Flickinger has suggested.[82] Apparently, a puppet was present on stage in the place of Polydorus' eidolon, which is referred to as ἀσώματος and winged (30–2, 53f.), while an off-stage actor was reading the prologue. At the same time, Polydorus' real body, as indicated by the tragic character himself, lies on the shore; hence, the audience could see Polydorus' corpse along with Polydorus' replica which was given voice through an off-stage actor (28–30).[83]

Euripides' predilection for mediated, artificial speech is further attested in the *Suppliants*: at vv. 433–7, Theseus states that '[w]hen the laws are written, both the powerless and the rich have equal access to justice, and it is possible for the weaker man to address the same words to the fortunate man whenever he is badly spoken of and the little man, if he has right on his side, to defeat the big man'.[84] At this point Euripides pays tribute to democracy by highlighting precisely the fact that democracy can be enhanced through a technical mediation of speech. Isocrates, in his *Antidosis*, makes a roughly similar argument, though from a different perspective: that of the lawgiver. He argues that while both barbarians and Greeks proved able to write down laws (80), and thus later generations who make laws have access to past written laws from which they could choose (83), orators (81) should constantly try to invent new discourses (83, καινὰ δὲ ζητοῦντες ἐπιπόνως εὑρήσουσι). The reason for this is that if orators repeat something that has been already said and written by a different person, they would be accused of being 'shameless babblers' (83, λέγοντες μὲν γὰρ ταὐτὰ τοῖς πρότερον εἰρημένοις ἀναισχυντεῖν καὶ ληρεῖν δόξουσι). On the other hand, easy access to knowledge, guaranteed by the written text, 'persuades' the lawgiver to abandon innovation, καινότης.

Writing, as a technologized representation of live speech, is similar to the case of artificial bodies discussed above; it demonstrates the complexities involved in establishing an interaction between the artificial and the living and motivates the development of a systematic approach to mixed, hybrid types of delivery. Alcidamas, the fourth century BC author of the treatise *On the Writers of Written Speeches, or, On Sophists*, brings out this issue with his use of the terms εἴδωλον, σχῆμα, μίμημα and the notion of statues and pictures (fr. 1.161-4): he identifies these concepts with written speech (described as ἀκίνητος, 'immovable', 'unchangeable', fr. 1.169) which is opposed to oral speech.[85] Alcidamas describes oral speech as being ensouled, ἔμψυχος (fr. 1.173). Writing is considered to be ῥᾴδιος, easily used by anyone (τῇ τυχούσῃ φύσει πρόχειρον, fr. 1.12.), in contrast to oral speech, a painful endeavour employed only by educated people of exceptional nature (fr. 1.17f., οὔτε φύσεως ἁπάσης οὔτε παιδείας τῆς τυχούσης ἐστίν). Written speech, moreover, lacks spontaneity and, thus, truth (τὸ μὲν αὐτόματον καὶ πλέον ἀληθείαις ὅμοιον ἀποβεβληκότες); that is why, he argues, speeches seem more convincing when they are extemporaneous (fr. 1.77-9, τοὺς αὐτοσχεδιάζοντας).[86] In general, the habit of writing weakens the ability to deliver a speech (fr. 1.94f., καὶ γὰρ ἡ μελέτη τοῦ γράφειν ἀπορίαν τοῦ λέγειν πλείστην παραδίδωσιν) and presents an obstacle to the advantages that would have otherwise emerged 'naturally', 'automatically' had the speech been conceived orally (fr. 1.160f., καὶ τοῖς αὐτομάτοις εὐπορήμασιν ἐμποδών ἐστιν).

Writing, nevertheless, is used for the reason that it makes more visible:

> the progress which it is fitting that there should be in thinking; for it is not easily discernible whether my extemporaneous speeches are now superior to those I formerly delivered, as it is difficult to remember speeches spoken in times gone by. Looking into the written word, however, just as in a mirror, one can easily behold the advance of intelligence.
>
> Fr. 1.200f.[87]

The idea that the improvement of intelligence can be reflected in written speech is, according to James I. Porter, 'a remarkable concession'.[88] A similar point is made in Gorgias' *Encomium of Helen*. While Gorgias praises the truth associated with oral speech, he argues that a speech written with *technê*, 'artfully', could also be persuasive (13) and serve as proof of a certain accomplishment. In the end, Gorgias reveals that this is a speech that he has written (21). Thucydides argues against oral speeches which deceive the audience, and implicitly praises also the written word that is the result of an effort (πόνος) to find the truth (ζήτησις): the written word has the qualities of ἀκρίβεια, accuracy, and σαφήνεια, clearness (1.22) which helps to reveal hidden things (1.23). Thucydides' remark has to do with the fact that the technology of writing allows for the recording and storing of data, rendering the latter invulnerable to the passing of time.[89] Writing by functioning as technical means which reproduces and improves mental activity, can affect and eventually inform identity, subjectivity and agency.[90] The hidden moral concern here, however, relates to the restricted accessibility to technical means and writing; to the illiterate herdsman in Euripides' *Theseus* fr. 82, for instance, the text appears to consist of mere drawings, that is, circles and lines.[91]

2.4 Tools for prosthesis: Automated bodies and minds

Sigmund Freud, in his work *Das Unbehagen in der Kultur*, argues that modern man is defined by the technological means which liberate him from the limitations imposed upon his body and mind by nature.[92] Freud calls this type of man a prosthetic god, 'der *Prothesengott*'.[93] Prosthesis is defined in this context as a process of addition to the human body and it functions as a means for the fulfilment of certain needs.[94] On the other hand, Katherine Hayles, in *How We became Posthuman: Virtual Bodies in Cybernetics, Literature, and Informatics* (1999), argues that there is no essential distinction between the natural body and its artificial extensions. As she puts it, starting with language, one of the most basic early prosthetic tools, human beings are, from the moment they are born, prosthetic beings.

Ancient prosthesis is understood both in terms of augmentation, assemblage but also as something that forms a continuum with the human body.[95] Building on the work that has been done by Alex Purves, Melissa Mueller and Anne-Sophie Noel on prosthetic imagination in the ancient Greek world,[96] this part will explore two cases where prosthetic means and human bodies become interweaved with each other. In the first part, I will discuss cases where weaponry is used to empower the warrior's body skill and agency, thereby forming or transforming his identity. In the second part, I will discuss techniques which are employed to rejuvenate the body and mind of characters. This second type of prosthesis reproduces and enhances natural, automatic mental and bodily processes, while the first case depends on a prosthetic means which serves as an explanatory paradigm of both agency, selfhood and identity.

2.4.1 Case 1: Smart weaponry: Heracles, the bow and his arrows

Euripides' *Heracles* gives rise to a sense of uncertainty about the value of weaponry as prosthesis and, generally, about the fusion between the technological and the living in Athenian drama.[97] In negotiating weapons/body issues, the play, on the other hand, thematizes how the living, breathing body and its material extension or replacements can coexist. The play suggests eventually a reconciliation between the model of technological warrior and the idea of ἀνδρεία, bravery that works for the benefit of a community.[98]

The bodies of epic warriors, on the other hand, seem to exist *ab ovo* in a continuum with their weapons. The archaic body is the result of a merging of its parts with intention as well as with forces imposed on it by the gods (see *Iliad* 13.541 where Poseidon makes the limbs of the Ajaxes agile); it is also merging with materials like clothing, weaponry and adornments.[99] Commenting on the notion of prosthesis in terms of weaponry, for instance, in the *Iliad*, Alex Purves explains that Ajax's enormous shield essentially functions as a second skin that covers the warrior's entire body. Ajax's body does not stop at the apparent boundary of the skin, but it incorporates external objects into his self-image, extending it prosthetically;[100] for this reason, he is described as the only one who has the strength to operate the shield (*Iliad* 11.572, 23.820 but see 18.192f.). Likewise, Achilles' spear, because of its exceptional weight, cannot be handled by any other warrior (*Iliad* 16.141–2, 19.388–9).[101] The same is true for Achilles' armour made by Hephaestus, which, as described in *Iliad* 19.386, lifts him into the air. This type of enhanced warrior forms part of a selected class of warriors which Homer calls πρόμαχοι, that is, strong and expert in the use of their weapons warriors, who tend to fight in the front ranks and in one-to-one battles, in contrast to the λαός, common soldiers.[102] But the rise of the early *polis* saw the emergence of a new type of warrior, the hoplite, whose *aretê*, courage was defined not so much by his physical individual strength combined with the use of individual weapons, but by his skilful use of weapons, such as the spear, the shield and a body armour along with their decisiveness not to give ground but to remain in formation under any circumstances.[103]

Euripides' play *Heracles* is to some extent sceptical towards weaponry as a prerequisite to courage, especially when this does not appear to complement the bodily strength of the warrior as it does in the case of epic warriors. In the play Heracles' famous prowess, by means of which he is believed to establish order in the world, is conceived as a product of both Heracles' body and of his weapons, particularly his bow.[104] The fact that Heracles' descendance from Zeus is disputed in here adds to the bow's value (see v. 148),[105] which endows him with self-sufficiency and excellence that extend beyond his divine heritage.[106] A choral song extols the 'bloody bow' (367) and the 'winged arrows' (367), and admits that Heracles' aretê, excellence acquired through the weapons with which he killed the Centaurs, Cycnus (392), the Lernaean hydra (422) and Geryon (423),[107] surpasses his divine birth (696–7, τᾶς δ' εὐγενίας/ πλέον ὑπερβάλλων <ἀρετᾶι>). At the time of Heracles' labours, the bow and arrows often switched places, harmoniously, with Heracles' hands with which he stole the golden apples of the Hesperides (*Heracles* 396–7, χερὶ καρπὸν ἀμέρξων [...]) and held the firmament (403–7). By combining natural strength with weapons, Heracles succeeds in annihilating evil and freeing the world from monsters. This is why he is called the best, ἄριστος, of humans (150; see also 183, 208, 1306) and is declared a national hero (359–424) and benefactor (222–8, 877, 1254, 1309–10, 1334–5). It is in this capacity that Heracles joins forces with the gods against the giants (*Iliad* 14.250–61), and he later celebrates his victory with them (*Heracles* 177–80, 1192–4).

By contrast, in Sophocles' *Trachiniae*, in an ode delivered by Heracles the bow is absent. Emphasis is given instead on Heracles' hands, which are praised as having the leading role in his triumphant life (see 1090–1102, esp. 1090 ὦ νῶτα καὶ στέρν', ὦ φίλοι βραχίονες, 'O hands, hands, O back and shoulders, O dear arms,' and v. 1102).[108] Artificiality in this play is deemed, in general, to be a force that threatens the body. Deianeira's attempt, for instance, to master Heracles' body and desires through Nessus' drugs results in utter disaster and in the death of her beloved husband. Deianeira dips the robe she weaved for her husband in a love poison that was given to her by the Centaur; as soon as

Heracles puts it on, he dies. Heracles' body struggles against the χιτών, the robe which clings on his sides at every joint as if glued by a τέκτων, a craftsman (765–9, 1052–7) and attacks his body as an outer force (cf. 1027, 1083).[109] When he realizes that his body has been conquered by the χιτών, he takes the situation into his own hands: against the flesh-eating cloak, he puts his 'former bodily glory', as Nancy Worman puts it (1089–1102),[110] and finally, orders his own death, an act that leads to his apotheosis (1056–7, 1255–6).[111]

In the same spirit, in Sophocles' *Philoctetes*, the protagonist, who is in constant pain, instructs Neoptolemus that he should take a sword and cut his sick leg or put him on fire (732–90; cf. 796–801).[112] The Sophoclean body-in-pain affirms the physical body;[113] it does not seek for artificial alternatives or extensions but becomes, in a way, enhanced through suffering and pain.[114] The importance of the body's resistance against external artificial interventions and attacks can be taken as part of a general reluctance, on Sophocles' part, to use theatrical devices in his plays.[115] Technological achievements, on the other hand, which are clearly the result of the human mind which is described as δεινόν and as such provide solutions to life's difficulties, as listed in a famous ode in *Antigone* 332–83, are not rejected, since they do not claim any autonomous value on their own.[116]

Aeschylus equates the idea of an attempt to externally control and manipulate the living body with the concept of autonomous technology and tyranny. Consider, for instance, the Danaids' endeavours in *The Suppliant Women* to escape from their Egyptian cousins who pursue their bodies (see, e.g., 839, 925; cf. *Prometheus Bound* 853–9): the incident is depicted in the play not only as an assault against the maidens themselves but, moreover, against the entire city of Argos. In his reply to the Egyptians, at 946–9, the Argive king, Danaus, proudly defends his city's spirit as this is embodied in its free-minded citizens, and declares through an analogy which recalls Hephaestus' understanding of his *technê* in terms of βία, violence in *Prometheus Bound*,[117] that his words 'are not written down on tablets, nor sealed up in the folded sheet of papyrus; you hear them plainly from the lips and tongue of a free man'.[118]

Euripides, on the other hand, discusses technology for its own merit: in this context, he acknowledges the significance of the life-sustaining power of technology along with its consequences. As said above, in Euripides' *Heracles*, the bow is featured as an artificial extension of Heracles' hands (1098–1100).

As an extra limb, the bow constitutes first the basis for a discussion on cowardice, as opposed to courage, εὐψυχία (140–203). Lycus, who rules Thebes in an unlawful manner in the place of Heracles' father-in-law, argues that if Heracles is ever deprived of the bow, he will prove to be merely a coward (160–4).[119] He suggests that because Heracles has never learned to face the enemy's spear in a close battle, he could never win without the bow in his possession. In a similar manner, the significance of Heracles' labours is also belittled. Lycus observes that Heracles only strangled the lion of Nemea after he caught the beast in nooses, i.e., through a trick, not with his own hands (152–4). He omits, however, the well-known reason behind Heracles' decision to strangle the Nemean lion, which occurred, according to other sources (see, e.g., Bacchylides 13.46–54; Theocritus 25.153–281), because Heracles knew that the lion's skin was impervious; hence, any piercing-weapon would be useless against it.

Amphitryon, speaks in favour of his son's well-deserved reputation as the best of all men (183, ἄνδρ' ἄριστον), however, not by praising his extraordinary skills attributed to his divine origin, but by paying tribute to the advantages conferred to Heracles because of his bow.[120] As he argues, this device gives the archer the opportunity to confront his enemy from a safe distance (170–94), that is, to injure without being injured. If all that really matters in the battlefield is that a warrior should achieve his goal, it is of little importance whether the warrior has a weapon that could protect him and defeat the enemy or brave and strong hands. After all, Amphitryon, whose bodily weakness due to old age is emphasized throughout the play (see for example 42, 108–29, 230–5), has every reason to underline the benefits that result from fighting with a weapon which is not used in a face-to-face, close battle and in a way compensates for the lack of bodily strength (316–18; cf. 436–41). Moreover, according to Amphitryon (170–203), this device provides the warrior with a kind of autonomy that eliminates the factor of chance (203, σώιζειν τὸ σῶμα, μὴ 'κ τύχης ὡρμισμένον). This occurs because the archer is not a slave to his weapon, unlike the infantryman is to his spear, but the one who wisely and skilfully guides it (195). Besides, if a spear breaks, the soldier is unprotected and cannot defend himself, but if an arrow is lost, it can rapidly be replaced by countless other arrows; and though the arrows themselves are 'blind' (v. 199, τυφλὰ τοξεύματα), the archer has an overview of the battlefield, since he stands on the backline (195–203). Hence, for Amphitryon, the best type of weapon is the one which guarantees best the warrior's success during a battle (cf. *Iliad* 23.315–18).[121] For Lycus, on the other hand, only a weapon that allows a face-to-face battle could be considered to be an aid to bravery.

The same issue is discussed in the Platonic *Laches*, which poses the question whether ἀνδρεία can be taught. Here, Nicias argues that young men should be trained in fighting in armour. He claims that training for war improves the body's condition, it is fitting for free citizens, it gives an advantage in battle, it impels one to fulfil his military duties and it gives warriors a martial appearance which causes fear to the enemy (εὐσχημοσύνη, 181e–182d). Laches argues against fighting in armour by claiming that the Spartans, who are superior in military practice, do not use it (181e–184c); moreover, cowardly warriors take risks by using it. He then goes on to tell the story of Stesilaus and his invention, the δορυδρέπανον, half spear half scythe, and how its use in a battle turned into a fiasco when his owner lost control of it.[122]

Like the δορυδρέπανον of Stesilaos, the use of Heracles' bow could have unintended consequences. Upon Heracles' return to Thebes, his weapons and hands still operate as interchangeable and on a cooperative basis. He cries that he will punish Lycus with his bare hands (565) and take vengeance for the cowardly Thebans who turned against him and his family, despite the fact that he had benefited them in the past by using his 'gloriously conquering weapon' (570). However, as soon as Heracles is driven mad by Lyssa and, subsequently, loses authority over his body, his bow cuts itself from the physical hand and acts autonomously.[123] Under these circumstances, the bow loses its beneficial capacities and turns into something vile. Bows and arrows neither know how to interact in the environment in an autonomous manner nor have the ability to change their mode of action in response to the changing circumstances; navigation and manipulation of the bow lie strictly within Heracles' command, who, however, goes mad. He, now, thrusts aside his father who begs him to stop his frenzy, as he thinks he is the father of his enemy, Eurystheus, and he aims his arrows against his children, imagining that he is going to murder Eurystheus' children, and his wife. His weapons, on their part, keep performing tasks with the sole purpose of completing their assigned mission, that is, to eliminate Heracles' every enemy.[124]

When Heracles defies Amphitryon, Athena appears and throws a stone at him, which puts him to sleep. Theseus, the king of Athens, who is told that

Heracles' family is threatened by Lycus, arrives at Thebes to help his friend who has previously freed him from Hades. In the meantime, when Heracles wakes up and is informed by his father about his deeds, he feels ashamed and assumes a sitting position with his head covered. Amphitryon, by arguing that it is not only his son but also the bow and the gods which are responsible for these deeds (1135, σὺ καὶ σὰ τόξα καὶ θεῶν ὅς αἴτιος, later on at 1139, all these are blended into one hand), tries to present some mitigating factors that might result in reduced charges.[125] According to Pausanias 1.28.10–11, there was an Athenian law against lifeless things, 1.28.10–11, and, as a result, the court in the Prytaneum could prosecute irons and other inanimate things for murder (ἔνθα τῷ σιδήρῳ καὶ πᾶσιν ὁμοίως τοῖς ἀψύχοις δικάζουσιν). On the other hand, inanimate objects inflicted punishments upon men of their own accord, *automata*, for instance, in Cambyses' case, when his sword struck his thigh as retribution for hiding the Egyptian god Apis (Herodotus 3.64).[126] Heracles imagines the bow and arrows as being animated too, punishing him by clashing against his ribs and speaking to him with their own voice. They scream: 'With us you killed children and wife; you keep the slayers of your children!' (1380f.). Their voice conveys a heightened sense of agency,[127] and it reminds us of epic scenes in which warriors are depicted as talking to their *thymos* (see e.g. Odysseus in the *Iliad* 11. 404–10).[128] The behaviour/response of the *thymos*, as Christopher Gill puts it in the context of refuting Bruno Snell's conception of the *thymos* as deriving from a post-Cartesian conception of subjectivity and the concept of the unified mind,[129] is formed according to the values of an ethical community and individual psychological thinking.[130] Like the Homeric *thymos*, bow and arrows are part of the self expresssing individual and social needs and concerns. When Heracles' hands and bow blend with each other, they become indistinguishable. A new agent or 'actor', as Bruno Latour would have described it, is created: a hybrid composed of both human and bow.[131]

Upon his recovery, Heracles is, at first sight, forced to assume a completely new identity in order to go on with his life. At first, he feels appalled by his weapons;[132] they are no longer the symbol of glorious deeds but 'of tragic suffering and of unending disgrace'.[133] He feels that he does not have any reason to live (1146–7). Theseus tries to dissuade him from committing suicide by appealing to his glorious past, without referring to any technical aids (1250–4). This probably has the purpose of convincing Heracles that he could have a second chance, away from his bloody bow and arrows. He asks Heracles if he has faith in their friendship and invites him to accompany him to Athens. Interestingly, the way Theseus offers his help is by offering his hand to Heracles. He says, 'Give your hand to your helper and friend' (1403; cf. 1171). His caring presence replaces the bow and arrows; in this context, Anne-Sophie Noel is right in pointing out that the bow and arrows suggest 'the absence of any human being that could bring assistance to the distressed hero'.[134]

However, by the end of the play, Heracles cannot help but returning to his original self: 'Shall I strip myself of the weapons with whose help I performed my glorious exploits in Greece, put myself at the mercy of my enemies, and thus meet a disgraceful death? I must not let them go but must in misery keep them' (1382–5).[135] The bow elevates him to a higher plane of existence, towards an ideal conception of himself, and thus, reminds him that without it, although it is just a lifeless object, he is just a common mortal.[136] Heracles' final decision not to leave his weapons and commit suicide illustrates to the audience Euripides' attempt to offer a consideration of a shared agency between humans and technological artefacts. The bow and arrows express who Heracles believes that he truly is: they represent a certain status, and thus, they will contribute to the re-establishment and maintenance of his self-image. The Sophoclean Ajax, by contrast, both buries his sword in the ground and chooses death over life after the disgraceful massacre he has committed (*Ajax* 657–63): Unlike Ajax, Heracles' decision to keep the bow clearly suggests his decision to maintain his identity as a warrior and bowman.[137]

The afterlife of the Heraclean bow is also interesting in this regard. In Sophocles' *Philoctetes*, the bow is in Philoctetes' hands, in Lemnos. Deserted by his companions during the campaign against Troy because of a malodorous wound caused by a snake bite, Philoctetes does not use the bow to kill enemies at war but carries out, instead, ordinary tasks, such as hunting (287–8, 708–11, 931, 955–8, 1154–7). The bow is presented, at the same time, as a prominent artefact which everyone admires and wishes to 'conquer'. At some point, Neoptolemus, who comes to Lemnos with Odysseus to recover the bow of Heracles, asks Philoctetes: 'Am I allowed to look at it, to handle it, salute it as divine, to touch it?' (654–61). Philoctetes concedes to Neoptolemus' request but the latter seems now unwilling to let it go, at which point Philoctetes starts crying: 'I am now without power' (1094, 1109–11).[138]

In Sophocles, the bow's function is determined by Philoctetes' benefaction to Heracles; it is something that is given to him as a present for accomplishing what had to be done when others refused to light the fire that would lead to his *apotheosis* (662–70, esp. 670). Hence, although it is vital for Philoctetes' survival on the island –this is the reason why he mourns its loss (1004f., 1128f.) – it does not constitute a fundamental part of his identity. Philoctetes is merely the 'lord of the bow of Heracles' (262), his carrier (655). The bow is described as modular, that is, it can answer to the different needs of different people and it does not exhibit any exclusive links to Philoctetes. The Greeks must acquire the bow to conquer Troy (68–9, 113), but they do not need to take Philoctetes with them as well. According to Odysseus, anyone can use the bow, for instance, Teucrus or himself (1055–62). That said, Neoptolemus and, later, Heracles, who appears as *deus ex machina*, argue that, according to an oracle, not only the bow but also Philoctetes must go to Troy for the city to be conquered by the Greeks and for Philoctetes to be healed (1332–9, 1433–8). Even so, the bow and Philoctetes are understood in this play as being two separate entities; the one is not integrally linked to the other.

For the remainder of the play, and especially in the end, Philoctetes, in anger, turns the bow against Odysseus, who disgracefully tries to take his weapons away, but Neoptolemus, who is acting now as Philoctetes' friend, prevents him from shooting an arrow (1301, 1308–9). Neoptolemus does so in an attempt to ensure that the bow will operate upon a friendship's agreement and for the wellbeing of the bowman and his comrades.[139] While in Sophocles' play weapon technology is used in a way that does not overshadow its users, in Euripides' *Heracles*, by contrast, the audience is witnessing the threat that technological means can overtake the body, when the latter, for instance, lies weakened and exposed to a sickness that has put it out of balance. Weaponry, nonetheless, provides Heracles with a type of identity which derives from its merging with the warrior's physical body.

2.4.2 Case 2: 'Nootropics' or the thinking school of Socrates[140]

In the first scene of the *Thesmophoriazusae*, Euripides tries to explain to the kinsman the relationship between sense organs, such as ears and eyes (ἀκούειν, ὁρᾶν), and learning or knowledge. As Euripides puts it, speaking under the influence of philosophical trends, the whole process involves a sort of cosmogony. Ether assumes the role of a craftsman, creating parts for living beings whose eyes are manufactured as an ἀντίμιμον, a counter-image, to the wheel of sun and whose ears are perforated as a funnel for hearing (17f.[141]). The technical analogy which Euripides brings into the discussion to explain hearing and sight aims at heightening the distinctive faculties of these senses which are regarded as knowledge providers (11). Yet the kinsman is confused: is he supposed to hear or see new knowledge (5–10) and, most importantly, has the funnel which drilled the ear eventually destroyed the ability to hear (19–21)? What the kinsman cannot conceive is the heuristic function of the technological analogy used by Euripides; thus, he takes it literally.[142]

For the kinsman, two different types of knowledge seem to exist: an inherent knowledge which does not need mediators – knowledge which mirrors nature or, simply, what is 'out there' – and an acquired knowledge offered by the σοφοί, the wise (21, οἷόν γέ πού 'στιν αἱ σοφαὶ ξυνουσίαι, they are quite something these wise conversations), which can be taught.[143] This latter type could complement, according to the kinsman, our inherent knowledge of things (20, προσμαθών, 24, προσμάθοιμι) and might be useful for fulfilling private needs; for instance, the kinsman needs to learn how to limp so that people should feel sorry for him and leave him to rest, since he is tired from walking (22–4). In a different context, Democritus at fr. 33 notes that such a transformation process is called φυσιοποιεῖν and is the result of διδαχή, instruction. To create nature, as the term suggests, means to create, or correctly alter and supplement one's inherent *physis*. This μεταρυσμοῖ τὸν ἄνθρωπον, 'changes' or 'reshapes the human'.[144] This is, for example, what the orators and teachers of gymnastics offer to their pupils, according to Isocrates (*Antidosis* 191, 207–15). The orators, however, help their pupils to advance to a certain degree, but they certainly cannot force an inclination to rhetoric or gymnastics in everyone (*Antidosis* 183).[145]

The idea of cognitive augmentation found in rhetorical and philosophical contexts, is also discussed in the *Clouds*, where Aristophanes refers explicitly to technology as an instrument of intellectual production. At first, Strepsiades is described as offering both his body and mind to Socrates, the grand teacher, διδάσκαλος of the Thinkery, the φροντιστήριον, allowing him to manipulate them as he sees fit (439–41); this he does in the hope that he would learn how to deceive his enemies. In 478–80, Socrates asks Strepsiades to enlighten him about the ways of his mind (for instance, if he has a good memory) so that he, Socrates, can design new devices as replacements for the old ones (καινὰς μηχανάς; cf. *Acharnians* 445, πυκνῇ γὰρ λεπτὰ μηχανᾷ φρενί, for you think finely with your dense mind[146]). If Strepsiades accepts these new devices, he will become a new man, enhanced beyond his inborn characteristics (502f.): 'You and Chaerephon are going to be very much alike,' Socrates replies (503). Sterpsiades is upset as he does not want to look like Chaerephon. The joke here lies in the fact that Strepsiades is afraid that this procedure will change him into something that will resemble the half-dead, ἡμιθνής, Chaerephon. Acquired knowledge will manage to remove all of his blood, that is, the seat of life, out of his body. Socrates, of course, refers to character improvement, not to his external appearance.[147]

The weakness of Strepsiades' intellectual capacity due to his old age is crucial in this context. Strepsiades' body and mind are treated like a device that could improve its defective parts by having them replaced. However, similar to what is discussed at the beginning of the *Thesmophoriazusae*, the *Clouds* suggests, too, that processes of knowledge production can be found in all parts of society and they are not monopolized by a group of wise teachers, a superior social class or the state. Similar to the kinsman in the *Thesmophoriazusae*, Strepsiades believes that there are two kinds of knowledge. First, we have a type of knowledge that is not so easily transferable, such as everyday facts, like, for instance, the fact that we know that the sun shines every morning.[148] Second, the acquired knowledge which can be articulated, codified, stored and accessed. Strepsiades wishes to conquer the latter and this is precisely why he goes to the Socratic 'Thinkery'. Socrates, on the other hand, tries to teach him about facts of nature and provide him with the knowledge of even the smallest thing, for example how one can observe how high a flea can jump (143–52). At the same time, Socrates demonstrates how knowledge and evidence are produced. Various scientific instruments reveal things which would have otherwise remained unapproachable by the senses (see, e.g., 200–17, where Strepsiades discovers various measuring instruments and maps offering a panoramic view of the earth).

This is also what is debated in the *agôn* of the *Clouds*, although in a different form: on the one side, valuable information is described by the 'Unjust' speech as the subject of an ongoing process of construction and interpretation. According to the Just speech, on the other hand, 'good' knowledge is transmitted by the gods to humans; it is inflexible and internal, that is, it persists through time. Or, to put it differently: the two types of knowledge addressed in the play can be explained as follows: the first type of knowledge is the knowledge linked to and offered by scientific elites. This type of knowledge lies at distance from everyday life and from every day and inherent knowledge; it can only be accessed and attained through observation, by means of various tools, and it makes common people look 'silly'. The second type of knowledge is traditional knowledge which derives from the gods and is developed, preserved and passed from generation to generation within a community. These two types of knowledge create a polarized encounter between Strepsiades, a bumpkin, and Socrates, the master of the Thinkery, as well as between a 'technical', laborious acquisition of knowledge, on the one hand, and the effortless inheritance of knowledge on the other.

Aristophanic characters often mock various types of knowledge which are transmitted through painful and redundant instructions. Philosophers, scientists, politicians, religious representatives, poets and everyone who is portrayed as an instructor of knowledge is often scorned in Aristophanic plays: in this context of mockery, knowledge is presented as the result of incomprehensible discourses or corrupted institutions and users. On the other hand, the knowledge that the Aristophanic citizens praise and dream of is associated with nature's patterns. This is not to be confused with the slogan 'be natural', uttered by the Unjust Speech in *Clouds* v. 1078: 'kick up your heels, laugh at the world, take no shame for anything' and which Eric R. Dodds labels as the *physis* school, which, as he puts it, 'provided human weakness with a fashionable excuse by declaring that the passions were "natural" and therefore right, morality a convention and therefore a shackle to be cast off'.[149] The type of knowledge which Strepsiades longs for is related to what is known in old comedy as *automatos bios*,[150] where every good is provided to humans without requiring an effort. This automatic knowledge is not the result of teaching but comes of its own accord, that is, it requires no labour.[151] To be naturally capable of acting in a specific way, for instance, as the Unjust speech argues in the verses mentioned above, clearly differs from the idea of automatic information processing which is fast and requires little cognitive effort. Moreover, the concept of nature which Naturalists, like Socrates, discuss can be taught for a fee and, as a concept, it is designed along the same lines of the type of knowledge that is, for instance, produced to be used in court (*Clouds* 98, 245, 1146). Such knowledge not only can be reproduced; what is more, it can challenge the boundaries between the social and the natural world.

Strepsiades, however, fails to become better, i.e. to learn; he remains, according to Socrates, rustic, inept and brainless (δυσμαθής, 627ff.). From Strepsiades' point of view Socratic education does not look particularly useful: 'How would all this help me get my daily bread?' he asks at 648, and then again, at 658, 'I just want to learn the very worst argument.' 'But,' Socrates warns him, 'there are some other things you must learn first . . . you cannot acquire things automatically' (636f.). At the end, Socrates says: 'Get lost! I'm not going to be your teacher any longer' (784). [152]

Whereas Strepsiades dreams of an improved mind, other plays in Greek drama explore rejuvenation stories of ageing bodies desiring a new, young body through divine help.[153] We might consider Cadmus and Teiresias, in Euripides *Bacchae*, who acquire a new pair of legs, a gift from the god Dionysus, and become stronger: 'Where shall our dance steps take us, where shall we set our feet and shake our aged heads?' (184),[154] asks Cadmus of the seer Teiresias, who, being the wiser of the two, is in charge of the expedition leading to Cithaeron and to the Bacchic ceremonies (178–98). A scene of body enhancement takes place here and the fact that two old men are moving their newly acquired young limbs is not without comic effect, as Bernd Seidensticker argues (187–9 cf. the old Paedagogus in Euripides, *Ion* 739f.).[155]

The chorus of old men in Euripides, *Heracleidai* 673–86, experience a similar rejuvenation. Here the old singer, in singing for the goddess Mnemosyne, praises Heracles' victories and dances in the presence of Dionysus, the giver of wine and the Libyan pipe, whereas before he could barely move his old feet (107–30, cf. 312f.).[156] In this way, he celebrates the opportunity he has been given to reverse the aging process (657f.). Later in the play, Iolaus' rejuvenation (848–66), which is conveyed through the youthful form of his muscular vigour, particularly his hands in the battle against his enemies, is construed in the same way, that is, as a divine miracle, this time directed by Heracles and Hebe (856f.).[157] With these references to divine intervention and body enhancement, I will now move on to the final part of this chapter, where I discuss divine madness in relation to the notion of the technical automation, by placing special emphasis on Dionysus and his central role in body enhancement.¹⁵⁸

2.5 To err is human, to automate, divine¹⁵⁹

So far, I have been discussing the reproduction or improvement of bodily and mental activity with reference to artificial bodies, body parts and cognition as the result of human *technê*. In this section, I will explore cases of humans acting under the influence of divinely inflicted madness: these humans only appear to act autonomously, since the divine forces behind their actions are hidden. Oliver Taplin, in *Greek Tragedy in Action*, discusses briefly mad characters in drama, and underscores the plasticity of the mad body. According to Taplin, 'never, except perhaps in mad scenes, are the characters of Greek tragedy portrayed as automata or marionettes'.¹⁶⁰ A similar comment is made by Ernst Jentsch in his essay *Zur Psychologie des Unheimlichen* (1906). Jentsch discusses the impression which waxwork figures, dolls and automata make on people. He talks about the uncanny effect produced by epileptic outbursts and cases of insanity, that is, an emotional response, this could be horror or laughter that happens when we encounter an entity that is almost, but not quite, human. Similar to the case of insanity, these artefacts suggest a disconnection between mind and body, since their movements are governed by an external force – a force which the audience – although probably aware of its existence – cannot see.

Madness is often associated in Greek tragedy with a divine cause – which, though, cannot always be identified as the sole factor and as the sole reason behind a madman's wrongdoings. For instance, Athena punishes Sophocles' Ajax with madness (*Ajax* 51–73, 172–81, 216, μανία, 407, 447, 450–3) because of his boast that he can win fame, κλέος, without divine help (756–61).¹⁶¹ His madness only lasts for a day (756, ἡμέραν μόνην, 778). However, Ajax is portrayed as being mad even before and after the end of his punishment (see e.g. v. 77). This type of madness, which is not the outcome of an external divine force, is related to Ajax's obsession with his reputation as a brave warrior: it is a kind of madness, in other words, that is strongly linked to his self-perception, and ultimately to his own identity (cf. 19, 430–80). With this we can compare the character of Agamemnon in Aeschylus' *Agamemnon*. The goddess Artemis and ἀνάγκη, divine necessity, lead Agamemnon to madness, but they are not the sole reasons. Agamemnon's θράσος, over-boldness, is also to blame, since the king goes to extremes and he even considers sacrificing his daughter for the sake of the Greek alliance, so that they can all march together against Troy (218, ἀνάγκας ἔδυ λέπαδνον; 219, φρενὸς πνέων δυσσεβῆ τροπαίαν, 223, παρακοπά).[162] This is confirmed later in the play, when his character alone is held responsible for the shameful destruction of Troy and its temples (119f., 131–7, 338–47, 527). This type of 'inborn madness' ceases and can then reappear, which makes the person who has it dangerous. By contrast, an externally inflicted, divine madness is a one-off event; as such it indicates a breach between the individual who is affected by it and the criminal conducts and acts to which he is exceptionally lapsing.[163]

In Euripides' plays, on the other hand, there is often an obvious divine force that influences or controls mad actions.[164] Heracles' madness, for instance, is caused by Hera's attendants, who are not convinced about the rightness of this deed. In other words, Heracles' madness is not linked to his character. The massacre of his family is not his fault, οὐδὲν ὢν αἴτιος (1310, 1393). This view is advanced by Iris, who voices her strong disagreement over Hera's harsh punishment of the innocent man (843f., 1307f.).[165]

In Aeschylus' and Sophocles' plays, insanity is, moreover, linked to delusion, that is, to damaged perception (cf. Sophocles *Ajax* 51–60, 85; cf. Orestes in Aeschylus *Choephoroi* 1048–62).[166] In Euripides, on the other hand, it is clearly stated that the loss of control, caused by madness, involves the body as well. Mad characters' activity in Euripides is being usually expressed through rush movements.[167] Phaedra, for instance, being madly in love in Euripides *Hippolytus* lets her hair down and longs for the mountains (198–202, [...] ἄφελ᾽, ἀμπέτασον βόστρυχον ὤμοις, 215–22, πέμπετέ μ᾽ εἰς ὄρος [...]). The Euripidean Heracles, being under the influence of madness, is forced to dance (Euripides *Heracles* 871, τάχα σ᾽ ἐγὼ μᾶλλον χορεύσω [...], 878 f., 861–5) and sings a chant of death (895, δάιον μέλος ἐπαυλεῖται).[168] Madness also causes his muscles to contract violently (953). According to Lyssa, he tosses his head, rolls his eyes and cannot control his breath (990). In v. 931, it is stated that 'he wasn't himself anymore' (ὁ δ᾽ οὐκέθ᾽ αὑτὸς ἦν). Both during his madness and after this is over, he stands in silence, ἔστη σιωπῇ (867–71; 929f.). In contrast to the Sophoclean Philoctetes or Heracles in the *Trachiniae* (971–6), who fall silent because they are exhausted and because they have suffered excruciating pain, here, Heracles' silence indicates his complete loss of consciousness; he is neither present nor can he perform any action.

In verses 943–9, Heracles envisions the beginning of a new journey. He is going to Mycenae to challenge the Cyclopean foundations. At the beginning, he claims that he has a chariot and servants with him – which, however, is not true. They are terrified and laughing at his deeds at the same time (950, διπλοῦς δ' ὀπαδοῖς ἦν γέλως φόβος θ' ὁμοῦ).[169] Subsequently, Heracles imagines himself going to Isthmus to fight an invisible enemy and then he supposedly returns to Mycenae (953–63). Heracles' maddened body is eventually saved by Athena who petrifies him (1004; cf. 1395, 1397).[170] Moreover, she binds Heracles' body to the pillars, in a way that alludes to animated statues that were similarly bound to be restrained and prevented, as it was believed, from walking away (1009–12, 1035–8, cf. Herodotus 5.85–7).[171]

As soon as Heracles wakes up, the first words he utters are: 'I am ἔμπνους' (1089; cf. Pentheus in *Bacchae* 1132); that is, he describes himself as 'breathing'[172] like the ἔμπνους eidolon of Helen (Euripides, *Helen* 34).[173] Heracles' murderous action takes place involuntarily, whereby the only memory that could exist after the incidence is a sort of somatic memory – here breathing. It appears that he has no knowledge of his deeds (1108) – a hypothesis which is confirmed when he forces his father to tell him everything that happened (1105–8, 1122, 1109–45). When he recovers consciousness, he conceals his face in silence, ashamed of his deeds (1159–227) and prepares to die (1241, τοιγὰρ παρεσκευάσμεθ' ὥστε κατθανεῖν). Theseus advises Heracles to uncover his head in order to confront him and his father (1227, βλέψον πρὸς ἡμᾶς; cf. 1205) and, in this way, to re-establish contact with the surrounding environment. Even though Heracles decides to put aside the veil and follow Theseus' friendly words, he wishes to return to his previous unconscious state and be like a stone without memory (1397; αὐτοῦ γενοίμην πέτρος ἀμνήμων κακῶν; cf. 1395).[174]

The same is evident in the case of Euripides' Orestes, who is mad in a dreamlike state, partially aware of what is going on but incapable of consciously controlling his behaviour. In *Orestes*, actions are not defined by a complete lack of consciousness. Madness is here linked to λύπη, sadness[175] and σύνεσις

(43f., 396[176]), i.e., to a personal sense of responsibility for his mother's murder which defines his actions as an internal force.[177] As Orestes explains, Apollo only persuaded him to kill his mother and her lover; he was not commanded or forced (29f.). He accuses Apollo of getting him into trouble (cf. 285–7, 579f., 591–9), but, simultaneously, he insists on his own agency and responsibility for the act of matricide.[178] Orestes preserves, however, all the typical traits of mad characters that we examined above: after the mad crisis that provokes rapid movement (44f.; cf. 277f.), he is merely a breathing image (155), a living corpse (385f.), with weak disjointed limbs, ἄναρθρος (228), in need of his sister's help in order to walk (218f., 231–4; cf. Sophocles, *Philoctetes* 879–81); his sick body descends into a state of formlessness, ἀμορφία (390f.; cf. 468f.). According to Electra, he is weakened (218, 227f.), he has not eaten, drunk or washed himself for six days and jumps around when madness seizes him (44, 263–5). When he recovers his sanity, he covers himself with bedclothes and cries (39–45).

In the *Bacchae*, the god Dionysus, who is constantly present on stage, not only maddens the women of Thebes (33, 36, 1295, ἐμάνητε, πᾶσά τ' ἐξεβακχεύθη πόλις), but he gradually contrives Pentheus' death by leading queen Agaue and her sisters to kill the young prince (1079–81).[179] Dionysus is presented here as an inspiring religious leader but also as a theatre instructor who teaches his actors (cf., e.g., 847–61; cf. also the role of Athena in Sophocles, *Ajax*).[180] Pentheus is driven by Dionysus to change his mind and appearance (he drives him out of his wits and sends upon him a light-headed madness, 850f.: πρῶτα δ' ἔκστησον φρενῶν,/ἐνεὶς ἐλαφρὰν λύσσαν, cf. also *Bacchae* 999),[181] and to approach the maenads, whom he had previously followed up to Cithaeron in order to spy on them and learn their practices. In this context, Pentheus allows Dionysus to dress him (934: ἰδού, σὺ κόσμει· σοὶ γὰρ ἀνακείμεσθα δή), and instructs him how he should hold the thyrsus (941–4) and, ultimately, turn into a maenad (915: σκευὴν γυναικὸς μαινάδος βάκχης ἔχων, cf. also 828, 830). As a result, Pentheus becomes interested in hair care (831, 928) and asks Dionysus how he looks in his maenadic dress (925, τί φαίνομαι [...]; see also 914). Ultimately, he is sent to Cithaeron where, even though he hides in a tree, the maenads discover him, rip off his limbs and head and tear his body into pieces. Shortly before his death, Pentheus impulsively throws away the maenadic headband from his head, hoping that this gesture will restore his inborn male identity (1115–21).

However, it is too late since his mother, Agaue, maddened by Dionysus, cannot recognize her son, even after he removes his female insignia. By the time of his death, he is left without a body (1137, κεῖται δὲ χωρὶς σῶμα). In the final scene of the play, what once was Pentheus' body is now butchered limbs: Cadmus, his grandfather, finds the head, then the hands, the limbs ... and he reassembles them (1300, ἢ πᾶν ἐν ἄρθροις συγκεκλημένον καλῶς; 'Are its joints laid properly together?'; cf. the dismemberment scene in 1125–47).

But Dionysus forces also the women of Thebes to flee to the mountains in a state of madness (34, ἠνάγκασ', 32–8, ᾤστρησ', 119, θηλυγενὴς ὄχλος [...] οἰστρηθεὶς Διονύσῳ, 665, 979, 1229). Agaue, who is possessed, in κατοχή, thinks that her son's head (1122–4), which she holds in her hands, is that of a lion which she has killed during hunting (1272–8). Remaining untouched by her son's pleas (1124, οὐδ' ἔπειθε νιν), she tears him into pieces and impales his head on the tip of her *thyrsos* (1139–42). Even though for a moment she addresses the head with motherly tenderness (1185–7, νέος ὁ μόσχος [...]), she generally seems incapable of recognizing her own child (1277, τίνος πρόσωπον δῆτ' ἐν ἀγκάλαις ἔχεις). After Pentheus' slaughter, she returns alone, without her sisters, from Cithaeron, (1168) boasting about her personal success (1233–43) while demanding at the same time that her father and son should hang her prey on the gable of the palace (1239f.). Agaue's crime is indicated as the result of ἀφροσύνη, of the loss of her mind (1301, cf. 1123f., οὐ φρονοῦσ' ἃ χρὴ φρονεῖν,/ ἐκ Βακχίου κατείχετ', οὐδ' ἔπειθέ νιν).[182] In order to return to her senses, she must follow her father's indications. First, Cadmus makes her aware of the natural environment; shortly after, she looks at the sky, which appears to be cheerful (1264–6). Then, he forces her to remember her marital and maternal role (1273–6), until she finally recognizes what she thought was the lion's head as her son's (1279–4).[183] Nevertheless, she still needs more time to understand how the head of her son has ended up in her hands in the first place (1284–6), how she killed him (1290) and what she was doing in Cithaeron (1292–4). One could even argue that she wilfully resists recalling the whole murder scene (1286), perhaps so that she could avoid taking responsibility and being punished (1269f., οὐκ οἶδα), or to maintain her new enhanced female body as Dionysus' devotee, instead of the traditionally subjugated female one (cf. 1235–7).[184]

The Dionysiac skills which the Theban women had acquired as ἐμμανεῖς, maddened by the god (1094), include the development of excessive speed

(731, 977) the acquisition of animal features (748, 957, 1090), generally, of a power which exceeds the limits of their physical strength, or what is normally expected from a female body (764-6, [...] οὐκ ἄνευ θεῶν τινος, 1127f., [...] οὐχ ὑπὸ σθένους /ἀλλ' ὁ θεὸς εὐμάρειαν ἐπεδίδου χεροῖν). Their hands and thyrsus, like shovels, can dig the ground; the maenads tear the limbs of men solely with their bare hands (734-47, 1095-1115, 1125-8, 1245), without using battle tools such as lances (1104 ἀσιδήροις μοχλοῖς, 1173, ἔμαρψα τόνδ' ἄνευ βρόχων, 1205-10; cf. μοχλοὺς φέρωμεν ἢ χεροῖν [...], 949).[185] At the maenads' hands, the holy *thyrsus* also transforms into a weapon (762, 1099). Their bodies are further elevated through hyper-motion (731, 746-52); the maenads can cross over the villages at extremely high speed (977, 1090f.). In a way, envying the improvement of the maenads' female bodies, Pentheus asks Dionysus, after he is forcefully persuaded to approach the maenads, whether he should lift up Cithaeron with his hands or with the help of a lever (949); however, in contrast to the maenads' bodies, his is not endowed with such a power, as he is not initiated into the Dionysian *thiasos*.

Whereas Pentheus, Agaue and the other women of Thebes are transformed into kind of puppets, natural automation in the play is entirely mastered by Dionysus, who turns it against Pentheus and his restraining measures as the god automatically overrides walls and chains (cf. 443-8, esp. 447f., αὐτόματα δ' αὐταῖς δεσμὰ διελύθη ποδῶν/ κλῇδές τ' ἀνῆκαν θύρετρ' ἄνευ θνητῆς χερός, 498; cf. Xenophon *Anabasis* 4.3.8).[186] The Bacchic body, too, in contrast to the mad automata, reflects the automatic plan of nature; Aristotle, in his *Metaphysics* where he talks about self-moving matter, refers to a form of improvised dancing (1034a 9-18), which, according to Emanuela Bianchi, could be a sort of Bacchic dance. Its movements do not have a particular direction or rhythm, i.e., it is escaping every conscious and intentional processing of taught information.[187] Indeed, the Bacchic body, specifically the Bacchic leaping body (ἔκπεδος), could be associated, as Marcel Detienne puts it, with the αὐτοφυής, sudden and spontaneous power of nature, i.e. the autonomous power of spurting associated with Dionysus (see, e.g., 142f.). What characterizes the Dionysiac cult, Detienne argues, is both the immediacy seen in the women's sudden possession by the god, in his sudden epiphanies, and the spontaneous production of wine from the soil (Pausanias 6.26.1) – they all occur ἐξ αὐτομάτου, spontaneously.[188]

2.6 Conclusions

Dramatic automata are categorized in this chapter as follows: Statues and eidola, which reproduce bodily automatisms, and human beings, which imitate statuesque *schemata*, reveal both the limits as well as the potentials of each type of body. A second category relates to enhanced bodies through prosthetic tools, such as weaponry, which function as supplements to the human body. These help to expand the human body beyond its limits. Once a tool user, however, a human body could be transformed into a device – which could compromise its human agency. Finally, mad automata can be read as the result of divine processes of automation. In this case, mental disorder and its misdeeds are associated with manipulated, automatic bodily activity. All three categories of dramatic automata ask whether artificial mental or bodily automatisms could replace, complement or improve the human body and mind: at the same time, while they depict the 'collapse' of the physical body and mind into the artificial, they remind the audience that manufactured or enhanced bodies and minds can be subjected to the whims of an uncanny manufacturer who is pulling the strings.

3

Mechanical Automation

3.1 Introduction

With the emergence of mechanics in the Hellenistic period a new automation age begins, an age which is primarily concerned with a type of automation inherent in the machine itself: from the Hellenistic period onwards, we witness a shift of focus from the manufacturer who is manipulating the automation process to the automation process itself – of which the manufacturer is just a part.[1] This new type of technical automation is premised on the principle that the mechanical procedure is realized through the use of various hidden tools, materials and techniques, all of which contribute to the creation of artificial automatisms, especially bodily movements. It does not, however, appear as overcoming nature and its forces as some scholars have argued in the past.[2] In the post-classical era, the mechanical art is not conceived as being in opposition to nature but as supplementing the natural.[3] Moreover, this type of art cultivates a new kind of audience, one which is led to search for the well-hidden cause behind mechanical operation or inside the machine, and which is not carried away by the wondrous effects of mechanical automation.[4]

*

This chapter falls into three parts: the first part explores the meaning of technical automation in the fourth century BCE which depends on an external force, that is, the operator of the technical automatic procedure. The second part deals with mechanical automata, their manufacturing and performance: in particular, this section looks at the work of Hero of Alexandria and discusses how hidden tools, techniques and materials are used to essentially replace the skills and labour of the engineer; in this context, automatisms are reproduced by the activities of internal mechanisms. Finally, the third part turns to the impact of mechanics on *art making* and *perceiving*. Being part of the public, i.e. of the religious and political sphere,[5] automata in particular and machines in general start being employed as a new visual mode. The notion of mechanical automation becomes a fitting tool and provides an appropriate conceptual framework for defining the way of perceiving and describing an artefact, that is, by making the audience appreciate what lies behind and within the latter. Essentially, the focus shifts here from a mere lifelike art towards the techniques and materials that reproduce liveness.

3.2 Automation in the fourth century BCE

Before proceeding to the discussion of specific cases of technical automation in Plato and Aristotle, it is useful to explore briefly how technical automation is generally understood in the fourth century BCE. Apart from some unclear cases of ingenious devices dated back to early fifth century (such as Cleotas' eagle, Pausanias 6. 20.12, and Canachus' stag, described by Pliny at *Natural History* 34.75) and Archytas' flying dove which is briefly described, among others, by Favorinus in Aulus Gellius' *Attic Nights* 10. 12.8–10,[6] and seems to balance with weights and to move by a current of air enclosed and hidden within, automation in this period depends on the skilful operation by a human being. Isabel A. Ruffell has recently argued that the automatic snail which Demetrius of Phalerum had displayed at the Dionysia festival in Athens (308 BCE) described by Demochares and quoted by Polybius 12.13.11 (= Democh. FGrH 75 F 4), similar to the Hellenistic Nysa statue that participated in Ptolemy's II grand procession and described in Athenaeus, *The Deipnosophists* 5.28.25–7 as standing up by means of a mechanism οὐδενὸς τὰς χεῖρας προσάγοντος, without anyone touching it, probably functions on the basis of a man operating inside the automaton.[7]

To this type of automata that function on the basis of a human agent hidden inside or behind a device belong also the νευρόσπαστα, that is, puppets with moving limbs operated by puppeteers which existed already before the fourth century, as well as the so called θαύματα, wonder tricks of an unclear nature. While the latter do not involve a hidden agent instilling liveness in inanimate matter, they seem to share with νευρόσπαστα their ability to be performed in a simple way; nonetheless, these θαύματα seem to differ from νευρόσπαστα to the extent to which they captivate the audience. On the one hand, the puppeteer's skilful hands, his strings and the special kind of puppet (one with moving limbs), are clearly responsible for the puppet's allegedly spontaneous motion; on the other hand, in the case of θαυματοποιία, the juggler is an expert in concealing human effort and technical agency completely when performing and this increases the audience's sense of wonder.[8] What is important in both cases is to deceive the audience into believing that what they witness is merely the result of an uncomplicated procedure, although in reality it requires an enormous amount of effort and technique.[9]

Athenaeus, in the *Deipnosophists*, refers at 1.35 to various entertainers, among them an Athenian named Potheinus, who was a famous marionette-player (νευροσπάστης); he also mentions some miracle workers (θαυματοποιοί):[10] Xenophon, his student Cratisthenes of Phlius, who could create fire spontaneously (αὐτόματα), and the juggler Nymphodorus.[11] Later in the text, at 4.13.155f., quoting Matro's parodic poem *Attic Dinner Party* 121f., Athenaeus talks about two female slaves, called θαυματοποιοί, who are 'driven like swift birds by Stratocles' ([...] ἃς Στρατοκλῆς ἤλαυνε ποδώκεας ὄρνιθας ὥς).[12] Xenophon, in his *Symposium* 2.1 and 7.2, explains how the work and success of miracle workers depend on the audience sharing in the illusion of a dangerous spectacle being performed easily. He specifically refers to a dancing girl, skilled in acrobatic tricks, as a maker of wonders (2.1, τῶν τὰ θαύματα δυναμένων ποιεῖν) and a boy who also provides a wondrous show. Their expertise, according to Socrates, lies exactly in the way they offer the maximum pleasure to the audience (7.2, ἡμεῖς δ' ἂν μάλιστα εὐφραινοίμεθα θεώμενοι αὐτούς), which is watching them while putting in, or at least looking as if they are putting in, the minimum effort in e.g. twisting their bodies to imitate hoops, τροχοί (7. 2, [...] ἡ παῖς ἡδέως ῥᾷστα διάγοιεν) and using the most ordinary equipment, such as a potter's wheel (7.3).

Engineers appear to be associated with both miracle workers and puppeteers precisely because of the alleged effortlessness and simplicity which characterizes the performance and demonstrations in all these cases. Ps.-Aristotle in *On the Cosmos* 398b 11–21, a text probably dated in the first century CE, describes the divine in terms of μηχανοποιοί, engineers, and νευροσπάσται.[13] According to the text, the former initiate automatic motion by using a single release-mechanism of a device (διὰ μιᾶς ὀργάνου σχαστηρίας); the latter make their puppets move automatically by pulling a single rope (μίαν μήρινθον ἐπισπασάμενοι);[14] hence, they both seem to practise their art easily, in a single motion (τὸ μετὰ ῥαστώνης καὶ ἁπλῆς κινήσεως). Later in the text, the ἀόρατος, invisible divine, is compared to a μηχανοποιός because it moves things in a concealed manner (399a–b).[15] On the other hand, according to Pappus, a mathematician of the fourth century CE (*Synagoge* or *Collection* 8.1024, 24–30), people in the past call a group of engineers θαυμασιουργοί, wonder-makers, since they are able to produce lifelike motion while concealing its cause.[16] Pappus divides these wonder-engineers into three categories: those who generate wonders through air; those who generate wonders through cords and sinews and can thereby reproduce the motions of animated beings (8.1024. 27, ἐμψύχων κινήσεις δοκοῦσι μιμεῖσθαι); and those who create mechanical wonders through water, specifically by using bodies which float in water, or by using water to tell the time.[17]

In Plato θαυματοποιία, juggling is specifically associated with the deceptive aspect of θαύματα (see *Republic* 514b, 602c–d, 804b).[18] The jugglers are responsible for performing the θαύματα in such a way that they disorientate the audience, making it believe that what it sees is the result of spontaneous activity and effort; hence, here θαῦμα reflects the bedazzlement of the viewers and is not used as a word of definition for the ways in which wonder-making is accomplished. This is clearly also the case in *Laws* 658c, where θαύματα are considered to be children's favourite show.[19] But in *Laws* 644d7–645b1, the εἰκών, the example that is deployed for discussing self-control as a central principle of the spirit of the laws, makes use of the notion of θαῦμα in order to describe an unspecified toy which is designed, among other things, for amusing the gods (παίγνιον). Human passions are discussed here as being analogous to the sinews or cords which force the toy to move in various directions. Hence, the term θαῦμα highlights here the performative aspect of imposing self-motion to inanimate matter, that is, the toy or the body.[20] True spontaneous movement, on the other hand, is explained in Plato through the notion of 'automaton' and stands, as Michael Naas has recently argued, often in contrast to predetermined, puppet-like activity which follows a pattern of instruction.[21]

Aristotle, on the other hand, uses the term θαῦμα on many occasions to refer to technical automation in a way that lies, as we will see, closer to Hero's understanding of mechanical automation. Different from the puppet-like automation seen above, what Aristotle discusses in these cases presupposes the interaction of an external force and a coordinated internal collaboration of mechanisms, tools, cords or sinews.[22] Hence, the automatic wonders in Aristotle do not merely point towards the relationship between an external force and its results, i.e. the production of bodily automatisms, especially motion. When the cause of motion cannot be directly perceived by the senses, it produces wonderment: not a bedazzlement which leaves the viewer dumbfounded, but a sense of wonder which leads them to further inquire what is going on. Aristotle explains that automatic motion is not simply the result of an external force but depends on internal forces, too. And while external forces could be separated from the actual space and time of the automatic activity, the ἐνοῦσα κίνησις, which refers to moving forces within the moving body or artefact, is constantly present. This is what Aristotle argues in *On the Soul* 406a31–406b26 when he says that the soul, though moving of its own accord, cannot move the body on the basis of the motion of its material parts, in the way that Democritus thought it could, i.e. in an automatic, spontaneous way, or as Daedalus' statue which is moved by the quicksilver with which it is filled (according to the comic poet Philip). Instead, the soul effects change in animals through a certain choice and thought (διὰ προαιρέσεώς τινος καὶ νοήσεως). This becomes clearer in Alexander of Aphrodisias' *Mantissa* 106. 13–17, where the metaphor of the νευροσπαστικόν is employed by way of underlining the principal role of the soul's power and role in locomotion: the soul resembles a νευροσπάστης who controls the puppet by tightening and releasing the strings attached to their wooden limbs (105.32); the νευροσπαστικόν itself, on the other hand, describes the pneuma which like the tendon of the puppet is pushed and pulled by the soul.[23]

In the same way, at *Generation of Animals* 734b and 741b, where Aristotle talks about reproduction, it is explained that the external agency of the semen's producer, as in the case of an automaton, eventually causes the embryo's movement by having been only once in contact with the same. Similar to the technical automaton, semen has a specific δύναμις, potentiality; once the principle of movement is applied from the outside, this becomes actuality, ἐνέργεια, which then develops without interruption (741b, συνείρεται τὸ ἐφεξῆς).²⁴ At *Motion of Animals* 701b, the animal's motion is compared by Aristotle to that of an automaton, which moves after a very small movement of the strings which then strike one another,²⁵ or a toy wagon, ἁμάξιον, which a driver pushes straight or in a circle because its wheels do not have the same size.²⁶ An animal's activity is conceived as being the response to a power which is being applied to it from the outside; in the context of this association, the animal's sinews correspond to the automaton's strings and its bones to the automaton's pegs, wood, iron. Moreover, both automata and carts can transform an initial steering into a different kind of motion: the automata, when jerked, move their limbs in various directions and the cart, while being pushed forward, moves in a circular manner because of its wheels.²⁷ However, animals, in contrast to automata and carts, are not only self-movers but also self-changers; hence, not only can they adapt their body limbs – some parts become larger and others smaller – to environmental conditions; more importantly, they can also change their behaviour and activity – including locomotion – according to factors such as intellect, imagination, purpose, wish and appetite, i.e. mind and desire (*Motion of Animals* 700b 17–19, διάνοιαν καὶ φαντασίαν καὶ προαίρεσιν καὶ βούλησιν καὶ ἐπιθυμίαν. ταῦτα δὲ πάντα ἀνάγεται εἰς νοῦν καὶ ὄρεξιν; 701b, ἀλλοιοῦσι δ᾽ αἱ φαντασίαι καὶ αἱ αἰσθήσεις καὶ αἱ ἔννοιαι).²⁸ Again, what is important for an animal's locomotion is pneuma which turns the qualitative change into locomotion (*MA* 703a4–25).²⁹

Despite the similarities between technical and natural automation described above, certain differences between the two can still be noted. In *Metaphysics* 1032a–b and 1070a, Aristotle differentiates between four modes of generation: that is, natural generation, technical manufacture, spontaneous generation and generation by chance.³⁰ The first two are defined through the principle (*logos*) of change (μεταβολή), which is positioned both in the generator, i.e. in nature or artist, and the final product, for instance, an animal or a statue. In the case of technical manufacture, tools, the materials which are being used, and, eventually, the form and the final product have different dynamics (*Generation of Animals* 730b15–23, 740b24–34, *On the Soul* 407b 23–6; see also *Physics* 200a 31–4). Materials, for instance, do not relate to form in the case of technical generation – a sphere is a sphere both in a wooden and bronze form (*Metaphysics* 1033b 8–11), in contrast to the relationship between materials and form in the case of natural generation. Moreover, at *Generation of Animals* 735a, we learn that heat and cold can soften and harden the iron, but they do not actually produce the sword; this is produced by the *kinesis*, movement or energy, of the tools which are being employed – tools which contain the '*logos* of the Art' (ἀλλὰ ξίφος ἡ κίνησις ἡ τῶν ὀργάνων ἔχουσα λόγον [τὸν] τῆς τέχνης). Art in its turn constitutes the principle and determines the form of what is being produced (ἡ γὰρ τέχνη ἀρχὴ καὶ εἶδος τοῦ γιγνομένου). This '*logos* of Art' is not only being employed by the craftsman. As Aristotle claims at *Generation of Animals* 743a, while the form of the product does not relate to its materials, decisions on materials are related to elements such as manufacturing, function and use: for example, for a chest to be produced, apart from the carpenter who is considered the appropriate motive agent, one also needs a specific material, i.e., in this case, wood (ὥσπερ οὔτε κιβωτὸν μὴ ἐκ ξύλου ὁ τέκτων ποιήσειεν ἄν, οὔτ' ἄνευ τούτου κιβωτὸς ἔσται ἐκτῶν ξύλων). In the same way, in the *Parts of Animals* 642a 9–11 the axe or saw should be made by a hard material. As far as the automatic, i.e. spontaneous generation, and generation by chance are concerned, what is missing is what James G. Lennox calls a 'formal replication model', whose absence prevents the final product from having similarities with its generator.[31]

The intellectual engagement with the meaning and scope of technical automation in the fourth century BCE, the inquiry into the similarities and differences between natural generation and technical manufacture, and the parallel investigation of the intentions of a generator, and of the relationship between material, artefact and function – all these philosophical questions give rise to new attitudes towards the manufacturing of automata, and they foster the beginnings of a new art of self-moved artefacts whose construction would be eventually pursued by the Hellenistic engineers. This is the subject to which I shall now turn.

3.3 Mechanical automation

Similar to the νευρόσπαστα and θαύματα of the fourth century BCE, Hellenistic automata, by pretending to require no effort in their convincing representation of liveness and automatisms, create the illusion that movement results automatically. However, in the case of mechanical automata, what must remain hidden is not so much the effort of the external force, as in the case of θαύματα and νευρόσπαστα, the juggler and puppeteer, but the workings of the internal force resulting from the interconnection of various mechanisms and materials. The engineer, on the other hand, does not directly participate in this process; he stands rather behind his engineering plan which should secure technical efficiency through prediction and control of mechanisms and materials. External forces such as heat and air, moreover, complement the mechanical plan of automation in a way that does not threaten to expose its allegedly natural, automatic character. In this context, the wonder resulting from the mechanical reproduction of liveness is not associated with deception but with mechanical efficiency and clarity.

Machines and mechanical operations which are designed to be αὐτόματα, spontaneity-driven, are clearly described by the engineers as the outcome of three interrelated parameters: (1) design or the engineering plan, (2) tools and (3) materials. To start with the latter: specific materials are chosen by engineers because of their ability to adapt to the engineering plan of automation; such adaptation means that they can solve various technical problems, and thus be functional. These materials have some of the automatic, self-sufficient properties of natural organisms which means that they can perform in similar ways, especially with regard to their inherent capacity of reacting to changes in their environment (see, e.g., Aristoteles, *Meteorologica* 389a11–13). Materials serve what Hero calls a complex design, διάθεσις ποικίλη (*On Automata Making* 1.8 and *Pneumatics* 1 proem 15)[32] which corresponds to a προκείμενη πρόθεσις, a prearranged [engineering] plan (*On Automata Making* 1.2), and to a μῦθος, a scenario or plot that is being performed by the automata (*On Automata Making* 1.2, 1.4. 2.4, 2.12, 21.2).[33] Pneumatic automata, for instance, work with air and it is exactly because of this material, as Hero in his *Pneumatics* 1 proem 65–85 puts it, that they can respond in a controllable and reversible way to an external stimulus, such as certain mechanical stresses or a certain temperature (1 proem 75f., πάλιν εἰς τὴν αὐτὴν τάξιν ἀποκαθίσταται τῇ τῶν σωμάτων εὐτονίᾳ [...]).[34] A similar result is noted to the shavings of horn and dried sponges: 'when compressed and released, they return to the same space and return to the same bulk' (Hero *Pneumatics* 1.75–8, [...] πάλιν ἐπὶ τὴν αὐτὴν χώραν ἀποκαθίστασθαι καὶ τὸν αὐτὸν ὄγκον ἀποδιδόναι).[35] Again, the cords in Hero's *On Automata Making* are possibly made of flax or hemp,[36] which gives them elasticity and the ability to be wound around screws, hubs, axles, to be bound to counterweights, to be extended, etc. For instance, in the case of the mobile automata, Hero argues that the origin of motion lies in the tension, τάσις, of the cord while the end of motion has to do with its loosening, ἀπόλυσις (2.9). As Courtney Roby points out, the elasticity of the cord 'runs the risk of derailing the automaton's careful sequence of timings ... The lively elasticity of the cord's natural material must be eradicated if the automaton is to function properly.'[37] On account of this, at *On Automata Making* 2.4–5 Hero recommends a stretching process, while at 2.6 he suggests that one should better avoid using sinews since they stretch and shrink according to atmospheric conditions. The control of material elasticity in automatic technology emphasizes the link between the aesthetic perception of materiality (materials support the wonder of mechanical liveness) and the measurable physical properties of the materials.

Metals, on the other hand, while they can support larger forces, at the same time, have mechanical constraints; for instance, their rigidity cannot easily be controlled in a reversible manner, and probably for this reason they are not used in this way in mechanical automatic technology. However, in different contexts, this is considered an advantage. Philo in his *Belopoeica*, for example, referring to spring catapults, argues that the bronze plates of the springs, while they bend, can also retain their curvature, since bronze cannot return to its original position (71.7–10, καμφθέντα μέντοι ὑπό τινος βίας εἰς τὸν μετὰ ταῦτα διαμένειν τὴν καμπὴν ἔχοντα καὶ μὴ δύνασθαι ἑαυτῷ πάλιν ἀπορθοῦσθαι).[38]

For similar reasons with elastic materials, and although there is no extensive discussion on the 'service performance' of wood in mechanical automatic technology, Hero at *On Automata Making* 2.2 states that mobile automata, in order to move easily, should be made out of light and dried-out wood (ἐκ κούφων τε καὶ ξηρῶν ξύλων).[39] Moreover, in another context, Hero argues that wood is used in constructions not only because of its light weight (machines should be easily dismantled and transferred) but also because it is inexpensive (*Belopoeica* 102.9–10; cf. 90.3f.). Materials are thus chosen not just because of certain fixed mechanical properties that satisfy functional criteria and specific design but also with regard to cost.

From the fourth century BCE onwards, innovations in material processing led to increasingly refined artefacts.[40] For instance, thermal processes were used to alter a range of materials. As an example of resilient material, Philo refers to the iron of 'the so-called Celtic and Spanish swords' (*Belopoeica* 71.9); he explains that when it is pure and is worked extensively after it has been melted, it is neither too hard nor soft but something in between (*Belopoeica* 71.17–35). Theophrastus, in his treatise *On Stones*, discusses the ways stones are being produced through fire. According to Theophrastus, the whole process is 'the same as the one followed by nature or very similar to it' (54f., αὐτόματος ἡδὲ τεχνική or μὲν αὐτοφυὴς ὁ δὲ σκευαστὸς). As he adds in paragraph 60, art imitates nature but only for creating its own, ἴδια, products. In the *Plant Explanations* 1.2, Theophrastus brings forward a similar argument regarding the generation of plants: there are two types of artificial generations (in contrast to natural generation which could be *automatos*, spontaneous, or through a seed, σπέρμα). The first type involves external, technical interference which, however, collaborates with the plant's *physis* in order for fruits to be produced (see also 3.1.1, συνεργεῖν τῇ φύσει πρὸς τὸ τέλος); the second type leads to the production of fruits of a special and extraordinary type, i.e. beyond the plant's *physis* (for instance, grapes without seeds; see also 2.1.1). At 1.16.10–13, Theophrastus essentially describes the first type of artificial generation, the κατὰ φύσιν one, as natural: although this generation is premised on an external cause (a cause that is not 'natural'), it still helps the plant to achieve its *telos*, without interfering with natural principles.[41] For novel material processing technologies to be easily and successfully adapted, they had to be presented in analogy to the way nature creates or transforms matter. Let us take here the case of glass: the fact that glass, although a man-made material, was often classified among natural materials (see, e.g., Aristotle *Meteorologica* 389a 7–9) might have informed stories like the one of the unbreakable glass told by Pliny and others (*Natural History* 36.66, 36.196).[42] In these stories the unbreakability of this specific glass suggests that the glass possesses the type of resilience observed in natural materials. In other words, the unbreakable glass is admired for its biomimetic features.

In addition to materials, engineering processes integrate also tools and technologies which amplify the ability to automate artefacts. Along with the well-known wheel and axle as well as the lever and wedge, already used in the archaic and classical periods, in the Hellenistic period two further tools are introduced, i.e. the gear wheel and the screw (Hero, *Mechanics* 2.1–5).[43] Hero in his *Mechanics* explains the use of windlass, lever, pulley, wedge and screw (2.7–20), and provides details for the reason why they are supposed to move large weights despite their small force (7–19).[44] At 2.20–34, he explains how these five tools could be combined for moving a large weight with small force – a fact which causes wonderment – while in Book 3 he describes how they could be more effective when being combined and working together with other implements.

The function of the mechanical automata, starting from a single external movement which comes from a hydraulic, pneumatic energy or depends on a falling weight or an ὕσπληγξ, a spring,[45] often relies on the use or combination of these tools. To give one example: at *On Automata Making* 26.6–9, Hero refers to the stationary automata, and explains how the scroll (which has sky and sea painted on it) may roll on its own; this must be taken into consideration in advance (δεῖ προμηχανήσασθαι ταῦτα) in order to include various mechanisms and techniques: we have a bar (κανών) around which the scroll is rolled, cords (σπάρτος), a bobbin, a drum, axle, pulley and a weight. When these move the aforementioned mechanisms which unroll the scroll are set in motion (see also *On Automata Making* 13.8). A correct management of materials and mechanisms could result, according to Hero, in a spontaneously driven mechanical motion of automata called ὑπάγοντα, mobile (1.2), and στατά, stationary, i.e. figures which give the impression that they move, although they do not actually change their position (1.5, ἐν κινήσει δύναται φαίνεσθαι). The latter is an older version of an automaton called θαῦμα, because it could admit more types of arrangements than the mobile one (1.7). In the same manner, as in the case of mobile automata, here, one can cause motion without getting close to the figures (1.6, καὶ ἁπλῶς, ὡς ἄντις ἔληται δυνατόν ἐστι κινεῖν μηδενὸς προσιόντος τοῖς ζῳδίοις), thus creating, once again, the impression that everything happens in a natural, automatic way.

Design would be the last parameter on which, as I argue, mechanical automation relies. Size and form, specifically, are important to a design's aesthetic qualities, its non-complexity and safety.[46] As Hero puts it, both στατά and ὑπάγοντα automata hide their working mechanisms behind the machine's performance, by placing these mechanisms where they cannot be observed, thus making them 'invisible', ἀφανῆ (*On Automata Making* 17.120.2–3, 28.2–

3).⁴⁷ The invisibility of mechanisms is interconnected with the concept of 'smallness' in mechanical technology.⁴⁸ The automaton's small size highlights the technical skills of the engineer who manages to get ever more power into an ever smaller space, and subsequently appeals to an audience which will hopefully understand the causes behind the automatic motion. For this reason, *On Automata Making* 4.4, Hero advises future automata makers to build automata that should be small enough to eradicate the suspicion that someone is sitting inside the automaton and operating it.⁴⁹

The design of the automaton is further connected with the easiness with which it is operated. Hero admits that his contemporaries developed further the art of automata-making: they introduced, so he says, a more complicated *diathesis*, arrangement, which could present ἀστεῖοι, elegant stories and involved many, disparate movements (22.1–2) – unlike an older arrangement which could only present a succession of three scenes and allowed only a limited number of movements. However, Hero does not abstain from criticizing Philon's construction of Athena's epiphany via a crane as being ἐργωδέστερος, that is, very difficult and complicated, whereas, as Hero advises, it would have been more appropriate to have an Athena that could be moved on a hinge, laid down on the scene and, when needed, be drawn up and down by cords (thus being made visible, φανῆναι, and invisible, ἀφανῆ γενέσθαι, respectively, 20.2; cf. 22.1–2). An engineering plan should be designed to direct even an ignorant user towards an uncomplicated process and safe result. This is what Hero states at *On Automata Making* 20.1 when he refers to his description of methods regarding mobile automata which, compared to those previously described, are easy to handle, riskless and, at the same time, unusual (εὐκόπως καὶ ἀκινδύνως καὶ ξένως παρὰ τὰ πρὸ ἡμῶν ἀναγεγραμμένα).⁵⁰ The qualities of simplicity and safety have to do with the construction's technical effectiveness; the latter requires the designer's thinking about where – and how much – the construction will be able to automate.⁵¹ Hence, although Hero suggests some technical improvements for stationary automata (20.1; also when he proposes a different and simpler mechanical solution for Athena's epiphany), originality or novelty are not that important (2.12). Rather, as Francesco Grillo has recently argued, the construction's technical effectiveness is what matters for Hero, unlike his peers.⁵²

Technical effectiveness is brought up by Alfred Gell as well, in his seminal paper 'The Technology of Enchantment and the Enchantment of Technology'.⁵³

Gell discusses here art as the product of techniques, and he introduces the notion of technical wonder, which increases as the audience becomes familiarized with the technical challenges involved in the process; in Hero's case, this is related to the automata's mechanical realization and functionality. Gell's technical wonder lies close to what Gilbert Simondon describes as *technoaesthetics* – a term which underscores the reciprocal implications between aesthetics and technics, and brings out the allure of technical operations which do not fully reveal themselves.[54] A technical analysis of Mona Lisa, as Simondon argues, would stress and decode the technical mystery behind her smile and increase its technical mastery. In a similar way, the Heronean wonder is, in principle, indistinguishable from the technical means which have been used in its construction. Hero's *Pneumatics* and *On Automata Making* provide the reader with the opportunity to gain an insight into the technical challenges faced by the engineer while he was manufacturing the automaton, and allows them to appreciate the designer's technical skills.[55] More importantly, the audience gets to know that the movements of the automata, apart from being the product of an engineer's skill, are also the result of tools, materials and design or arrangement. This type of wonder persists even when it has been rationally explained: it is a display of erudition on the designer's part (for ἐπίδειξη see, e.g., Hero, *On Automata Making* 4.4, 21.1).[56] Wonder, in this case, is not only related with the hidden causes of operation and motion; while it is being explained, it increases by instilling an unfailing sense of appreciation for the final product (cf. ps.-Aristotle, *Mechanics* proem 848a 34–7).[57]

The engineering process, designed by an expert, aims to construct a mechanical reality which presents inanimate matter as moving (Hero, *On Automata* 1.5, 22.4, καθάπερ <ἂν>ἐπὶ τῆς ἀληθείας γίνοιτο).[58] The sense of wonder emerging from this process is not about leaving an audience astonished and bewildered; it is directly linked with the physical outcome of the mechanical process, the mechanical device, its complexity, ποικιλία, and the way it functions (see Hero, *On Automata Making* 1.1–4, 1.7, *Pneumatics* 1. proem 16f. αἱδὲ ἐκπληκτικόν τινα θαυμασμὸν ἐπιδεικνύμεναι).[59] This is what Hero tells us in *Mechanics* 2.33, when he argues that we will be wondering how things which we thought were known to us will prove to be different when we study their principles and causes. In contrast to the technical θαῦμα of the fourth century and the one traced in Greek drama (discussed in Chapter 2), which draws a line between σοφοί, wise technicians, who know how to produce automatic motion, and the ignorant spectators, Hero posits no such distinction. Wonder is still dominantly present in the context of technical explanation which is constituted by the characteristic qualities of the materials, techniques and design.

3.4 Automated artworks or what lies within

My imagination rose, unbidden, possessed, and guided me, gifting successive images that arose in the mind with a vividness far beyond the usual bonds of reverie. I saw—with shut eyes, but acute mental vision—, I saw a pale student of the unhallowed arts kneeling beside the thing he had put together.
Mary Shelley, Preface to *Frankenstein* (1818)

Mary Shelley's appeal to the creative force of imagination reflects the blending of science and literature in the nineteenth century. Mechanical automation in antiquity, I suggest, and its principal premise of reproducing liveness through materials and hidden mechanisms, influences how artefacts are generally represented: the crucial element added by mechanics in this case is the fact that the audience's imagination is energized towards thinking about and around what is seen, what remains hidden from the senses and what had never existed.[60] This is different from the way *phantasia* works in oratory or theatre: in that case, we speak about the orator's or actor's capacity to only generate visual images of something known and seen which in turn are transferred to those who are listening.[61] In her study of the relationship between ekphrastic and mechanical thought, Roby argues that in both contexts imagination is expected to be mobilized as a creative force.[62] The interplay between imagination and reality in engineering procedures is also acknowledged by Hero himself. In his *Pneumatics*, acoustic details add to the vividness of his description and enforce *phantasia*. At 1.29.1–5, we are told that positioning a cup and producing the noise of running water in front of a drinking animal will make the audience imagine the feeling of thirst ([...] ὥστε φαντασίαν ποιεῖν δίψης [...]; see also *On Automata Making* 30.5).[63]

Mechanical automatic technology, however, does not merely represent or enhance what already exists and is visible. It discloses, at the same time, what could lie inside or behind a device or suggests an image that does not reflect the reality and in this way questions classical theories of artistic representation.[64] Consider, for instance, how the famous bronze cow of Myron is depicted as animated in a number of epigrams. The cow wanders off, joins the herd, ploughs the field, suckles a calf and is mounted by a bull.[65] However, according to Pliny the Elder (*Natural History* 34.57–8), even Myron – most likely, a fifth-century BCE sculptor – 'although very careful in relation to bodies, did not represent inner feelings' (34.58, *et ipse tamen corporum tenus curiosus animi sensus non expressisse*).[66]

The difficulty in depicting what lies or should lie behind an artefact's animative potential is overcome by engineering and the technical explanation itself. This explanation extends beyond the mere spectacle of the living artefact and duels on its inner technical and material causes.[67] There is now a technical and material side to artefacts: for instance, in the case of Aristonidas' statue of Athamas after he had hurled his son Learchus from the rock, the intense emotion of shame is fleshed out 'by the rust of the iron shining through the brilliant surface of the copper' (Pliny, *Natural History* 34.140). This material and moreover technical information increases rhetorical vividness and acts as a technique through which things become alive for the listener.

The view, moreover that engineering serves art in such away that it might even surpass nature's constructing skills is attested most clearly in the sixth-century writer Cassiodorus Senator. In a letter to Boethius, Cassiodorus emphasizes that '[o]nly engineering tries to imitate it [i.e. nature] by contraries, and, in some things, if it is proper to say so, even seeks to surpass it. For this art, we know, made Daedalus fly; it suspends the iron Cupid without support in the temple of Diana; it daily makes dumb objects sing, inanimate live, immobile move. The engineer, if it is proper to say so, is almost a partner of nature, unlocking her secrets, changing what she reveals, playing with wonders, and making such exquisite counterfeits that we take for truth what is certainly artificial' (Variae 1.45. 10–11).[68]

In the second chapter of this book, in my discussion of *technomimesis*, I investigated a type of mimesis, which is close to what is described in Plato as phantastic imitation (e.g. *Sophist* 264a–b3), according to which an image could be represented not in real terms but based on a certain viewpoint of the perceiver and through various instruments. This type of mimesis is being further cultivated through the mechanical art and is paired with a type of *phantasia* which specifically reveals what is not being represented, that is, the unseen or the non-existed. We come across this type of *phantasia*, for instance, in Horace's famous description of unreal creatures such as centaurs, mermaids at the beginning of his *The Art of Poetry* 1–15 (see also Vitruvius, *On Architecture* 7.5.3). This is also explicitly displayed in Philostratus' *Life of Apollonius of Tyana*. There, *phantasia* stands in contrast to mimesis which imitates only what can be seen through the eyes (6.19).[69] This type of *phantasia* and the mechanical art by expanding the number of possibilities that a human designer can use in reproducing or transforming reality, consider, are increasing the reach mimesis.

*

I will now to late antique sources of automation, specifically to the depictions of artworks by Callistratus,[70] an orator of the fourth or fifth century CE.[71] The reason for doing so is not just the fact that technical causes behind artefacts' liveness, and their influence on art perception become especially apparent in late antiquity;[72] it also has to do with the increasing emphasis, in this period, on materials. This is probably due to what Patricia Cox Miller calls the 'material turn' which occurs between the fourth and seventh centuries and defines the religious materialism of the Neoplatonic theurgists and the Neoplatonic ideas on art perception,[73] where matter is positively evaluated.[74] This material turn has three distinctive characteristics which facilitate the deployment of the concept of automated artwork in artworks' descriptions: first, late antique art perception-theory is grounded in sense perception, *aesthesis* and *phantasia*: the late antique notion of *aesthesis* describes, as Eyjolfur Kjalar Emilsson puts it, 'a cognitive power in its own right and not merely an instrument of cognitive powers';[75] *phantasia* as a faculty of the soul plays in this period an active role in shaping the objects of its perception, rather than passively receiving the information of sense experience (that said, associations between *phantasia* and 'passive intellect' features were still active in late Antiquity and Byzantium).[76] Moreover, *phantasia* is linked by some

Neoplatonists with inspiration: thus, it is considered that it opens up the possibility to imagine the unseen, the divine or the supernatural (see e.g. Iamblichus *On the Mysteries* 3.2–3 and 3.14), as in the case of the mechanical concept of *phantasia* mentioned above.[77]

The second feature of this material turn is related to the artist-genius which can have access to the principles of nature and thus imitate them and consequently improve nature.[78] The last characteristic, which relates to theurgy, supports the active cooperation between the material and the demiurge and how the former is made accessible to the divine.[79] As Iamblichus claims in his *On the Mysteries*, the divinized *demiurge* conceives matter as being connatural (συμφυής) with Soul, the Intellect and the One (5.23). What is more, aside from the influence of the contribution of Neoplatonic metaphysics on the conception of matter and consequently *technê* and the artist's capacities, technological development in late antiquity allowed mechanics to refer, as Proclus states, to 'the entire art of moving matter' (in his commentary on the First Book of Euclid's *Elements*, p. 41, 18, καὶ ὅλως πᾶσα ἡ τῆς ὕλης κινητική).[80]

3.4.1. Callistratus' description of automatic statues

By employing the figure of the technical automaton, Callistratus manages to go beyond the suggestion that the sculpture's vivid presence is a by-product of the spectator's imagination and the orator's skills. He takes the audience back to the very beginning of the artwork's manufacturing process and presents the wonder of art's agency by explaining how this is made possible. In this context, the artefact's animated features are not linked to the artist's alleged magical powers,[81] nor are they defined as a 'mistake' of the viewer's perception.[82] Rather, the fascination of the animated artefact lies, as in the case of the mechanical automaton, in the technical and material conditions of the artefact itself and, consequently, in the orator's ingenuity to present these in a clear and vivid way. Consequently, the sense of wonderment sparked by Callistratus' allegedly animated sculpture, similar to the wonder inspired by mechanical automata, engages the senses in a constructive way: the audience stares at the moving statues, and widens its eyes in front of the technical excellence of the artefact in order to learn how this could be accomplished (see, e.g., 3.4 καὶ ἦν θαυμαστὸς οἷος ὁ χαλκός, 5.5 τοῦτον θαυμάσας, ὠνέοι, 6.4 καὶ τὸ μὲν ἡμῖν θαῦμα τοιοῦτον ἥ, 9.1, Ἐθέλω δέ σοι καὶ τὸ Μέμνονος ἀφηγήσασθαι θαῦμα).[83] By contrast, in the absence of a technical explanation, listeners and spectators of art face the risk of being distracted by an arresting spectacle, and become enslaved by its sight (10.2, δουλοῦται τὴν αἴσθησιν).[84] A close examination of a statue can reveal its techniques and tricks, as in the case of the statue of a youth (11.3, ὡς δὲ καὶ κατὰ μέρος ἐξητάζομεν τὴν τέχνην καὶ τὰ ἐν αὐτῇ δαιδάλματα).[85] These techniques, if they remain unexplained, could make viewers fall into a state of ἀφασία, speechlessness (11.3, ἀφασίᾳ πληγέντες εἱστήκειμεν; see also 2.3, ὑπὸ ἀφασίας ἔστημεν).[86] The most renowned victim of such an encounter is Narcissus; the love he develops for his own image (σχῆμα), due to its aliveness (ζωτικός and ἔμπνους), proves fatal (5.4).[87] Art lovers must develop an exploratory approach towards art in order to discover its truth and thereby enjoy it without taking any risks. If there is trickery in this kind of art, it only tricks the ignorant observer who is unaware of the true explanation behind the moving image.

An art expert can decode the artisan's techniques and avoid the dangerous effects of such a spectacle. In the depiction of the Kairos-statue of Lysippus, Callistratus notes that there was a man who knew how to trace the craftsman's mechanisms, and thus he could provide logical explanations (λογισμὸν ἐπῇδε) on how art could deceive the senses of the viewers (6.4; cf. 7.2, ὡς ἀπατᾶν τὴν αἴσθησιν, 8.4, ὁδὲ θύρσος ἠπάτα τὴν αἴσθησιν [...]). This man is called by Callistratus a 'tracker of wonders' (ἀνιχνεύειν θαύματα). The wonder-tracker is in a position to appreciate the δύναμις, the force, stored inside the statue.[88]

Callistratus explains that the feathers on the statue's feet, πτέρωμα, imply (αἰνίττεσθαι) the feature of swiftness, while conveying, at the same time, the impression of the passing of time throughout the seasons (ἐποχούμενος).[89] This movement communicates a sense of circular movement around the axis of the statue (ἀνελίττων) which is situated on a sphere (6.2, εἱστήκει δὲ ἐπί τινος σφαίρας).[90] As far as the statue's beauty is concerned, the art expert explains that this depends on the moment in which the viewer encounters the spinning statue.[91] Hence, κατὰ τὸν δέοντα καιρόν, in the ideal moment, one would meet the statue during its youth and ultimate beauty. That is, as the statue turns around, one must be careful not to disregard it and be deprived of such a manifestation of beauty (6.4, προσιόντος [...] παρελθόντος).

Behind a statue's activities lies the artisan's ability to 'implant' mechanisms inside the sculpture in order to give the impression of liveness (cf. 2.5, Scopas ἀπετυποῦτο τὰ θαύματα). The lack of technical ingenuity, on the other hand, constitutes, according to Callistratus, a sign of superficial art. This is what we learn, in Depiction 4, concerning the statue of an Indian, where Callistratus claims that, because of his lack of means, the sculptor fails to portray drunkenness and to make the cheeks of the statue look red (4.3, οὐ γὰρ ἦν αὐτῷ μηχάνημα τὰς παρειὰς φοινῖξαι σκέποντος τοῦ μέλανος τὴν μέθην); thus, the pathos – i.e. the drunkenness of the Indian – can be indicated only through his outer schema and form. The statue of the drunken Indian, according to Callistratus, lacks delicacy (4.4, εἶχε δὲ ἁβρὸν οὐδὲν) and charm (4.4, χάρις), and consequently liveness.[92]

By highlighting the artist's skill to construct statues, Callistratus downplays, as I mentioned above, the idea that, allegedly, moving art in general is the product of divine, magical or even theurgical power.[93] For example, Eros' statue made by Praxiteles, as described by Meleager (*Greek Anthology* 12.56, 12.57),[94] is evidently animated by the god Eros' magical capacities (ὁ δὲ νῦν ἔμψυχα μαγεύων).[95] In contrast, Callistratus' description of the same image suggests that the bronze was mastered and 'brought to life' by Praxiteles: on Callistratus' interpretation, the material meets the artist's demands and is consequently made fit to convey the emotional reality of the depicted character (3.2).[96] More specifically, Callistratus states that when Praxiteles manufactured Eros' statue, not only did he provide the statue with movement and sensation, but, more importantly, he almost gave it the ability to think (3.5).[97] He then says at 3.5 that 'by admiring Praxiteles' statue one could indeed believe the myth, Daedalus made living statues'.

When referring to the mechanisms of artificial liveness, Callistratus becomes especially vivid sometimes. He notes, for instance, that Scopas' statue of the Bacchante is stimulated by a sense of breathing (2.1, ὥσπερ ἔκ τινος ἐπιπνοίας κινηθείς).[98] This impetus is conveyed into the statue, filling it with Bacchic frenzy (2.1 [...] τί δὲ ὑμῖν οὐκ ἄνωθεν τὸν ἐνθουσιασμὸν τῆς τέχνης διηγοῦμαι; cf. 10.2). The statue then, by setting the instrumental element of *pneuma* into motion, creates further interactions: activated by breathing, it becomes eager to go to Cithaeron and live the Dionysian experience (2.4; cf. 5.4).[99] Seen from this perspective, Scopas' pneumatic artworks, according to Callistratus, differ from the images created by Demosthenes' words, which, in order to come to life, require the help of νοῦς and φρόνησις, the mind and intelligence, and the 'spells' of rhetorical art (2.5, τέχνης φάρμακα).[100]

The notion that air under pressure can make matter move is also used in relation to the Satyr's statue (1).[101] Callistratus observes here how the artist has made the stone of the statue able to convey the feeling of the depicted flute-player (1.3), by transforming the air in the Satyr's lung into *pneuma*, air, which is vital for the production of music;[102] he then concedes that the allegedly talking statue of Memnon, manufactured by the Ethiopians, could actually have a voice (1.5, τοῦτο θεασάμενοι τὸ εἴδωλον καὶ τὸν Αἰθιόπων λίθον ἔμφωνον Μέμνονος ἐπιστεύομεν γενέσθαι, cf. 9.3).[103] Callistratus believes that the Ethiopians, when constructing this particular statue, must have discovered the way to make it talk; they must have found a solution to the same *aporia* with which Daedalus was faced with regard to speechless stone (9.3).[104] Even though Daedalus is capable of creating lifelike statues (explicitly defined as θαύματα in 8.1), he still is, in contrast to the Ethiopians, unable to give to marble statues one of the most important characteristics of liveliness, i.e. voice.[105] By contrast, Memnon's statue is even capable of changing sounds according to light and brightness:[106] when sunbeams move across the surface of the statue, it becomes filled with voice (9.1).[107] A similar phenomenon is described by Hero at *Pneumatics* 2.13. Here, by means of sun and heated air, a fountain, probably designed to be placed in the outdoor area of a sanctuary, trickles. Thus, rejecting the assumption that the sound which the statue makes is the result of a natural, sonic phenomenon, as described by Pausanias (1.42.3) or an epiphanic phenomenon, as explained by Philostratus (*Life of Apollonius of Tyana* 6.4, the statue rises and makes obeisance to the Sun),[108] Callistratus thinks that the technical skills of the Ethiopians are responsible for the talking statue of Memnon (9.3).

Now, the technical explanation of the spectacle of the *living* artefact influences the way viewers experience artistic materials, too. As already noted above, automatic technology emphasizes the link between the perception of materials and their physical properties. This, again, turns out to have an impact on the way materials and the behaviour of materials are being depicted in relation to artefacts. In the case of Callistratus, the materials, i.e. their hardness, ductility or shine, do not just passively register the emotions and external features of the sculptured images but actively represent them. On many occasions, for instance, the hard and dry stone becomes soft and wet in order to allude to femininity (3.2, 6.3, 3.4; cf. *Diseases of Young Girls* 1, Aristotle, *Parts of Animals* 648a 9–18 on female wetness and softness).[109] In the depiction of the statue of the Youth in 11.4, the bronze makes itself erotically desirable by simulating the radiant flesh and the curling of the hair. Moreover, in 14.3–4, the wax, in its attempt to imitate the sea, appropriates the sea's qualities, beguiling the senses and giving the impression that the artefact is being tossed by the wind. In the depiction of Dionysus' statue, the bronze blushes, expressing gracefulness and desire (8.2–3). At 8.5 τὸ βακχεύσιμον ὁ χαλκὸς ἐνεδείκνυτο, 'the bronze exhibited the Bacchic madness' (see also 2.2–3).[110] In depiction 5, stone appears as though it was struggling to simulate Narcissus' story, as his watery reflection dissolves from solid to liquid (5.4–5, esp. τὸ δὲ οὐ λόγῳ ῥητὸν λίθος εἰς ὑγρότητα κεχαλασμένος καὶ ἐναντίον σῶμα τῇ οὐσίᾳ παρεχόμενος). Likewise, the bronze in the depiction of the god Eros reduces its hardness and becomes plump and supple in order to match the god's female traits (3.2, cf. 8.2, 11.1 on void, i.e. lack of matter). In depicting this statue, Callistratus recounts that the bronze responds to the touch,[111] creating the impression of interaction. He says specifically that the statue's hair moves when touched (3.4, ἁψαμένῳ δὲ ἡ θρὶξ ὑπεξανίστατο μαλθακιζομένη πρὸς τὴν αἴσθησιν, see also 7.2, καὶ πρὸς τὰς ζεφύρου πνοὰς σειομένη [sc. the hair of Orpheus' statue] δονεῖται).[112]

Matter's ability to reproduce bodily automatisms such as motion, health, sickness, as well as emotions, is further emphasized in cases of artefacts which host divine figures. By praising, for example, Paean's statue (Depiction 10), Callistratus praises the artistic material hosting the god's figure, health and youth, as well as the artist who proves able to manipulate it; at some point, however, the material, ὕλη, of Paean's statue decides to obey not the logos of art but the god whom it resembles and supports, for instance, the moisture and vitality of the god's curly hair (10.3).[113] This idea is bolstered with an analogy. As Callistratus puts it, since we accept that the divine dwells in some humans and becomes embedded in their vulnerable flesh, we should be ready to accept that certain materials, which do not have the weaknesses of human flesh, are worthy of hosting a god (10.1).[114]

*

In a similar way, Triphiodorus, a contemporary of Callistratus,[115] describes the Trojan Horse in the *Taking of Ilios* by laying special emphasis on its makers (Epeius and Athena, 57f.), the material which has been used (59–61) and the method of construction (62–102).[116] By highlighting the motion of the Horse (74, 79, 84–6) via the description of its wheels (99–102), as well as through the references to the construction of its bodily parts such as the belly, the neck, the limbs, the teeth, the eyes and ears, or to its functions like breathing and hearing, Triphiodorus encourages the audience's conscious awareness of the technical qualities and principles of the Horse's function. Eventually, the various techniques applied to the horse for bolstering its lifelike qualities arouse amazement (247f., οἱ δ' ὅτε τεχνήεντος ἴδον δέμας αἰόλον ἵππου,/ θαύμασαν ἀμφιχυθέντες).

This type of marvelling at the technical details of material liveness becomes even more obvious in Quintus Smyrnaeus' fourth-century epic description of the Trojan Horse (12.105–12). Similar to Triphiodorus, Quintus also refers to the Horse's maker, Epeius (with the divine help of Athena), to the material of the Horse's construction, and, finally, to the way every bodily part of the Horse is fashioned, particularly its feet, belly, back and loins behind, the throat in front, the towering neck, the crested head, the streaming tail, the ears and the lucent eyes. The people of Argos marvelled at this construction, or, as Quintus puts it, they marvelled at how the wood was forced to express vigour, the speed of the feet and how the horse seemed to neigh (πολὺς δ' ἐπεγήθεε λαὸς Ἀργείων, θαύμαζε δ' ὅπως ἐπιδούρατι θυμὸς καὶ τάχος ἐκπεπότητο ποδῶν, χρεμέθοντι δ' ἐῴκει).

3.4.2. Some examples of automatic art in Early Byzantine *ekphrasis*

The notion of the automatic artefact continued to be attested later, during the early Byzantine period. Along with the descriptions of real automata, such as cisterns,[117] weathervanes[118] and mechanical clocks,[119] the concept of automatic artefact is also adopted in descriptions of churches and in secular art, demonstrating the continuation of classical and late antique thought into the early Byzantine world.[120] The horologion of Gaza, for example, pictured Heracles accomplishing his twelve labours in the course of twelve hours. Its description survives in Procopius, who, while remaining true to classical models of representation, just as his fellow orators from the school of Gaza, reflects also contemporary ideology. According to Hermann A. Diels, Procopius pays no attention to the clock's mechanical construction since he does not wish to reveal the mechanism's secret and thus destroy the workings of the παράδοξος *kinesis* of the figures which surprise the spectators (5.8f., Ἀλλὰ προέλαβε τῆι παραδόξωι τ<ι> κινήσει <, ὅ>τ<ι> φοβεῖ τοὺς θεατάς, ed. Amato, Ventrella, Corcella and Maréchaux 2014).[121] Hence, wonderment here does not stem from the technical exploration of automation; rather, it is associated with a type of wonderment which, as Christine Hunzinger has shown in a number of papers,[122] prefers to leave the audience astonished rather than enlighten it about the techniques behind the θαῦμα (see, e.g., proem lines 1–7). Specifically, Procopius seems to build on the notion of the Herodotean wonder, which is connected with monuments that survived through time due to their extraordinary construction and required labour.[123] It is precisely for this reason that he describes the clock's overall creation as the wonderful outcome of the technician's labour (proem 3, θαῦμα τοῦ ποιήσαντος).

Later in the text, however, Procopius goes beyond the use of classical oratorical techniques by assigning mechanical features to the sensorial reality of the moving figures. He attempts to explain wonders like the Egyptian Pyramids, which were already depicted as θαύματα in Herodotus, the temple of Bal Zeus in Babylon and the Hephaestean automatic artefacts (including Alcinous' dogs), in juxtaposition to the clock's real construction (15–52). As he puts it, all of Hephaestus' automata belonged, until now, to the realm of fable (*mythos*); but if one looks at the moving images of the horologion (particularly that of Heracles), one has to admit that some degree of reality should be granted to Hephaestus' moving images (6). Moreover, near the end of the *ekphrasis*, Procopius describes how sound is produced by a trumpet in honour of Heracles' last labour. Sound has also been detected earlier in the text, during the slaughter of the lion of Nemea; here, the sound of the bronze sword mingles with the roaring lion and manages to surprise the god Pan who then starts moving. By calling attention to the acoustic elements of this scene, the text reflects on how the encounter with this spectacle could offer an experience which involves more than one senses; one both listens and sees, and this has an amplifying effect.

The spectacle of an automated artwork that is revealed through technical and material details is more emphatically attested in relation to the description of church interiors. According to Ruth Webb, '[t]he movement attributed to the architectural features may also be a means of suggesting the actual experience of the visitor who is moving around the church and for whom the architecture is an intricate and ever-changing pattern of forms'.[124] This is true, but one should also consider how engineering and science, which influenced the decorative and architectural design of the churches, might be reflected in their descriptions. Nadine Schibille, for instance, has recently explored the significance of optics and catoptrics for indicating and explaining the animative power of Hagia Sophia. Schibille contends that one major concern in the sixth-century architectural design of this church was exactly the visual effects of its sacred interior, specifically the luminosity within the church (cf. Vitruvius 1.2.7, 6.4, 6.6.6 generally on light in buildings).[125]

The author, Paul the Silentiary,[126] in his *ekphrasis* on the Hagia Sophia, a poem recited early in 563 soon after the church's second consecration (on December 24, 562), emphatically echoes this approach. He first describes how the work of the church's skilful architect, the mathematician Anthemius of Tralles (267–73), actually saved the church from total destruction (265–72), then, how this 'scientific building' should be perceived as a marvel (see v. 70, τὸ πάντα νικῶν θαυμάτων ὑπερβολῆι),[127] and continues by explaining how the church becomes technically automated: the arches seem to be roaming in the air (401, ἁψὶς ἠερόφοιτος), conches (κάρηνον) spring up into the air and the piers of the church 'rise up' (463–5; cf. 353, 367, 374); the material's movement is schematized through circles and triangles. Towards the end of the poem, the author employs a type of engineered animation that is non-mimetic and performative and which is associated with the church's illumination: he describes how the cunning craftsman pierced silver discs, attached them to chains around the church's central confines and decorated them with glass so that they provide light for people at night (light stems also from the cross-shaped πολυκάνδηλα);[128] those are suspended circle-wise in the air. The circling choir of bright lights gives the impression that the believers are outside, gazing at the moving stars (806–33).[129]

Procopius of Caesarea, a sixth-century scholar, in his *On Buildings* is also interested, as Michael Roberts notices, in 'construction rather than decoration, insofar as a distinction is possible, and it emphasises the marvellous craftsmanship rather than brilliant effects of light'.[130] He thus explains how the engineers Anthemius and Isidore used many devices to give stability to the church, making it a θέαμα κεκαλλιστευμένον, the most beautiful sight (I.1.27). This building – which is, according to Procopius, 'wonderful in [...] beauty yet altogether terrifying by the apparent precariousness of its composition'[131] (I.1.33, τῇ μὲν εὐπρεπείᾳ θαυμάσιον, τῷ δὲ σφαλερῷ τῆς συνθέσεως δοκοῦν τι εἶναι φοβερὸν ὅλως) – has many amazing features: the domes of the church seem to float in the air; the columns are placed on the ground as if they are dancing; the piers, from which the arches spring, are elevated (I.1.32–6). In the same period, Choricius of Gaza, however, in his description of the church of St Stergius, argues that the exterior of the church is so wonderful that it prevents him from stepping inside (1.17). As in the classical/traditional type of *ekphrasis*, here wonderment signifies the audience's bedazzlement when encountering the incomprehensible beauty of the monument, which is materialized through the orator's literary virtuosity. Ekphrastic θαῦμα can, thus, be explained in two ways in late antiquity and early Byzantium: as part of a nostalgic return to an old classical pattern of representing artefacts, buildings and figural decoration; and as a response to the scientific discourse and practice especially embedded in ecclesiastical architecture.

At any rate, the technical explanation of the church-building is seen as necessary for the spiritual understanding of the believers; it helps them to turn their attention from the material and the technical to the spiritual. By employing the trope of technical explanation of the scientific wonder, an orator overcomes the risk of distracting the audience through a spectacle caused by the church building itself. In this way, the audience does not run the risk of failing to reach the divine glory.

3.5 Conclusions

From the fourth century BCE onwards, the technical automaton played a crucial role in the philosophical, mechanical and artistic discourse. Hence, I have started this chapter by referring to various meanings of the technical automaton in the fourth century and how this is used as a means for explaining and describing motion and animation. Then, I moved on to investigate the automaton's mechanical transformation, mainly in Hero of Alexandria, and, finally, I turned to the deployment of mechanical automation in art description. I have argued here that the mechanical automaton opens up a new dimension in the creation and perception of artefacts; it reveals new aesthetic possibilities, marking a general shift in aesthetic style or preference: more specifically, the wonderment one experiences when encountering an artefact that is allegedly animated appears to change after the introduction of automatic machinery. In this last part of the chapter, I focused on late antique and early Byzantine *ekphrasis*, and I have outlined the animated artefact's mechanical explanation by presenting the importance given by *ekphrasis* to the valuable role of the artistic mechanism and the properties of the materials in the production of moving images and in the cultivation of an educated audience which is able to appreciate a technological miracle without being dumbfounded by it.[132]

Conclusions

The book argues that understanding how natural automatisms, such as motion and processes such as growth, intermingle with technology requires to travel along three interrelated axes: by positioning automatisms and automation at the core of nature, human body and the material and mechanical, this book explores: first, up to what point operation patterns of natural automatisms serve as a source of inspiration for technical automation; second, it discusses the social consequences of natural automatisms' technical reconstruction, especially in relation to human skills and capacities; and, third, it examines the relationship between automatisms, the mechanical automaton and techniques of artistic animation. In doing so, this book opens the study of automation, natural, technical and mechanical, to types of questions which relate to the fantasies associated with artificiality, the notion of liveness, the utopian motif of automatic *bios*, the shifting of agencies from bodies to tools and devices and the unstable boundaries between the organic and the non-organic where limbs are perceived as tools or weapons, and tools and weapons as artificial limbs.

The first chapter deals with technical automation in the archaic period. It observes that this directly reflects nature's automatisms, while in the classical period, as presented on the Athenian stage, it is established as a distinct power, further defined through the intention of its manufacturers and users, and thereby often conveyed as a threatening force towards the natural and its automatisms. This development is explored further in the second chapter, where I examine the way in which the figure of automaton in Athenian drama serves as allegory for the various outcomes of the porous boundaries between mimesis, *technê* and reality. The merging of the human, with artefacts and devices is evident in this case. More specifically, the chapter considers the cultural malleability of the figure of the automaton, asking how the automaton is put into dialogue with mimesis, theatrical liveness, the use of weaponry, the wish for replaceable body parts, the results of divine and educational practices. The chapter also explores whether readings of the automaton as 'uncanny' apply to cases of mad characters in drama. Finally, it proposes ways in which we can examine how to include the metaphor of the 'dramatic automaton' in technological discussions, not least because real mechanical performances as well exploit the co-presence of constructed, animate characters and audience.

From the fourth century BCE onwards, technical automation is used as a heuristic device for illustrating ideas about motion and liveness. The introduction of the mechanical automaton in the Hellenistic period, on the other hand, allows for the actual representation of technology as a life-giving force. Mechanical automata are defined by mechanical feasibility which is based on design or engineering plan, tools and materials. The automatic process determines the automaton's movements and, once actualized mechanically, is invariable: the automaton will reproduce the body's automatic functions, for instance, stand up, walk, dance, sing and so on. Successful automation obscures its mechanical control. Nevertheless, mechanical treatises and especially Hero's treatises on automatic devices give the opportunity to the audience to look inside them. A self-powered device whose mechanisms are designed to remain hidden causes wonderment which increases through the explanation of its workings. This is best described through what Alfred Gell calls technological wonder and Gilbert Simondon calls *technoaesthetics*.[1]

The last part of this chapter explores the ways in which ekphrastic techniques use experiences of the automatic to constitute modes of explanation of the mechanisms of animation. Inanimate matter is transformed in this context into live matter: the materiality of the artefacts which are being described activates a sensory response, while their alleged motion suggests a certain aliveness which is explained as dependent on mechanical principles and processes and the engineer or artist who function as the animating agents. The sense of fascination and wonder, which accompanies the imaginary animation of the artefacts, cannot be elucidated without explaining first the ineffable material dimension and mechanical processes which lie behind technological animation.

What I hope to have shown in this book is that technical automation in classical antiquity holds both a mirror to nature and opens a window for human artistry, depending on its historical and scientific environment. The book argues that natural automatisms function as a kind of conceptual umbrella which covers both the possibilities and the consequences of the collapse of the distinction between the categories of the natural and the technical or artificial, the animate and the inanimate. Technical automata in classical antiquity that use principles from nature to provide inspiration for technical applications could inform contemporary cases of biologically inspired devices with improved and enhanced capabilities over traditional ones. In other words, natural patterns are used in both antiquity and the contemporary world as suggestions for the search of effective technical designs and solutions; these are applied, modified or even rejected with aim at improving the quality of human life and natural world.

Notes

Introduction

1 See on that Naas (2018), ch. 2, esp. p. 61, and cf. Plato's *Phaedrus* at 245e on autokinesis.
2 Schürmann (1991); Pugliara (2002); Berryman (2003, 2009); De Groot (2014); Bianchi (2006) and (2014), ch. 2; Roby (2016); Mayor (2018). See also Chapuis and Droz (1958); Price (1964); Cambiano (1994a); Tybjerg (2003); Bosak-Schroeder (2016); Ruffell (forthcoming a–b).
3 See, e.g., in Descartes' *Treatise on Man*, vol. VI 55–6, and vol. VII 32 (Adam and Tannery 1904) and in the *Discourse*, vol. I, 139–40, and vol. II, 21 (Descartes 1988). See further, among others, Huxley (1874) and Janet (1889) on the notion of the automatic as describing non-intentional human action. See also the results of the Research Training Group Automatisms at the University of Paderborn (available online: https://www.uni-paderborn.de/en/research-training-group-automatisms, accessed 15 March 2022). They argue that automatisms are generally positioned between conscious actions and completely involuntary acts. See specifically, Bublitz, Marek, Steinmann and Winkler (2010).
4 As Emanuela Bianchi argues in her analysis on automation in Aristotle: explained in relation to the Indo-European root *men-* which could mean either 'to be very eager to do' or 'to think', the automaton could be explained as if it is 'self-moving because it appears to be possessed of a mind' (2014), 68.
5 Dudley (2012), 50–3.
6 See e.g. *Places in Man* 33; *Internal Affections* 33; *On Articulations* 46.27f.
7 Holmes (2010b), 142–7, and (2013).
8 Specifically on spontaneous generation in Aristotle biological works, see Balme (1962); Lennox (1982) and (2001); Gotthelf (1989).
9 On that see Bianchi, Brill and Holmes (2019); Chesi and Spiegel (2020).
10 I shall not explore here this topic, since previous scholars have already discussed extensively the meaning of *technê* in the Graeco-Roman word: see e.g. Kube (1969); Löbl (1997, 2003, 2008); Zhmud (2006); Cuomo (2007). Aristotle argues in *Nicomachean Ethics* 6.4, that art, in general, is concerned with bringing something forth which cannot do it by itself and does not yet lie here before us

(cf. Plato *Symposium* 205b). See also Heidegger (1977) who claims that ancient *technê* – belonging to the realm of *poiesis* – brings 'forth' and reveals the real while modern technology (based on exact sciences) challenges the truth.

11 See, among others, on technology in the archaic period Heinimann (1961); Kube (1969), Schneider (1986); Löbl (1997) and Chapter 1 in this book. What I argue here and in the first chapter is in line with what Vernant (1991b) observes about archaic art as something that is deprived of the concept of the image or the notion of the copy; but see Neer (2010a–b) on this.

12 Zhmud (2006), 45f.; see also Holmes (2010b), 142–7 and (2013) and Chapter 1 in this book.

13 Löbl (2003); Zhmud (2006), 28, 45–54 on *technê* in this period and Chapter 2 in this book.

14 Cuomo (2007), esp. ch. 1. On the role of *technê* in the taxonomy of knowledge, see most recently Johansen (2021).

15 Bensaude-Vincent and Newman (2007).

16 Blumenberg (2000), 18; the essay was first published in the journal *Studium Generale* in 1957.

17 On that see Berryman (2009), ch. 6, and (2020), 245; and Gerolemou (forthcoming b).

18 De Groot (2014), 17.

19 Benjamin (1935).

20 On mimesis and automation see Reilly (2011).

21 See especially Berryman (2009), 50–3 and Chapter 3 in this book. But see Tybjerg (2003).

22 Gell (1992).

23 Simondon (2012). He says: 'The techno-aesthetic feeling seems to be a category that is more primitive than the aesthetic feeling alone, or than the technical aspect considered from the angle of functionality alone (which is an impoverishing perspective)' (p. 7).

24 On Homeric automata as robots, see Mayor (2018); on Homeric automata and magic, see Faraone (1987). For Homeric automata as ekphrastic material see, among others, Kokolakis (1980); Francis (2009a). On the Iliadic automata and their relation to a kind of material energy and force see Bielfeldt (2014).

25 In contrast to Kenaan (2008), 36; Lather (2018).

26 On that, see Berryman (2003, 2009).

27 On the relationship between ekphrastic and mechanical writing, see Roby (2016).

28 Given the centuries-long period covered in this book, there are many themes I could not elucidate to their fullest extent, also because of the practical consideration of this book's length.

29 Cf. Kakoudaki (2014) who cautions against a '"time-line" approach' (p. 16), in which contemporary stories of automata are provided with premodern equivalents.

Chapter 1

1. On gestural autonomy and kinetic spontaneity specifically in Homer, see Purves (2019).
2. But see: Kenaan (2008), 36; Lather (2018), 339: 'She [sc. Pandora] models the triumph of *technê* over physis.'
3. This might be true for the Hephaestean chains as well, which are described as falling around Ares and Aphrodite of their own accord (*Odyssey* 8.296f.); see Cullhed (2014), 202.
4. Amato et al.
5. See Amato and Maréchaux (2014), 139: 'dans un movement d'automate'; similarly, Diels (1917), 28 translates: 'in selbstständiger Bewegung'.
6. Merry and Riddell (1886), 284, following Wilhelm Nitzsch (1831), 143f., refer to Homer's tendency to use 'hyperbolical expressions about works of imitative or mechanical art. Such expressions are intended to be a tribute to the skill of the artist.' See also Steiner (forthcoming), arguing that the animation of the *Hephaestoteukta* could also be attributed to their anthropomorphism (see, e.g. the emphasis on their ears 18.378).
7. Frontisi-Ducroux (1975), 101; Morris (1992), 10f.; Berryman (2009), ch. 1; Delcourt (1957), ch. 3; Faraone (1987).
8. Lather (2018). But see Liveley and Thomas who argue that the Iliadic automata possess a 'simple mind model akin to that of the slave who obeys the spoken orders of a master' (2020: 31).
9. Krafft (1972), 364; Schneider (1986), 23; Humphrey, Oleson and Sherwood (1998), 61; Irby-Massie and Keyser (2002) 150; Kalligeropoulos and Vasileiadou (2008); Mayor (2018,) 144–50.
10. Faraone (1987); cf. Delcourt (1957). See also Lather (2018), adopting Faraone's idea on Hephaestus' animate artefacts as operating by magic, adding to the idea that these are an extension of the god's mind (in terms of EMT: extended mind thesis).
11. Graf (1997) 14. On an anthropological approach to the relationship between religion and technology, see Frazer ([1890] 1889); Malinowski (1948), esp. p. 67; Simondon (2017), 174. See also Gell (1988), 9, and (1992) who suggests, in a

relevant context, to particularly see magical production as a flattering image of a production that is achievable through technical means and principles. See a case of magical automation in Euripides, *Cyclops* 646–8: ἀλλ' οἶδ' ἐπῳδὴν Ὀρφέως γαθὴν πάνυ / ὥστ' αὐτόματον τὸν δαλὸν ἐς τὸ κρανίον / στείχονθ' ὑφάπτειν τὸν μονῶπα παῖδα γῆς; 'But I know an incantation of Orpheus which is so beautiful that the firebrand on its own accord will march up to his skull and set on fire the one-eyed son of earth.' 35 Cf. Eusebius, *Reply to Hierocles* 18, 22, 27, 38, where automatic tripods are considered to be tools of wizardry not wisdom.

12 Lather (2018); see also n. 7.

13 Generally, on ekphrastic, descriptive animation, see, among others, Webb (2009); Bussels (2012); van Eck (2015).

14 See Eustathius of Thessaloniki at *Iliad* 18. 373–7, vol. 4, p. 194 and p. 208. See also the Iliadic *scholion* T18.483–606 (IV 530.13–15) and Cullhed (2014), 200f.

15 Kokolakis (1980); Francis (2009a) 11. See further Becker (1995), 80, 139, and De Jong (2011) with further bibliography, esp. in fn. 4. See also Cullhed (2014), 198, 200–19.

16 Delcourt (1957), 48–64; Faraone (1992), ch. 2; see also West (1997), 423f., and Corso (1999), 99; an ancient *scholion* describes Alcinous' dogs as mere πλάσματα, fiction (IV 530.15–17), and Cullhed (2014), 204. See further the V-scholia to *Odyssey* 7.91 and Eusthathius, vol. 1, p. 263, as cited by Cullhed (2014), p. 213f. and 205. Compare Hephaestus' four ever-flowing springs that present a seasonal variation in water temperature and his moving bronze bulls that breath fire which appear, among other ancient authors, in Apollonius Rhodius, *Argonautica* 3. 221–31, where they are presented as the outcome of Hephaestus' artistic genius, i.e. they seem as if they are moving (see also on the bronze bulls *Argonautica* 3.409–13, 495f., 1052, 1282f.; Ovid, *Metamorphoses* 7.210).

17 Halliwell (2002), 153f.

18 Daedalus is mentioned once in the *Iliad* as the designer of a dancing floor for Ariadne in Knossos; we are told that the divine smith, Hephaestus, is pictured as imitating Daedalus' art (18.590–2).

19 The stories of Daedalus' animated statues were apparently so famous that they became tropes for mocking rhetorical hyperbole as well as epistemic uncertainty and 'non-stationarity'. In Plato's *Meno* 97d, Socrates and Meno agree that ἀρετὴ can be taught only as long as it derives from knowledge and not if it comes from true opinion (ὀρθὴ δόξα). Socrates compares the latter to Daedalus' unchained, mobile statues: although these are beautiful, they may disappear at any moment, leaving their owners with absolutely nothing. See further on Daedalus' statues Euripides' *Eurystheus* fr. 372N; Aristophanes' *Daedalus* fr. 194; Cratinus' *Thracians*

fr. 74; Plato, *Meno* 97d, *Euthyphro* 11d; Diodorus Siculus 4.76. 1–3; Pausanias 2.4.5. Morris (1992), esp. ch. 9; Spivey (1996), esp. ch. 3; Corso (1999), 97f.; Frontisi-Ducroux (1975); Neer (2010b), 71, 81. Esp. on talking Daedalic images, see Kassel (1983); Steiner (2001), 143, 156, 181–4 and Chapter 2 in this book.

20 See on that Stern (1996), 7–9, and Hawes (2014), esp. 49–53. Cf., likewise, Pausanias, on the golden singers of Hephaestus, at 10.5.12. Diodorus Siculus draws, too, on how statues could trick the viewers into thinking that they are alive (4.76.1–3). See on that Corso (1999), 106, and Bur (2016), 47.

21 Cf. Philippus' description of a Daedalus statue moving with quicksilver cited by Aristotle in *On the Soul* 406b17–22. Further on automation in Greek drama and specifically in relation to statues, see Chapter 2 of this book.

22 On mechanical automation and material automatisms see Chapter 3 in this book.

23 See e.g., Herodotus at 2.66, [. . .] αἰέλουρος ἀποθάνῃ ἀπὸ τοῦ αὐτομάτου, 8.138, ἐν τοῖσι φύεται αὐτόματα ῥόδα.

24 Further on the *automatos bios*, see Chapter 2 in this book. On spontaneous generation, see, among others, Balme (1962); Lennox (1982); Gotthelf (1989); Henry (2003); Dudley (2012), ch. 5; Totelin (2018); Brockliss (2019), chs 4 and 6, on Homer and Theophrastus; Wilson (2020); Kress (2020), and Chapter 3 in this book. The heat and air which define the workings of the bellows are considered, at a later stage, to be necessary ingredients for and the physical causes of spontaneous generation. According to Anaximander, spontaneous generation of animals occurs 'from heated water and earth' (A30). Anaxagoras' doctrine of the spontaneous generation of plants makes mention of the air which carries seeds down with the rain (A117). Aristotle claims that plants and animals are generated spontaneously through the agency of psychic heat present in pneuma (*Generation of Animals* 762a18–32). Theophrastus explains spontaneous generation in similar terms: it occurs when the sun warms a mixture of earth and water (*On the Causes of Plants* 1.5.5).

25 Bielfeldt (2014), especially 24f., 31–8; on new materialism, see Grethlein (2008); Mueller (2016), ch. 1; partly Canevaro (2018, 2019); Telò and Mueller (2018); Hall (2018b).

26 Thales argues that magnets along with amber have an animating force; they give inanimate things (ἄψυχα) a soul (ψυχή); on that, see Aristotle, *On the Soul* 405a 19–21, Hippias B 7 and Diogenes Laertius 1.24; see also Damigeron, *De lapidipus* 30, *plenus enim spiritu* (ed. Brodersen). On magnets, see also Empedocles' A89. On their properties and effects, see further Lowe (2016). Cf. von Staden (1996), 87 on Herophilus, magnetism and the body, and cf. *Odyssey* 16. 294, αὐτὸς γὰρ ἐφέλκεται ἄνδρα σίδηρος, the iron itself draws the man.

27 Lloyd (1979), 50.
28 Cited by Brockliss (2019), ch. 6.
29 Cf. e.g. Hero, *On Automata Making* 1.1–4, 1.7. On mechanical wonder, see Chapter 3 of this book.
30 See Schneider (1986), 23, on Hephaestus' labour in this scene.
31 Berryman (2009) 26; cf. ibid. (2003).
32 Liveley and Thomas (2020), 31.
33 Cf. Apollonius Rhodius' *Argonautica* 4.35–42: the doors open automatically at Medea's incantations. See also Hermogenes in *On Types of Style* at 2.4.122f., 2.10.314f.: he refers to the automatic gates of the *Iliad* 5.749, 8.393 as a poetical trope that entertains the audience. On doors opening of their own accord see further Chapter 2 of this book.
34 The *automatos* Menelaus was part of a proverb in antiquity: 'good and brave men do not need an invitation to go to the feasts made by brave and just men'. On that, see Eupolis fr. 14, 289; Plato, *Symposium* 174b–c; Athenaeus, *The Deipnosophists* 5.5; see also Plutarch, *Table Talks* 706f. See also Sophocles, *Trachiniae* 391–4, Δη. μίμν', ὡς ὅδ' ἀνὴρ οὐκ ἐμῶν ὑπ' ἀγγέλων ἀλλ' αὐτόκλητος ἐκ δόμων πορεύεται. Λι. τί χρή, γύναι, μολόντα μ' space is needed Ἡρακλεῖ λέγειν; δίδαξον, ὡς ἔρποντος, εἰσορᾷς, ἐμοῦ (Deianeiara: Stay here – since this man is coming out from the house without calling him, but of his own accord. Lichas: My lady, what message shall I go and bring to Heracles? Instruct me, for, as you see, I am leaving); here, the term αὐτόκλητος is opposed to διδαχή and emphasizes on the fifth century BCE notion of *technê* as opposed to nature. See further on that Krafft (1967), 15–33; Krafft (1971), 46; Heinimann (1961); Schneider (1986), 84–103.
35 On Aristotle and technical automation see further Chapter 3 in this book.
36 A similar argument is brought forward by Crates, a comic playwright of the mid- to late-fifth century, in his *Theria*: if everything is made to walk by itself, no one shall need a man or a lady slave (Athenaeus, *The Deipnosophists* 267e); on that, see Devecka (2013), 63f.
37 On Aristotle and the Iliadic automata as artificial slaves, see Liveley and Thomas (2020).
38 Pugliara (2002), 94–6; Mayor (2018), ch. 1. Cf. Liveley (2006), 279–81 on Talos as a proto-cyborg, and Alexandridis (2017) as a figurative automaton. Cf. also the Sophoclean satyr drama perhaps called Talos, as cited at Hall (2006), 109 n. 41, in which Daedalus' gigantic bronze statue might have been operated by Medea. See also Heynen and Krumeich (1999), 389f. Hunter (1989), at *Argonautica* 1638–88 refers to the ps.-Platonic work *Minos* which rationalizes the story of Talos by arguing that he was a judge who travelled three times a year around Crete with laws inscribed in bronze tablets.

39 Mattusch (1988), 38, 42, 47. See also Ruffell (forthcoming a).
40 Ruffell (forthcoming a).
41 *On the Usefulness of the Parts of the Body* 3.268. See Berryman (2002a) 247, and ibid. (2003), 363–5.
42 Berryman (2002a).
43 Cf. on the importance of the craftsman behind motion Galen, *On the Usefulness of the Parts of the Body* 4.156 and Jones (2017), 245.
44 See further Eustathius at *Iliad* 18. 539, vol. 4, p. 245, on the mechanical explanation of fighting combatants engraved on Achilles' shield; he assumes that this case must be similar to the mechanical Sphinx fastened with bolts on Parthenopaeus' shield, at Aeschylus' *Seven against Thebes* 539–42; the same explanation is given by the scholion to Aeschylus, *Seven against Thebes* 542 g–h; see on that Cullhed (2014), 214f.
45 Vivante (1966). 47 On *physis* in Homer, see Benveniste (1948), 80–5; Naddaf (2005), 11–14. Heinimann (1945), 16–17, understands *physis* as 'form'.
46 The verb φύω and its derivatives in Homer indicate uncultivated, wild growth, both non-spontaneous and spontaneous (*Odyssey* 7.118f.; 9.109). On that see Brockliss (2019), ch. 6. By contrast, he argues, 'the stem φυτο/ε- [...] denotes managed growth, plants that have been grown by someone rather than simply left to grow'.
47 Kube (1969), 14–19. Specifically, Kube argues, 'τέχνη [sc. in Homer] gehört zur Person des Handwerkers wie sein θυμός [...]' (p. 17). See further Hieronymus (1970), 22; Schneider (1986), 14, 17, 25, 29; Romani Mistretta (2017). In Hesiod, moreover, *technê* is usually referring to cases of deception and treachery (often accompanied by the adjective δόλιος).
48 On the Phaecian ships, see Kalligeropoulos and Vasileiadou (2008); Tassios (2008); Liveley and Thomas (2020), 33f. who refer to the ships' 'natural' kind of (artificial) intelligence' (p. 33).
49 Finkelberg (1998), 54–7.
50 Eusathius, vol. 2, p. 285, explains αὐτοδίδακτος as θυμόσοφος, naturally wise. The *vetera scholia* at 8.491, on the other hand, referring to Demodocus attest that αὐτοδίδακτος means ὑπὸ θεοῦ ἐμπνεόμενος (inspired by the god). On the notion of αὐτοδίδακτος as equivalent to something like θεοδίδακτος see Luschnat (1962), 160, 164f; Thalmann (1984), 126–8. See also Aristotle, *Rhetoric* 1365a, where the case of the αὐτοδίδακτος Phemius is used to show how more desirable are natural characteristics from acquired ones. See further Sophocles, *Ajax* 700, ὀρχήματ' αὐτοδαῆ; the vetera scholia on *Ajax* 700 say about αὐτοδαῆ: αὐτομαθῆ, ἃ ἐκ φύσεως ἔχεις, οὐ διδακτά. Cf. also the term θυμόσοφος used in Aristophanes in *Wasps* 1280–3 and *Clouds* 877, meaning to be merely smart by nature

(θυμόσοφος). The automatos, natural and spontaneous, knowledge is contrasted several times in Plato with learning through instruction (see, e.g., *Alcibiades* 118 c 3–4, *Protagoras* 320 a 3, 323 c 6); I will return to this point in the third chapter of this book.

51 On διδάσκω in Homer see Hieronymus (1970), 19f.; Snell (1924), 72–4. Cf. Svenbro (1976), 187f., 193–5; Ford (2002), 113f.; Stewart (2016) on the archaic poet as a non-craftsman.

52 See Power (2010), part 3.

53 See *Lexikon des frühgriechischen Epos* s.v. αὐτοδίδακτος.

54 On Homeric wonders see Hunzinger (2018) and Gerolemou (2018b), 751f. with further bibliography.

55 See Becker (1995), 90f.

56 Fraenkel (1950), 2.446.

57 On a meaning of διδάσκω in Aeschylus as 'wissen lassen, erzählen, mitteilen, sagen' see Hieronymus (1970), 20. But see González (2013), ch. 7: he argues that αὐτοδίδακτος both in Homer and Aeschylus 'hardly entails a spontaneous singing devoid of craft and without knowledge taught by deliberate thinking'.

58 On *technê* from the sixth century onwards, see Kube (1969), who claims that *technê* designates the human sphere that stands in opposition to the divine or uncontrolled powers of *physis* and *tychê*. See also Hieronymus (1970), 22f.; Zhmud (2006), 45–54.

59 There are numerous examples of automatic agency in the Hippocratic corpus, and some of them are listed in Holmes (2013), esp. p. 3 n. 3. For instance, in an automatic, spontaneous way, health happens (*On the Articulations* 46.7, 46.49, *Generation, Nature of the Child, Diseases* iv 18.35; *On the Nature of Man* 12.33–5), or sickness attacks the body, the cavity is thrown into disorder (*Internal Affections* 21.8f., 42.22) or tumours appear (*Ulcers* 24.1). More precisely, according to Holmes, '[t]he medical writers often contrast these events to what the physician achieves with his drugs, thereby confirming a basic sense of difference throughout the otherwise disparate Hippocratic texts between what happens automatically and what is done deliberately' (pp. 3f.). See further Edelstein (1967a), 107f.; Holmes (2010b), 142–7, and Holmes (2017), 32–40, and Chapter 2 in this book.

60 τὰ μὲν καλὰ χρήματα τοῖς πόνοις ἡ μάθησις ἐξεργάζεται, τὰ δ' αἰσχρὰ ἄνευ πόνων αὐτόματα καρποῦται [It is by effort that learning produces fine things, but ignoble ones are reaped by themselves without effort, tr. Laks and Most]. See on this Johnson (2009). On μάθησις see Snell (1924), 75–81.

61 On the connection of the animated Pandora with the Iliadic handmaidens, see Edwards (1991), 195f.; Berryman (2003), 352, and (2009), 25f.; Francis (2009a).

62 See also the Promethean clay-humans on the basis that these are made and not born; on this see, for instance, Pausanias, 10. 4. 4; Apollodorus, *Bibliotheca*, 1.7.1; Ovid, *Metamorphoses* 1. 82–6; Juvenal, *Satire* 14. 35 and the statue brought to life by Venus in the story of Pygmalion in Ovid, *Metamorphoses* 10. 277–86. Cf. the case of the Spartoi, the earth-born warriors who sprang fully grown and armed for battle from the sown teeth of a dragon, see sv *Realencyclopädie der classischen Altertumswissenschaft* for relevant passages (see e.g. Euripides, *Phoenissae* 667–75).
63 See the *Sixth Tablet of Creation* l. 11–34 and the reference in l. 29 of the *Seventh Tablet* (ed. King); on that see Heidel (1951), 122–6; Lambert (2007), 24–6.
64 The handmaidens are swift – *Iliad* 18.417, 421 – in contrast to Hephaestus' slow, limping feet *Iliad* 18.410f., 417, 421, 4; cf. *Odyssey* 8. 329–32, the slow Hephaestus catches the fast Ares through *technê*.
65 See further Herodotus 3.37, Cambyses laughing at the dwarf-like statue of Hephaestus, and Hall (2018a).
66 Mayor (2018), ch. 8. Cf. Chesi and Sclavi (2020) on Pandora as a cyborg.
67 See Berryman (2009).
68 Wickkiser (2010) argues that there are two different Pandoras in Hesiod; there is the Pandora of the Theogony, an archaic terracotta statue in the form of a maiden that doesn't move, and which Hephaestus leads in front of the gods to be wondered at, an act that rather objectifies her. In the version of her story cited in the *Works and Days*, however, she becomes animated through human traits, such as a voice or a mind. See on that also Fraser (2011).
69 On the material and human nature of agency in contrast to intentionality, which has 'no counterpart in the material realm', see Pickering (1995), 17–19; Knappett (2005), ch. 2.
70 See Steiner (2001), 22–32.
71 Zeitlin (1995b); Iles Johnson (2008), 448; Francis (2009a) highlights this point in contrast to various entities in Hesiod's works that are either born or come into being naturally or spontaneously. Cf. the earthborn Pandora and her association with the Sophoclean satyr play Pandora or the Hammerers, and on that Harrison (1903), 283f.; Heynen and Krumeich (1999), 375–80; Bremmer (2008), 30; most recently, Uhlig (2020) with further bibliography. On the eminence of artificiality in Pandora's story see also Warner (1985), 213; Mulvey (1992), 60f.; Steiner (2001), 186–90; Francis (2009a); Vernant (2011), 411; Bianchi (2014), 69f.; Ridley (2016), ch. 3.
72 See further Arthur (1982, 1983).
73 Zeitlin (1995a–b): Zeitlin (1995b) argues that medical and popular sources imagine the uterus as resembling a jar. See further on the uterus-jar, Pucci (1977), 88f.; Marquardt (1982); DuBois (1988), 46–9; Sissa (1990), 147–56. Cf. the discussion on Campanian red-figure neck amphora on which a woman is depicted to be coming

out of a jar, esp. Harrison (1903), 282; Sissa (1990), 155; Grace Canevaro (2018), 258; see further Lissarrague (2001), 52, and Neils (2005), 41–4 who argue that the woman depicted as coming out of the jar could represent ἐλπίς itself.

74 Loraux (1978, 2000), 104f.; see also Purves (2004), 152; Grace Canevaro (2018), 250 arguing that Pandora introduces men to the Iron Age.

75 Bianchi (2006), 127. See further Wosk (2015); she argues that the process of manufacturing the female depicts women as assemblages of various parts. This is reminiscent of ancient, articulated Greek, Roman and Egyptian female votive figures or dolls, which, according to Wosk, 'embody socially constructed conceptions of gender and women themselves'. On ancient Graeco-Roman dolls, in particular, see Dolansky (2012), 278–80. He believes that specifically Roman dolls, apart from being emblems of manipulation and passivity, show potential for movement 'in ways their manufacturers never intended' (p. 279); for instance, they could run, jump, and thus challenge 'male stereotypes and expectations of the female sex' (p. 278).

76 For an overview of scholarship on feminist readings of Pandora's story, see Holmes (2012), 17–22. Cf. Sussman (1978) and Kenaan (2008), ch. 1.

77 Vernant (1990a), 196f., 199–201; and ibid. (2011). Steiner (2001), 24–6, 186–90 argues, too, that Pandora's artificial character informs her later human, gendered activity (i.e. the opening of the jar).

78 Faraone (1992), 102, for instance, notes that Hesiod never calls Pandora the first woman, or even a woman at all (she is like a virgin or a goddess, and from her is the race of women); see also Francis (2009a), 14–16.

79 Marder (2012), *passim* and p. 16. See also ibid. (2014); Decker (2016) and (2018), 90: 'Through the creation of Pandora, the maternal body as origin of life is effaced, and birth becomes a technical male achievement.'

80 Benjamin (1935). See on that Gerolemou (2020b) in relation to catoptric-technologies.

81 On the origin of the jar (*pithos*), see Musäus (2004), 28, 32–4, 67f. According to Wilamowitz-Moellendorff (1928), at v. 89, Prometheus told Pandora not to open the jar.

82 Jane Bennett's influential work on the 'vibrancy' of matter (2010) as well as Karen Barad's important work on 'agential realism' (2012) are well known among classicists. Latour (1993), and Deleuze and Guattari (2004) argue that, agential materialism attributes agency to materials that is beyond will-determination dualism.

83 See also Aristotle, *Physics* 193a 29–30; *Metaphysics* 983b7–27; *On the Soul* 405a19–20; 411a ff.

84 See, among others, on the Democritean notion of the automaton, Johnson (2009) and (2015).
85 On Eros, desire, etc., in Hesiod see Vernant (1990b) and DuBois (1992).
86 Vernant (1990a), 196f., argues that laborious birth that is introduced by Pandora is aligned to laborious agriculture. See also Zeitlin (1995a), 50; Marder (2012), 14.
87 The *automatos bios* returns as a motif in ancient comedy; see this book's Chapter 2.
88 See Evelyn-White (1914), 9.
89 Wilamowitz-Moellendorff (1928); West (1978); Verdenius (1985); Musäus (2004), 36f.; Most (2006) translates 'she wrought baneful evils for human beings'.
90 Musäus (2004), 30–41. But see Clay (2003), 125, arguing that 'the jar and the "gifts" of Zeus to mankind it contained accompanied Pandora as a part of her dowry'.
91 West (1978), at v. 94, p. 168. See also Wilamowitz-Moellendorff (1928), at 89; but see Musäus (2004), 35, arguing against the motive of curiosity. Wolkow (2007) argues that Pandora opens the jar because she is trying to steal what she believes is hiding inside.
92 Aphrodite's presence in an anthropogonic story is reminiscent of Empedocles' cosmogonic story where Love's role is bringing 'aimlessly wandering separated body limbs' together (B57). See on this, Sedley (2007), 55.
93 See also Origen, *Against Celsus* 4.38.63; Stobaeus *Anthology* 4.46.6.4.
94 Translation by Most (2006).
95 West (1978), at v. 99.
96 Clay (2003), 125.
97 See Holmes (2010b), 73f., on hands' actions that reveal hidden agency. On the omnipresence of hands in the *Iliad*, especially on Achilles' hands, see Robbins (1993). See also Chesi and Sclavi (2020), 307 on Pandora's hands and robotic autonomy. But see Mayor (2018), ch. 8, who claims that Pandora is an agent of Zeus with low intelligence (p. 160).
98 See Newmyer (2017), ch. 6. Further on the importance of hands, see Vitruvius *On Architecture* 2.1.2. On the interesting case of the *manus medicus* see Förg (2019).
99 On the social life of hands in Greek tragedy, see Worman (2021). In Aristophanes' *Birds*, the fact that the birds are presented as having human agency is underlined by the fact that they are able to execute their task, i.e. to build a city wall with their own hands, αὐτόχειρες (1133–5). On that, Gerolemou (2019c).
100 Wood (2002) argues that when men fall in love with androids, believing them to be 'perfect women', then, the mistake is usually 'fatal'. See, for instance, some modern cases of artificial women reproducing deceptively the real: Olympia in E. T. A. Hoffmann's story *The Sandman* (1816), or Maria in Fritz Lang's film

Metropolis (1926). See also Hammond (2018) on deception, Hesiod's Pandora and cyborgs (via the film *Ex Machina*). Cf. Warner (1985), 224f., who argues that women belong both to nature and art. Being part of the latter, women share the capacity of art to deceive through its lifelike products.

101 For a discussion on this play, see Chapter 2 of this book.

102 On the story of Apega see Mayor (2018), 193–5. The hidden *technê* in lifelike statues, images, dolls and automata characterizes what Jentsch (1906) and Freud (1919) describe as the 'uncanny'. Whereas, however, the former shows how the horror of the perceiver in such cases is related to lack of information regarding the cause of motion of inanimate matter, the latter argues that these might raise feelings of terror or anxiety exactly because of their ability to imitate something known, i.e. the living. See further on that Chapter 2 in this book, Royle (2003), 39–42 and 52; and Kang (2011), ch. 1.

103 See Mauss (1935), esp. ch. 2 on sexual/societal divisions of the body's techniques.

104 See Lendle (1957), 108f.

Chapter 2

1 On the automatic body in the Hippocratic corpus see Holmes (2010b), 142–7, (2013) and the Introduction of this book. See also Aristotle's *Physics* II, 197 b 18–22, Guthrie (1981), 238–9, and Schiefsky (2005), 5–13, on the difference between *tychê* (which is the result of choice of adults) and the automaton; see also Dudley (2012), 50, 53–7, 97f., and Gerolemou (2019b).

2 On art imitating nature, see e.g. *On Regimen* 1.16, φύσιν τε ἀνθρώπου μιμέονται, 'they [sc. carpenters] copy the nature of man'. See also 1.17, 1.24.

3 On this, see Webster (2014) and (forthcoming); Gerolemou and Kazantzidis (forthcoming). Cf. further on this Kranz (1938); Solmsen (1963), 477–9; Tsitsirides (2001), 62. Generally, on the scientific value of analogy, see Lloyd (1966), part 2. Cf. Aristotle, *Posterior Analytics* 76a37–40, 98a 20–3, and Wilson (2000), chs 2 and 3; Taub (2012).

4 On body modification technologies, see Draycott (2018); Gerolemou (2019a); Gerolemou and Chesi (forthcoming).

5 On mnemotechnics, see, e.g., Simonides of Ceos' method of loci, Cicero *de Oratore* 2.74.299f., 2.86.351–4, 2.87.357f. Quintilian 11.2.11–20.

6 What I call here *technomimesis* is close to Lawtoo's (2015, 2019) notion of *hypermimesis*. See also Gerolemou (2019a).

7 On *phantastic* and *eicastic* mimesis, see Halliwell (2002), 62–5, 127–9. On mimesis, see Lodge's classic study (1953), ch. 9; Koller (1954); Else (1958); Sörbom (1966); Pollitt (1974), 32–58; Vernant (1991a); Halliwell (2002); Stähli (2010).
8 See also *Republic* 10.596d–e and *Philebus* 38c–d.
9 The significance of the medium in art production has become associated with the Lessing's 1766 essay *Laocoon: An Essay on the Limits of Painting and Poetry*. Lessing emphasizes the fact that each medium has particular limitations and possibilities. Lessing's idea of a distinction between media was taken up by Clement Greenberg in his essay *Towards a New Laocoon* (1940) and in *Avant-Garde and Kitsch* (1939) where he contends that abstract painting is the ideal form of a painting since it uncontaminated by the influence of other media. See Michael Fried's response to this: in his essay *Art and Objecthood* (1967), he argues that minimalist art runs the risk of producing effects which do not derive from the work itself but are dependent on the viewer's encounter with the object and its 'objecthood'.
10 On ancient mechanics as acting παρὰ φύσιν and what this could mean, see Schiefsky (2007); Berryman (2009), 44–8 and Chapter 3 in this book.
11 Specifically for technological advancements in the classical period, see Kahn (1970); Löbl (2003); Zhmud (2006); Cuomo (2007), ch. 1. On various advancements in technology and the issue of advancement in Graeco-Roman technology, in general, see Diels (1924); Neuberger (1919); Kahn (1970); White (1984); Greene (2000, 2008); Oleson (2008), and Chapter 3 in this book. But see Finley (1959, 1965) on technological stagnation.
12 Steiner (2001), ch.1.
13 Vernant (1983), ch. 13, ibid. (1991b), ch. 10, esp. p. 187. On the ancient Greek notion of the double in general, see Zeitlin (1985), 79f. on the double dimension of role playing. On the 'ritual double', see Seaford (1981); Segal (1993), 37–50 (regarding Euripides' *Alcestis*). On mirror scenes producing double effect see Taplin (1978), ch. 8; Mastronarde (2010), 6–77.
14 On technology and religion, see Bur (2020); Gerolemou (2020b) 162–4.
15 See recently Worman (2021). As she puts it: 'Euripides' tragedies appear especially attuned to [...] post- or extra-human combinations.' See also p. 170f.
16 On the meaning of masks and theatrical machines, their use and manipulation see Marshall (1999), and ibid. (2014), 190; Arnott (1989), 77; Wiles (1991); Ruffell (2011), 349. On costumes, especially the comic costume, see Foley (2000); Green (2002), 93–105; Compton-Engle (2003). On the tragic costume, see Wyles (2011).
17 On Agathon's mimesis achieved through the imitation of bodily traits and manners, see Schwinge (2014), 69f. Cf. Sörbom (1966), 76; Muecke (1982), 55f.; Vernant (1991a), 175; Stohn (1993); Zeitlin (1996), 382–6; Stehle (2002), 381–5;

Duncan (2006), 27–46. See further Lada-Richards (1999), ch. 4, esp., pp. 169–72 and (2002), 402f., where she notes that 'mimesis cannot leave the imitator's own identity intact' (p. 403).

18 This is close to what we encounter later in regard to the excessive use of gestures. See e.g., Quintilian *Institutes of Oratory* 11.3. esp. 88–91. On the meaning, function and use of gesture and voice in oratory, see further Dionysius Halicarnassus *Demosthenes* 53 on Demosthenes; Athanasius' *Prolegomena* 14.177.4 on Theophrastus. See also Lada-Richards (1999), 169 n. 24, and Wiles (2020).

19 Walter Benjamin's *On the Mimetic Faculty* argues the same: 'the child plays at being not only a shopkeeper or a teacher but also a windmill and a train' (1986: 333f.)

20 Csapo (2002), 128, and (2010) 118.

21 Plutarch partly adopts a Platonic approach in this case (cf. Plato, *Republic* 397a). At the same time, however, he suggests that one should appreciate this kind of faculty and the kind of art that could accomplish such mimesis (διδασκέσθω τὴν μιμουμένην ταῦτα δύναμιν καὶ τέχνην ἐπαινεῖν). Cf. Xenophon, *Symposium* 7.3–4 where dancers imitate the wheels of potters.

22 On actors' vocal training see Porter (2010), 316, 359. Actors were generally judged by the quality of their voice. See e.g. Aristotle, *Rhetoric* 1404a, Lucian, *De Saltatione* 27, *Nigrinus* 11; Cicero, *De Oratore* 1.251. See Pickard-Cambridge (1988), 167–71, with further evidence on the topic and Arnott (1989), ch. 3; Wiles (1991), ch. 8, and Easterling (1999).

23 On improvizations, αὐτοσχεδιάσματα see Lucas (1968), 74f.

24 See e.g. Alcidamas on the use of written speech in oratory, in *On the Writers of Written Speeches, or, On Sophists* fr. 1 110–32.

25 See on that Wiles (1991), 22; Graf (1991), 39, 51; Porter (2010), 315f.; Dutsch (2013), 421–3.

26 See on that Hall (2002), 9f. For Sophocles as actor see the Suda (A.1.24–5) and the *Life of Sophocles* 58–63. On the question of tragic plays as written scripts, see Taplin (1977), 12–16 and (1986), 168; on re-performances of ancient drama, see Revermann (2006), 87; Hanink (2017). On improvization and oral poets see Purves (2019), 10, with further bibliography.

27 Fantham (2002).

28 Csapo (1999–2000), 404.

29 According to Pollux 4.128, the *crane* in tragedy is called μηχανή and in comedy κράδη. On the use of the crane in drama, see also Plato, *Clitophon* 407, Antiphanes fr. 191. 13–16, Alexis fr. 125–6. 19, Menander, *The Demoniac Girl* fr. 5, 227, Polybius 3.48, Cicero, *On the Nature of the Gods* 1.53 as cited at Spira (1960), 149, and Taplin (1977), 444 n. 5. Cf. also Müller (1886), 152–5 for further sources, and

Mastronarde (1990), 253, and Möllendorff (2017), 167; the latter argues that the crane in Greek tragedy serves as an open-end narrative technique.

30 See e.g. in tragedy, the Dioscuri in Euripides' *Electra* 1233ff., Medea in *Medea* 1371ff., Iris and Lyssa in *Heracles* 815-74, Artemis in *Hippolytus* 1289-1439; Athena in *Ion* 1553-1618; Castor and Polydeuces, *Helen* 1642-87; Athena at *Rhesus* 595 (but see Liapis 2017: 243: 'Athena probably appears at ground level'), the Muse at *Rhesus* 890. In comedy: Socrates in *Clouds* 218-38, Trygaeus in *Peace* 79-176, *Birds* 196-1261; see also Pollux 4.128, 130. But see below, n. 33.

31 On *ekkyklema* scenes in tragedy, see Sophocles, *Ajax* 344-594, Euripides, *Hippolytus* 808-1089, *Heracles* 875-1426. Neckel (1890), argues that the *ekkyklema* was not used by Aeschylus and Sophocles. Instead, it is Euripides that makes use of it as well as Aristophanes for the purposes of comic parody. Similar Pickard-Cambridge (1946), 109-11, and Hourmouziades (1965), 93-108. Cf. the *scholion ad* Aeschylus *Eumenides* 47, where the *ekkyclema* is described as Euripides' invention, as cited at Hourmouziades (1965), 98. Taplin (1977), 325-7, 442f. is undecided about the existence and use of the *ekkyklema* by Aeschylus *Agamemnon* 1372. Blume (1984), 72, argues that a *deus ex machina* was used in Sophocles, *Philoctetes* and *ekkyklema* in Sophocles, *Ajax* 346f., *Antigone* 1293f. and *Electra* 1458ff.; Pickard-Cambridge (1946), 50, argues against the use of a crane in *Philoctetes*. Melchinger (1974), 191, 195-7, doubts also the existence of a *deus ex machina* in *Philoctetes* but argues on the use of *ekkyklema* in some of Sophocles' plays. Newiger (1996), 99, argues on the use of *ekkyklema* in Sophocles and excludes the possibility that a crane could have been used in *Philoctetes* (only in Euripides, see n. 117; but see *Life of Aeschylus* 62); same Mastronarde (1990), 271, 286f. On the *ekkyklema*, see recently Brioso Sánchez (2006). Bodensteiner (1893), Flickinger (1922) and Taplin (1977), 443-7, deny the use of a *mêchanê* on Aeschylus' stage. But, on the 'mechanical' entrance of the chorus and Oceanus at 284, and Pickard-Cambridge (1946), 39f. See also Taplin (1977), 252-62. Barrett (1964), at *Hippolytus* 1283, and Taplin (1977), 443-7, argue against the use of *mêchanae* in the epiphany scenes of Euripides. For archaeological evidence on the use of the *mêchanê* in 5th century BC, see Papastamati-von Moock (2014) and (2015), 69-72; on its reconstruction see Chondros, Milidonis, Vitzilaios and Vaitsis (2013).

32 Möllendorff (2017), 169.

33 On the use of novelty, καινότης by Aristophanes and other comic playwrights see Wright (2012), ch. 3.

34 Cf. the comic Plato who according to Suda s.v. Καρκίνος was overusing the *mêchanê* and was called δωδεκαμήχανος; as cited at Spira (1960), 151 n. 146.

35 See e.g. Medea's triumphant re-entry on the stage in Euripides *Medea* 1317ff. and Möllendorff (2017), 173.
36 Möllendorff (2017), 171; Cf. Stiepel (1968), 252–63; he states that actually it was not a crane but rather other forms of machines that supported divine epiphanies.
37 See Ley (2005), 103.
38 On this: Rau (1967), 96f.; Melchinger (1974), 194; Blume (1984), 71; Lucarini (2016).
39 In the *Clouds*, at 205, Strepsiades, looking at the geometry tools which Socrates' pupils show to him, states: τὸ γὰρ σόφισμα δημοτικὸν καὶ χρήσιμον, this device is both democratic and useful. However, later, when looking at a map, he gets upset because Sparta is depicted as being too close to Athens (206–17). In general, the city seems to be unsuccessfully represented through this medium since it is furthermore portrayed without any law courts. On *Clouds*, devices and education see also later in this chapter.
40 Möllendorff (2017), 172, states that the metatheatrical comment might imply that the author-director was present on stage when the *ekkyklema* was being used.
41 Cf. Agathon on the *ekkyklema* in *Thesmophoriazusae* 95–265.
42 For 'αὐτόματος' in Aristophanes, referring to the absence of technical interventions, see *Acharnians* 976, *Peace* 665, and *Wealth* 1190. Cf. also *Prometheus Bound* 1282, ἀλλ' ἀπὸ σοφῆς φύσεως αὐτόματον ἐκμαθεῖν: Wilson deletes this verse, claiming that it has the same content with verse 1281, ὅντινά ποτ' ὤμοσε μαθόντα παρὰ μηδενός. However, verse 1282 draws on naturalness in the learning process and stands in contrast to 1281 where the term μαθών reflects mediated learning.
43 On the social role of technological artefacts, see the theories of Latour (1996, 2005); Ihde (1990); Verbeek (2005).
44 On stories of relationships between statues and humans, i.e. on the phenomenon of *agalmatophilia*, see Morris (1992); Steiner (2001), ch. 4; Hersey (2009); and O'Bryhim (2015). See also Neer (2010b) on the idea of animated statues in general. One of the first examples of this type of communication is found in the *Iliad* 6.297–311 where Theano prays that Diomedes will be defeated but Athena turns her head from her (ἀνένευε). See also Strabo 6.1.14 on the statue of Athena in Heraclia which closed its eyes when suppliants were dragged away by the Ionians; cf. e.g. Dio Cssius 46.43; Steiner (2001), ch. 3, and Hersey (2009), 13–17.
45 Platt and Gaifman (2018).
46 Stieber (2011), 130, argues that κεκίνηται *ad* 1226 'suggests more the movement of an inanimate object, like a statue, than an animate being [...]'.
47 Cf. the dead painted eyes of the immovable *kolossoi* in Aeschylus *Agamemnon* 416–18 which instead of comforting Menelaus remind him that his real wife, Helen, has gone. See on that Steiner (1995).

48 As Platt and and Gaifman (2018), 415, put it: 'Mimêsis, it turns out, can work both ways: not only do objects imitate living bodies, but living agents are repeatedly cast as objects.'
49 On a statuesque Andromache, see Worman (2021), 224. Generally, on materiality in Greek drama, see Mueller (2016); Telò and Mueller (2018). On material engagement in general, see Malafouris (2008, 2014).
50 Cf. Democritus' on 'empty', non-numinous god-statues at fr. 195; see on that Steiner (2001), 121f., and Wright (2005), 323f. On moving statues, see further Herodotus 2.48, at the festival of Dionysus in Egypt and Lloyd (1976), 222f., on mechanized *phalloi*.
51 See Kahn (1979), 266f.
52 Notably, her brother and Pylades, in the previous lines, could not handle the κλίμακες and μοχλοί to escape their helpless state, ἀμηχανία (95–102).
53 {Ιφ.} βρέτας τὸ τῆς θεοῦ πάλιν ἕδρας ἀπεστράφη. {Θο.} αὐτόματον, ἤ νιν σεισμὸς ἔστρεψε χθονός;/{Ιφ} αὐτόματον· ὄψιν δ' ὀμμάτων ξυνήρμοσεν;. See Steiner (2001), ch.2, esp. pp. 110, 159. Cf. vv. 216f., 273f., and Stieber (2011), 152f.; she argues that in these verses, Orestes and Pylades are regarded by the herdsmen as animated statues of nymphs.
54 This is what we also learn from Polyneices' first burial in Sophocles, *Antigone*. At first, the fact that the body was buried in a way that the security guard could notice nothing, indicates, according to the guardian and the chorus, a miraculous divine action that was completed without leaving any traces behind (250–4), i.e. without the signs of an external technical intervention, hence automatically. But eventually, it is revealed that Antigone, as the representative of the divine and, at the same time, a manifestation of autonomous will (821, αὐτόνομος ζῶσα), is the sole agent of this deed. Rouse (1911) argues that Ismene has conducted the first burial. Cf. Rothaus' response (1990), 209: 'in ancient drama such an important action cannot be attributed to a minor character' as Ismene. McCall (1972), argues that gods are the agents of the first burial; see further Adams (1931, 1955); Meiklejohn (1932); Messemer (1942); Margon (1969); Scodel (1984); Held (1983). According to Adams (1931), 110 Antigone conducts the second burial, coming as an automaton from the sandstorm. On that, see also Rothaus (1990), 211. On automatic miracles, see further, e.g. Herodotus 8.37.2: here weapons move on their and appear lying outside the shrine. Gerolemou (2018b), 762f. and Gerolemou (2019b). Temple doors opening of their own accord is one of the most common automatic miracle, see, for example, Homer *Iliad* 5.748–52 = 8.392–6, Plutarch, *Timoleon* 12.9 and Weinreich (1929) and Wessels (forthcoming).

55 Kannicht (1969), 27, on ἔμπνους. See further Steiner (2001), 191–3; Stieber (2011), 170, on the possibility that Helen is somehow a robotic statue. Cf. also *Helen* 1014–16 and again Kannicht (1969), 259–62, and Euripides, *Suppliants* 533f. where the term *pneuma* is related with ether and the body with earth, on that see Wright (2005), 264 n. 140.

56 Wright (2005), 322. Cf. Euripides, *Protesilaus* where, supposedly, a slave mistakes Protesilaus' statue lying in bed with Laodamia with a real lover; cf. Steiber (2011), 168, and Steiner (2001), 44–50, 191 on statues, art and ἀπάτη, deceit.

57 It is noteworthy in this context that the true Helen is in negotiation with her natural body throughout the entire play: she wishes to be an *agalma*, statue (705, 1219), whose colours she can erase in order to repaint a plain face instead of a beautiful one (262f.; cf. Aeschylus' *Agamemnon* 1329, Plato, *Laws* 6. 769c 3–8).

58 Kannicht (1969), 166.

59 On the metatheatrical role of the urn, see Segal (1986), 128; Ringer (1998), 185–99.

60 Vernant (1991c), 162, and Steiner (2001), 5–11, 151–6, on funerary monuments and the substitution of the dead. In Euripides' *Trojan Women*, Hecabe praises the mark, typos, that Hector's body left on his shield as he is now dead and this τύπος will serve as his μνημεῖον, remembrance signage (1196–7, ὡς ἡδὺς ἐν πόρπακι σῷ κεῖται τύπος).

61 On the substitution of living bodies with voodoo dolls, see Faraone (1991a–b).

62 'So all the arts share common ground with human nature.' On the concept of mimesis in this text, see, Bartoš (2014).

63 In Sophocles' play *Ichneutae* where the invention of the lyre is depicted (312; cf. *Homeric Hymn to Hermes* 25–54), voice clearly indicates livingness, both natural and artificial. The sound that the instrument is doing comes from an animal, the tortoise, which, while it was alive, had no voice, but acquired one once it died (299f.).

64 Helen is like her father who is πτανός, winged, too, 1145. Cf. the winged chorus in *Prometheus Bound* 135, 280, 129f. See further Euripides, *Heracles* 627f and the possibility that Heracles could be merely an eidolon. He says: 'Let go of my clothes. I have no wings and I will not go'; on that, see Rehm (2002), 203.

65 On Helen's copy, see Steiner (2001), 55f., 290f.; Hall (2006), 121.

66 On the Satyrs' eidola, see Morris (1992), 217f.; Sörbom (1966), 41–53; Zeitlin (1994), 138; Stieber (1994); Steiner (2001), 45–9, 141; Hall (2006), 109.

67 Wessels and Krumeich (1999), 135, and Porter (2010), 332 argue that 'Δαιδάλου μιμήματα' means 'in the style of Daedalus' and not 'the likeness of Daedalus' as Lloyd-Jones (1957), 547, states. According to Steiner (2001), 46, 49f., 144, the Δαιδάλου μιμήματα of the Satyrs as well as the *kolossoi*, gigantic statues, in

Agamemnon 416f., do not pose a threat to their originals; their importance rather lies in underscoring the ability of the artist 'to create a semblance of life' (46). The *kolossoi* in *Agamemnon* could resemble, according to Philipp (1968), the hateful Helena (p. 28). But see Fraenkel (1950), 218f., who thinks that it could be the statue of any female and not necessarily Helen's; cf. Stieber (1994), 104f.

68 On talking Daedalic images see Steiner (2001), 46, 48, 52f., 143, 181–4, and Kassel (1983). On Daedalus' animated statues, in general, see Morris (1992); Spivey (1996), esp. ch.3; Corso (1999); Frontisi-Ducroux (1975); Neer (2010b), 71, 81.

69 Morris (1992), 218; Steiner (2001), 51–4, 143; Hall (2006), 138, calls Hecuba a rhetorical automaton; cf. Stieber (2011), 123. See further Euripides' satyr play *Eurystheus* fr. 372 and Cratinus, *Thracians* fr. 75 K–A, where statues move and make sounds and are tied in a place in order to be prevented from escaping; on that see Morris (1992), 221; Faraone (1992), 37.

70 Cf. e.g. Euripides, *The Phoenician Women* 220–1, *Andromache* 246; Aeschylus, *Suppliants* 282f., *The Libation Bearers* 48–51.

71 On the woman–artefact analogy in drama, see, among others, Philipp (1968), 26–8, 31–7; Zeitlin (1994); Hall (2006), ch. 4.

72 On the objectification of Alcestis, see Rabinowitz (1993), 91–7; Wohl (1998), 126–31, 157–9, 164–75. See further O'Higgins (1993), 83–5; Segal (1993), 42–50, 54–6, 67–72, 80, 86.

73 On Alcestis' statue-like stupefaction: Segal (1993), 37–50; Steiner (2001), 149, 192f.; Hall (2006), 128; Neer (2010b), 60–1; cf. further Stieber (2011), 415f.

74 Montiglio (2000), 179.

75 Alcestis' silence might be explained by the fact that Greek dramatists never used more than three speaking actors. Alcestis' silent re-entrance in the play, if the play was meant to be performed by two actors as certain scholars have suggested, might have been necessary since the actor who was playing Alcestis is now playing Heracles. See on that Pickard-Cambridge (1988), 145; Arnott (1989), 46f. On the silent Alcestis, see also Trammell (1941); Rabinowitz (1993), 72f.; O'Higgins (1993), 78; Wohl (1998); Foley (2001), esp. 317. Furthermore, Alcestis' lack of speech, and generally the silence of humanlike statues, should not be confused with other cases of silence in Greek drama: there is the silence of the dramatic characters, like that of Philoctetes who wishes to hide his sickness and pain as part of a plot necessity (730f., 740). See further the case of Neoptolemus in Sophocles, *Philoctetes* 805f. and in 1066f., Agamemnon in *Iphigenia in Aulis* 1140–7, Phaedra in Euripides' *Hippolytus* 39f., 392–7 and Montiglio (2000), 225, on silent, sick characters in Greek tragedy. See further pp. 229–31 and n. 55: according to

Montiglio in the Hippocratic Corpus ἀφωνία heralds death and accompanies mental illnesses. See also the case of ritual silence, εὐφημία (combination of speech and silence), forced silence due to an oath (e.g. of Hippolytus in Euripides' *Hippolytus* 595, 1074f.), Montiglio (2000), ch. 1; Gödde (2011). See, finally, the case of silence as the result of a violent act (e.g. of Iphigenia in Aeschylus' *Agamemnon* 236f.); Montiglio (2000), ch. 5.

76 Cf. e.g. Euripides, *Medea* 230, πάντων δ' ὅσ' ἔστ' ἔμψυχα καὶ γνώμην ἔχει, Euripides *Electra* 372; fr. 291. In Euripides, *Electra* 387f., bodies with empty minds are like statues (αἱ δὲ σάρκες αἱ κεναὶ φρενῶν ἀγάλματ' ἀγορᾶς εἰσιν) and, according to Hippolytus, to be ἄφθογγος, voiceless, is like a wild animal (Euripides *Hippolytus* 645–8; cf. Sophocles *Philoctetes* 225–30). See on that Segal (1993) 96–9.

77 On the meaning of 'recording the voice' in the Graeco-Roman world, see Butler (2015).

78 On the notion of 'liveness' and whether it should be considered an essential quality of theatre, cf. Auslander (1999); Phelan (1993); cf. further Zeitlin (1985), 68–71, Hall (2010), 15, 18–20, 23f. Notably, Aristotle in his *Poetics* argues that tragedy could fulfil its purpose without being performed, that is, without being enacted (1461b 26ff., 1449b31–2). On Aristotle's inconsistent views on *opsis*, see Sifakis (2013) and Konstan (2013). But see Halliwell (1986), 337–43.

79 On this scene, see Arnott (1989), 75f. On the letter in *Iphigenia in Tauris*, see Wright (2005), 336. Cf. Euripides *Hippolytus* 842f., 856f., 877, Phaedra's letter is read silently by Theseus (although 877, βοᾷι βοᾷι δέλτος ἄλαστα, the tablet cries aloud, about grievous things), in contrast to the letters written and read by Agamemnon in *Iphigenia in Aulis* 34–40, 97–105, 107–14, 115–23 and the letter in *Iphigenia in Tauris* discussed here. On Phaedras' letter representing the failure of the written word, see Goldhill (1986), 135. See further the parody of Euripides, *Palamedes* in Aristophanes, *Thesmophoriazusae* 770–83 (on letter-carving) and the δέλτος in Sophocles *Trachiniae* 46f., 157, 492–6; on *staged* letters in Euripides, see Rosenmeyer (2001), 61–97; Mueller (2016), 155–89, inter alia on tragic letters as suggestive for the tragic plot, especially p. 183: 'The tablet's material presence underlines the mechanics involved in the production of dialogue on stage, a seemingly weightless, unmediated phenomenon.' Cf. further on that Torrance (2010).

80 Cf. *Prometheus Bound* 460f. on letters as bearers of memory (γραμμάτων τε συνθέσεις,/ μνήμην ἁπάντων, μουσομήτορ' ἐργάνην).

81 See Rosenmeyer (2001), 66 n. 15.

82 Flickinger (1939), 359f.

83 On off-stage voices, see Arnott (1989), 91–3.

84 Tr. by Kovacs (1998). Steiner (1994), 232, argues that, '[f]ar from guaranteeing full democracy, the existence of written law merely gives the impression of popular rule while supporting a traditional monarch'. See, by contrast, Aeschylus, *Suppliants* 946–9 and Sophocles *Antigone* (divine-oral vs the human-written law), where live speech is associated with the idea of a free born citizen.

85 On Alcidamas' written and oral speech, see Ford (2002), 234–5; Wright (2005), 318; Hall (2006), 121; Porter (2010), 335–9. On the adequacy of the written word as a means for reflecting reality, see Wardy (1996).

86 On αὐτοσχεδιάσματα, improvizations, in Alcidamas see Pfeifer (1968), 50f.

87 χωρὶς δὲ τούτων καὶ σημεῖα τῆς ἐπιδόσεως, ἣν εἰκὸς ἐν τῇ διανοίᾳ γίγνεσθαι, παρὰ τῶν γραπτῶν λόγων ἐναργέστατα κατιδεῖν ἔστιν. εἰ μὲν γὰρ βέλτιον αὐτοσχεδιάζομεν νῦν ἢ πρότερον, οὐ ῥᾴδιον ἐπικρίνειν ἐστί, χαλεπαὶ γὰρ αἱ μνῆμαι τῶν προειρημένων λόγων καθεστήκασιν· εἰς δὲ τὰ γεγραμμένα κατιδόντας ὥσπερ ἐν κατόπτρῳ θεωρῆσαι τὰς τῆς ψυχῆς ἐπιδόσεις ῥᾴδιόν ἐστιν.

88 Porter (2010), 338. Intelligence proven through writing is also reflected in the metaphor of the tablets of the mind, δελτογράφος φρήν (see, e.g., *Prometheus Bound* 789, *Eumenides* 273–5): on this, see Steiner (1994), 100–9; Gerolemou (2018c), 350.

89 Segal (1986), ch. 3.

90 See further Agathon, *Telephos* fr. 4; Theodectes, fr. 6. On that, see Wright (2016), 172f.

91 On material and technological mediation of human subjectivity, see Schraube and Sørensen (2013). On technological intervention and body enhancement as affecting subjectivity, see Zohny (2016).

92 At the same time, however, they can also release his destructive drives.

93 Freud (1930), 50. On prosthesis in antiquity, see Bliquez (1983); Garland (1995), 26f.; Wiesing (2008); Lee (2015), 83; and Draycott (2018). See further: Payne (2016) examines the relationship between human beings and animal body parts (and behaviour) and, also, technological means (e.g. devices such as κλεψύδρα, the water-clock, or πινάκιον, the voting token) which are related to the body as empowering prosthetics. This relationship is also examined by Samuel Durham Cooper in his doctoral thesis on post-humanism in Aristophanes (2016). In his discussion of Aristophanes' *Birds*, he uses the notion of *prosthesis* to describe the function of the wings in the play that were prepared and offered to desperate human consumers seeking to improve human activity (1277–1334; cf. 785–800). On wings as prosthetics, see also Gerolemou (2019c).

94 Sobchack (2006), 19, challenges this definition by arguing that prosthesis 'has become [a] tropological currency for describing a vague and shifting constellation

of relationships among bodies, technologies, and subjectivities'. Jain (1999) criticizes the vague trope of 'technology as prosthesis' as well, without rejecting, however, the impact that prosthetic technology could have on the body, i.e. that prosthesis transforms it by expanding its limits. See on that also Adams (2018).

95 See Webster (forthcoming). Following Bruno Latour's idea (2004) of the body as an 'interface', that is, as a constructed entity through its relationship with the objects that surround it, Webster argues how specific tools, devices and techniques shaped ideas about the corporeal interiors in antiquity.

96 See Purves (2015); Mueller (2016); Noel (2018).

97 On the relationship of prosthesis with issues raised in transhumanism, see Bostrom (2005); Badmington (2011); Sharon (2014), esp. ch. 1.

98 On the concept of ἀνδρεία see Sluiter and Rosen (2003), 14f.

99 See Snell (1975), 17f., on the composite structure of the human body in Homer; see further Vivante (1955); Fraenkel (1962), 83–94; Vernant (1991c), 28–41; Holmes (2010b), 1–83; Purves (2015), and chapter 1 in this book.

100 Purves (2015), 83–7, on the shield serving as a second skin. See also Mueller (2016), 222 n. 4, see also pp. 135 and 147; Noel (2018), 163f. On the 'shielded stature' of Ajax in general, see Worman (2021), 124–7. On huge shields and spears, see further *Iliad* 6.117–18; 7.222–3, 245–6; 11.485, 527; 13.803–4; 16.140–4. On warriors and their weapons as body extensions, see Vernant (1991c), 37f.; Longo (1996); Lissarrague (2008). See also Malafouris (2008), who argues that the conception of the Mycenaean sword as a body part, i.e. as a prosthetic attachment to the warrior's body, can be explained with a view to neuroscientific research on the systematic association between the body and inanimate objects (like tools or weapons). See further Gavrylenko (2012).

101 See also Odysseus and his bow in the *Odyssey* 21.404–12.

102 See, e.g., *Iliad* 3.21–37, on Menelaus, 13.284–91, Idomeneus arguing on braveness and the role of πρόμαχοι; see also Odysseus at *Odyssey* 18.376–81. See van Wees (1994), 7, and (1997). In the Hesiodic conception of the Bronze Age, warriors are conceived as technologically advanced, too. They are equipped with powerful bronze weapons (*Works and Days* 144–55, esp. 148–52). 'Upon their massive limbs grew great strength and untouchable hands out of their shoulders. Their weapons were from bronze, bronze were their houses, with bronze they worked.' Translated by Most (2006), 99. Talos in Apollonius' *Argonautica* is described as the last warrior of this Bronze Age (4.1641–4).

103 On this development, among others, Hanson (1995, 1996); van Wees (2001); Kagan and Viggiano (2013). On the hoplite panoply, see Snodgrass (1965) and (1967), 49–58, 77; Sekunda (2000), 9–17; Kagan and Viggiano (2013), esp. ch. 1. Cf. Foucault (1977), 135, on late-eighteenth-century soldiers: they have 'become

104 Euripides, *Heracles* 179–80, 188–203, 366–7, 392, 422, 472, 570; *Iliad* 18.117; cf. Sophocles *Trachiniae* 190–1102 and Holmes (2008), 252.
105 On Heracles' divine origins being disputed in the play, see Gregory (1977); Michelini (1987), 255–6.
106 In the *Odyssey* 11. 617–26 Heracles complains that, despite divine parentage, he has no benefit, and he was even made the servant of a terrible man who laid labours on him. On Heracles in the *Odyssey* 21.1–41 and as a foil to Odysseus, Liapis (2006).
107 Heracles tamed the man-eating mares of Diomedes by climbing on a chariot (380).
108 Cf. Heracles in Euripides' *Alcestis* 847, 1142.
109 Cf. Padel (1992) arguing on disease as a force which attacks the inside from the outside.
110 Worman (2021), 112.
111 The same happens with Philoctetes' body. Sickness succeeds in overtaking his body but not to replace it (740–69).
112 Heracles expresses the same thoughts in Euripides, *Heracles* 1146–52, though Theseus arrives and chases away his deadly plans, θανάσιμα βουλεύματα (1153).
113 See Valakas (2002).
114 Worman (2012), 353, describes the Sophoclean body as heroic and stubborn. See also ibid. (2021), 209.
115 See above, n. 33. See Pickard-Cambridge (1946), 51. As he puts it, '[h]e-sc. Sophocles may have been more sensitive than they – sc. Aeschylus and Euripides – to the least improbability or absurdity, such as these devices evidently suggested to some spectators, and among others to Aristophanes, and he probably felt that such things interfered with the austere and harmonious perfection of the play as a work of art'.
116 See Schiefsky (2007), 79: he reads this passage as providing evidence for the split between art and nature; on that see also the ps.-Epicharmean, *Politeia* 23 B 57.
117 Cf. *Prometheus Bound* 1–87, esp. 45, ὦ πολλὰ μισηθεῖσα χειρωναξία, Oh, this handicraft that I hate – says Hephaestus about nailing Prometheus on the Caucasus.
118 Tr. Sommerstein (2008).

(continued from previous page:) something that can be made; out of formless clay, an inapt body, the machine required can be constructed [...]'. See also Cavarero (2019) on, among other things, Hannah Arendt's concept of the human condition defined through spontaneity.

119 On the bow, a coward's weapon, see Dunn (1996), 124; Kirkpatrick and Dunn (2002), 45; Holmes (2008), 254. Cf. the words of Diomedes in the *Iliad* 11.385–95, condemning bowmen as 'unheroic' because they fight from a distance; see also *Iliad* 4.85ff. See further Lissarrague (1990), 97, 113f.; Cohen (1994), 696–715; D'Amato (2016), 803. The bow is often attributed to cowards, for instance, to the effeminate Paris (*Iliad* 11.385–7), to Scythians and Persian warriors, contrary to the Greeks who use the spear (Aeschylus *Persians* 147–9; cf. Aristophanes, *Acharnians* 707 and Thucydides 4.40); but see Skinner (2006). In Sophocles, *Ajax* 1120–2, Teucer defends the art of the bow by disassociating it from βαναυσία, handicraft. Further on the role of the bow in the play see Hamilton (1985); Padilla (1992). But see Odysseus and the bow contest in the *Odyssey* esp. v. 21 and 397–9, where the skill and technique of the archer are being underlined.

120 Dunn (1996), 124; Michelini (1987), 243–6.

121 As Holmes (2008), 255, argues: '[t]his new Heracles uses not raw force but *technê* to master the land'. Cf. further on the art of archery, Odysseus and his skillful management of his bow in *Odyssey*. 8.215, 8.223–5, 11.605–8.

122 Later on, in the Hellenistic period, with the introduction of military innovations and machines, around the middle of the fourth century BC, the discussion on ἀνδρεία becomes even more interesting. When, for instance, the Spartan king Archidamus II saw a catapult brought from Sicily for the first time, he cried: 'By Heracles, it is the end of manly virtue!' (Plutarch *Moralia* 191e) and Gerolemou (forthcoming b).

123 On the non-autonomous, mad body of Heracles, see Padel (1995), 17–21; Holmes (2008), 242–6, 273.

124 Cf. the case of military robots Campa (2015), 28 and ch. 5.

125 See on that Weiberg (2018), 76.

126 On the prosecution of a statue, also Pausanias 1.28.2, Aristotle, *Poetics* 1452a 7–11. See Hyde (1917).

127 On the talking bow, see Kirkpatrick and Dunn (2002). See further Michelini (1987), 265–8, and Dunn (1996), 125.

128 See further Menelaus' conversation with his θυμός at *Iliad* 17. 91–105, Hector's monologue at *Iliad* 22.99–130 and Lesky (1961), 9f.

129 Snell (1975), 15–37.

130 Gill (1990), 4, and ibid. (1996). See also Schmitt (1990), 13f., and Russo (2012); Long (2015), 15–50. On the multiple facets of the Homeric *thymos*, see Cairns (2014, 2019), Pelliccia (1995), and recently Zanker (2019), 187–200.

131 Latour (1999), ch. 6.

132 Gregory (1977), 275; Yunis (1988), 139–71; see also Kirkpatrick and Dunn (2002), 43.

133 Dunn (1996), 125.
134 Noel (2018), 172.
135 Tr. by Kovacs (1998).
136 See Kirkpatrick and Dunn (2002), 49f.
137 Chalk (1962) argues, like Wilamowitz-Moellendorff (1895), 127f., and Arrowsmith (1954), 14, before him, that Heracles demonstrates a new form of courage in choosing life over suicide at the end of the play. On this issue, see also Adkins (1966), 218f.
138 But see Noel (2018), 164. She argues that although the bow is not a prosthetic replacement for Philoctetes' impaired leg, 'it is conceived as a vital prolongation of Philoctetes' hands, which is his only means for survival on the desert island of Lemnos'.
139 See Gill (1980), 168, 'in this play the bow (and heroic achievement) is inseparable from genuine friendship'; Noel (2018), 164, remarks that in Sophocles' *Oedipus at Colonus* as well, the blind Oedipus, being deprived of any artificial device to help him, such as a stick, depends on filial love. As she states: 'Antigone lends him her eyes (34) and she and her sister are objectified when called "walking sticks" by Oedipus (σκῆπτρα, 848, 1109)'.
140 Nootropics are substances that enhance cognitive function.
141 Cf. Aphrodite fashioning of the eye in Empedocles fr. 84, 86f. On the philosophical influences of the *Thesmophoriazusae* 16–18, see Austin and Olson (2004), 14f.; Sommerstein (1994), 11–18; Tsitsirides (2001); Rashed (2007); Clements (2014), 24–7. See also Kovacs (1994), 81, who argues that the passage is a parody of the cosmology at Euripides fr. 484 (*Melanippe the Wise*).
142 As Clements (2014), 15, argues, and we will also see later in this chapter, his puzzlement is 'reminiscent of Strepsiades' mindless jumbling of snippets of Socratic theory in *Clouds*'.
143 On implicit knowledge in antiquity see Konstan (2015); on explicit knowledge, see Asper (2015). Also, see further Gerolemou (2018c).
144 Hawhee (2005), 93–8. See also Dodds (1973), 10, who notes in relation to Democritus' ambition to reshape humans: 'In the great days of the fifth century such optimism was natural.'
145 Cf. Plato's *Theaetetus*, which engages itself with the question of how many kinds of knowledge, knowledge producers and knowledge consumers exist. According to Protagoras in this dialogue, a good teacher can use arguments (or discourses: logoi) in the same way that a good doctor uses drugs: i.e. he can replace the state of the soul in which 'bad things are and appear' with a state in which 'good things are and appear' (165e4–168c5).

146 The adjective πυκνός could be referring to the artificial formation of Dicaeopolis' mind; φρήν could be seen in analogy to his artificial new appearance put together by various Euripidean costumes from several plays (cf. e.g. in *Iliad* 10.267 for πυκνός as a description of manufacturing quality); λεπτός is the result of the well-joined mind, here corresponding to a fine costume (for λεπτός describing mostly garments and the like cf. e.g. Euripides *Medea* 949, *Iliad* 23. 854). Cf. Hero, *On Automata Making* 25.2, ὀθόνιον δεῖ λαβεῖν λεπτὸν καὶ πυκνόν. Seen in this light, λεπτός and πυκνός are not necessarily juxtaposed as Olson (2002), 198, argues.

147 On that see Gerolemou (2018c).

148 Cf. *Regimen* 1.15: Ἡ φύσις αὐτομάτη ταῦτα ἐπίσταται· καθήμενος πονέει ἀναστῆναι, κινεύμενος πονέει ἀναπαύσασθαι, καὶ ἄλλα τοιαῦτα ἔχει ἡ φύσις ἰητρικῆς. Nature herself knows how to do these things. When a man is sitting it is a labour to rise; when he is moving it is a labour to come to rest. In other respects, too, nature is the same as the physician's art (translated by Jones 1931: 253f.).

149 Dodds (1951), 187.

150 Noted in passing in Chapter 1 in this book.

151 Cf. Plato, *Alcibiades* I 118c, Λέγεταί γέ τοι, ὦ Σώκρατες, οὐκ ἀπὸ τοῦ αὐτομάτου σοφὸς γεγονέναι, ἀλλὰ πολλοῖς καὶ σοφοῖς συγγεγονέναι [...] Socrates, they say he [sc. Pericles] did not get his wisdom automatically, but through his interaction with many wise men. See on the *automatos bios* in comedy Athenaeus who cites in his *Deipnosophistae*, a number of comic plays to show how in ancient times, probably during the Hesiodic age of Cronos, goods were provided automatically and there was no need for slaves or other intermediaries between natural production and human consumption (6.267e–270a). On the *automatos bios* in old comedy, see Ceccarelli (1996), 453–5; Ruffell (2000); Farioli (2001), 214f.; Konstan (2012). Generally, on the *automatos bios* in the age of Cronus, see e.g. Plato's *Stateman* 271f.; Aratus *Phenomena* 96–136; Ovid, *Metamorphoses* 1. 89–112, and Dodds (1973), 3, who calls this an 'anti-progressive myth'. See also Naas (2018), ch. 2, esp. on Plato's *Statesman* and Chapter 3 in this book.

152 Cf. the story told by Seneca in his *Epistles* 27 about Calvisius Sabinus who could not remember literary references and generally had a very bad memory. Instead of making an effort to read and learn the texts, he decided to use his wealth to obtain some specialized slaves, who knew Homer, Hesiod and the nine Lyric poets. Similar to Strepsiades' idea of automatic learning, Calvisius Sabinus claimed that having these slaves in his house was the same as having knowledge of the material himself, since anything a member of his household knew, he knew, too. Seneca of course criticizes this view, observing that there are no shortcuts to learning: Calvisius Sabinus still got his quotations mixed up; he would ask for a quote and then forget it as he was repeating it.

153 Often in Athenian drama, older characters are depicted as σκιαί, shadows and eidola, because their body is in the process of disintegration. On ageing bodies as shadows and eidola, see, e.g., Aeschylus, *Agamemnon* 81f., 1211–48, Euripides, *Troades* 191f., *Phoinissai* 1539–45.
154 Translated by Kovacs (2002).
155 Seidensticker (1982), 116–23. On the technical, mechanical, automatic and laughter, see Henri Bergson's essay *Le Rire* published in 1900 and Gerolemou (2020a).
156 In Plato's *Laws*, such freedom of speech and action is the product of the beneficial use of wine, as recommended to the older people of the chorus of Dionysus, cf. *Laws*, e.g., 2. 666b and Belfiore (1986), 426. Cf. also ps.-Aristotle, *Problems* 30. 1. 953b. See further Homer, *Odyssey* 14. 463–6, οἶνος γὰρ ἀνώγει, / ἠλεός, ὅς τ' ἐφέηκε πολύφρονά περ μάλ' ἀεῖσαι/ καί θ' ἁπαλὸν γελάσαι καί τ' ὀρχήσασθαι ἀνῆκε,/ καί τι ἔπος προέηκεν, ὅ πέρ τ' ἄρρητον ἄμεινον; see here also Aristophanes, *Lysistrata* 194–206, where women's revolutionary action against their men is inaugurated by wine (cf. *Ecclesiazusae* 136–43); see Bowie (1997), 12, 15. Cf. here also Aristophanes, *Wasps* 1476–81.
157 On Iolaus' rejuvenation see Zuntz (1955), 30f.; Conacher (1967), 117; Devereux (1971).
158 On Dionysus and automata, see briefly Csapo (2013), 25–7; Bur (2016). See also Grillo (2019), xcvii–c.
159 The title is taken from DiPietro's article (2016) on IT disaster recovery, cloud computing and information security.
160 Taplin (1978), 121.
161 Effe (2000), 53.
162 On Agamemnon as bearing responsibility for his own madness, see Lloyd-Jones (1962); Hammond (1972); Dodds (1974), 165f.; Gill (1990), 23f.
163 This kind of distinction – between, that is, an enduring and a momentary kind of madness – is not reflected in ancient Greek and Roman law; Robinson (2013), 19–21. However, crimes conducted by reason of insanity, when the perpetrator is found guilty, receive lighter penalties (see, e.g., Plato, *Laws* 864d).
164 See among others, Williams (1993), ch. 6; Gill (1996), 263f., esp. with reference to tragic madness. For the idea of madness as an externally inflicted malady, see Padel (1992, 1995).
165 On the lack of justification for Heracles' punishment, see Schlesier (1985); Effe (2000), 55f.; Hartigan (1987); Brückner (2007), 54. Like Heracles, Io is also unjustifiably punished with mania in Aeschylus *Suppliants* 562, 564; see also *Prometheus Bound* 541f., 581, 597, 673, 681, 878f., Sophocles *Electra* 5. See also Phaedra's divine madness in Euripides *Hippolytus* 141, 198ff., 237f., 240f., 248.

166 On that see Padel (1995), ch. 7.
167 Their hectic motion and the shaking of the head and hands come in opposition to the dignified, slow and calm gestures that the Athenians of the classical period had to display in order to acquire a certain status (cf. Sophocles, *Thyestes* fr. 257, although see Phrynichus fr. 10). See on that Bremmer (1991), 18f. On madness associated with extensive movement, see Mattes (1970), 63f.; Montiglio (2005), 27f.; also, see Becker (1937), 156f., esp. for Aeschylus; Gerolemou (2011). Certainly, in Greek drama, specific types of movement are associated with various health or emotional states. For instance, ill characters can be distinguished through slow motion or no motion at all (cf. the traumatized body of Philoctetes in Sophocles *Philoctetes* 207). Slow motion also characterizes older people (cf. e.g. Sophocles *Oedipus in Colonus* 19–20, Euripides *Electra* 489f.). On the other hand, angry characters are identified by sudden and speedy movement (cf. e.g. Sophocles, *Antigone* 766f. on Haemon, Euripides, *Bacchae* 214, on Pentheus).
168 On Heracles' mad dance, see Padel (1995), 139; Henrichs (1996), 62; Riley (2008), 36.
169 For the meta-theatrical perspective of the scene, see Kraus (1998), 151–6; Bassi (1998), 12–31.
170 Cf. the punitive petrification of the Phaeacian ship at *Odyssey* 13.163f. as cited at Steiner (2001), 138.
171 On binding as an apotropaic technique see Faraone (1991a–b) and (1992), 74; Graf (1997), ch. 5; cf. further Vernant on binding *xoana* (1991d), 156; Kindt (2012), 113–21.
172 Cf. Steiner (2001), 28, on breathing images.
173 This term is frequently used in tragedy to define a body on the verge of death (see Aeschylus *Agamemnon* 671, Euripides, *Alcestis* 205, *Hippolytus* 1246, *Phoinissae* 1419, 1442, *Bacchae* 1132; cf. Euripides fr. 936, ἀλλ' ἔτ' ἔμπνουν Ἅιδης μ' ἐδέξατο; Herodotus 7.181, Thucydides 1.134, 5.10; Plato, *Laws* 944a). Surprisingly, the term is not found in Hippocratic medical writings, except in one instance, in the *Breaths* 4.11, where it describes the process of inhalation. Cf. the Homeric term ἐμπνεόμενος, which is very common and describes the fury breath by the gods into the heroes (cf. e.g. *Iliad* 15. 262).
174 For more veiled characters, see in *Hippolytus* 133f., 243–5, *Andromache* 830, *Alcestis* 1020–69; cf. Aristophanes, *Frogs* 911–13, Euripides, *Phoinisae* 1485–92. See also Montiglio (2000), 176–80, who argues that the silenced man behind his veil is an invisible man, reinforcing the non-visual aspect of speech in contrast to theatrical visuality.
175 See on that Smith (1967), 297, 305f.

176 Cf. Aristophanes, *Frogs* 892f., καὶ ξύνεσι καὶ μυκτῆρες ὀσφραντήριοι,/ ὀρθῶς μ' ἐλέγχειν ὧν ἂν ἅπτωμαι λόγων, and consciousness and keen-scented nostrils, may I correctly refute whatever words I get hold of. As cited in Holmes (2010b), 248. Holmes argues that *On the Sacred Disease* 16, the word *synesis* is used, according to Holmes, 'to describe our alert awareness of the world' (p. 249).

177 On the causes of Orestes' madness in Euripides, *Orestes*, see Theodorou (1993), 33, 38: 'his madness comes from inside him and not of the gods'. Similarly, Gregory (1977), 301. On madness as the possible result of strong emotional states, see Aeschylus *Choephoroi* 233, [...] χαρᾶι δὲ μὴ 'κπλαγῆις φρένας (referring to Electra) and in *Trojan Women* 1284, ἐνθουσιᾶις, δύστηνε, τοῖς σαυτῆς κακοῖς (referring to Hecuba). See, further for this type of madness, Mattes (1970), 7.

178 He argues the same in Aeschylus *Choephoroi* where he states that he would have committed the murder regardless of Apollo's commands (300–5). However, in this play, this comment does not have any major role for the plot.

179 According to Stieber (2011), 157f., discussing Pentheus and the statue metaphor esp. as related to v. 934; according to Stieber, ἀνάκειμαι is the passive voice of ἀνατίθημι, i.e. to dedicate a statue.

180 On this role, see Taplin (1978) 76; Segal (1997), 225f., 257f.; Falkner (1999), 189; Dobrov (2001), 11, 58; Rehm (2002), 201; Valakas (2002), 86; Gerolemou (2016).

181 After this point, Pentheus appears not to be wholly sane; for example, he sees two suns and two Thebes (919f.) and wants to rip up Cithaeron with his bare hands (949). See Seaford (1996), 216.

182 Cf. Radke (2003), 72f., 169ff. She argues that this could be an indication that Agave's mad behaviour and crime could not be considered as entirely part of Dionysus' plan. See also Devereux (1970). The last scene with Cadmus at the place of a psychotherapist is, according to Devereux, a sign that Agave's attitude is not completely determined by others; the maenadic madness symptoms, such as foaming in the mouth and rolling back one's eyes (cf. 1122f.), according to Devereux, had disappeared before Agave's appearance on the stage, that is, before her encounter with her father. Her amnesia is not absolute; complete amnesia was not justified in Agaues' case, mainly because she could recognize her father (cf. v. 1233). On Agaue's madness, see also Simon (1978), 148; Gerolemou (2011), 366–76.

183 See Segal (1997), 97, 210. On one's failure to recognize relatives and friends (or even themselves) when one is seized with ἀθυμία see Thucydides 2.49.8.

184 Cf. Dodds (1960), 230; Mattes (1970), 88.

185 See Segal (1997), 65, 67. On the Maenad's mad hands, see Worman (2021), 82f.

186 See Scott (1975), e.g. p. 341. On Dionysus and automatisms, see Detienne (1989), 53–6.
187 Bianchi (2014), 79.
188 At the Aigai, the women's dance is conducted in parallel with the production of new wine; see also the feast known as Thuia. See Detienne (1989), 54–6.

Chapter 3

1 On scientific and technological progress in this period, see Sarton (1959); Edelstein (1967a), esp. ch. 4 on the Hellenistic period onwards; see also ibid. (1967b), 401–39, and Dodds' response (1973), 1–25, to Edelstein's notion of continuous progress. See also Zhmud (2006), esp. 16–22.
2 See among others, Krafft (1970); Tybjeg (2003); Newman (2004), 20–2.
3 On that, see Berryman (2003, 2009) and Schiefsky (2007). See ps.-Aristotle in *Mechanics* 847a 16–19, who argues that only engineering could provide a solution to paradoxical aporias which lie beyond natural law. Aristotle in *Physics* 199a 15–17, maintains something similar when saying that art completes and imitates the work of nature, ὅλως δὲ ἡ τέχνη τὰ μὲν ἐπὶ τελεῖ ἃ ἡ φύσις ἀδυνατεῖ ἀπεργάσασθαι, τὰ δὲ μιμεῖται.
4 Cf. Goldhill (1994), on the σοφός θεατής, educated audience of the second sophistic.
5 On the public character of automata, see Schürmann (1991), ch. 5; Millett (2001) 33; Schürmann (2002); Fragaki (2012); Caneva (2014); Gerolemou (2019a); Bur (2016); Grillo (2019), xcvii–cii.
6 On earlier automatic devices and the Archyta's dove, see Schmidt (1904); Schürmann (1991), 173–5; Huffman (2005), 571–9; Berryman (2003), 354f., and (2009), 96, argues that Archyta's dove could be referring to a kind of catapult; against this view see Grillo (2019) lxxxiii–iv.
7 Ruffell (forthcoming a). On the statue of Nysa, see further Fraser (1972), 413; Rice (1983), 62–8; Coleman (1996), 56–8; Koetsier and Kerle (2016); see further Pliny, *Natural History* 34.148 on Arsinoe's statue suspended through the use of magnetic stones and Lowe (2016), 7–13. See Rehm (1937); Schürmann (1991), 239f.l; Grillo (2019), lxxxviiif.; and Ruffell (forthcoming b).
8 See Berryman (2003), 354.
9 Θαυματοποιεῖν (here related to τερατολογεῖν and sophistic curiosities), according to Isocrates in his *Antidosis* 268f., attracts an empty-minded audience.
10 On νευρόσπαστα see Muratov's excellent study (2005), esp. pp. 2–4, 179–82; Herzog-Hauser (1936); Schröder (1983). See further on ancient clay dolls with

articulated limbs Elderkin (1930); Karageorghis (1992); Manson (1992); Muratov (2005). See also Chapuis and Droz (1958), 16f., who discuss a seated Aphrodite from the Hellenistic period, whose arms move with the help of metal pins. On the marionette analogy in Graeco-Roman antiquity, see Brumbaugh (1966), 46–58; Berryman (2009), 205–15. The metaphor of the νευρόσπαστον was also part of the imperial Stoic lingo in descriptions of the enslavement of the human ἡγεμονικόν to the 'passions that make a puppet of yourself', as Marcus Aurelius 12.19.1.1–2 puts it (cf. Michael of Ephesus, *Motion of Animals* 115.5–6 and *Mantissa* 105.33); see Alesse (2009), 256 on that.

11 On θαυματοποιοί see also Athenaeus, *The Deipnosophists* 1.35. 30–5, 4.3.28f., 12.54.24–7, 14.5.5f. On θαυματοποιοία see Pugliara (2003), 55f.; Roby (2016), 48f.; Lightfoot (2021), ch. 7. See also *Inscriptiones Graecae* I³ 757, a late archaic dedication for a prize in θαύματα, θαύμασι νικέσας, probably a contest (of uncertain nature); cited by Neer (2010b), 224 n. 223. Cf. Plato *Laws* 658b–c [...] ου θαυμαστον δε ει τις και θαυματα επιδεικνυς μαλιστ αν νικᾶν ηγοιτο, and it would be no marvel if someone who puts on a display of marvels thinks he could win.

12 Olson and Sens (1999), 143, argue that the humorous use of the term θαυματοποιοί suggests that these πόρναι are not simple dancing girls but are able to perform wondrous acts in bed. Cf. Xenophon, *Symposion* 4.55, the dancers are moved by the Syracusan like puppets.

13 Furley (1955), 390, reads μηχανοποιοί, while Lorimer (1933) has μηχανοτέχναι. Reale and Bos (1995) read μεγαλότεχνοι with most manuscripts and Thom (2014).

14 Nussbaum (1976), 147f. See also Grillo (2019), 143.

15 On the divine as a marionette player see also Philo, *On Flight and Finding*, 46.

16 Berryman (2009), 50–3, argues that Pappus wishes to maintain this wondrous aura for mechanics, however, only in relation to the way mechanical workings are displayed, and not as a significant part of its theory; see on that also Cuomo (2000), 106, 124. Finally, see Grillo (2019) *ad* Hero, *On Automata Making* 1.1. Further on θαῦμα and mechanics see below in this chapter.

17 Cf. a similar catalogue in Proclus' commentary on the First Book of Euclid's *Elements*, p. 41, 8–14.

18 See further *Sophist* 224a, 235b, 268d on sophistic jugglery.

19 Kurke (2013), 126, believes that θαῦμα here refers to a νευρόσπαστον. Moreover, as she puts it '[t]he designation *thauma* points us to something essential about puppets, focalised (as it were) through the credulous gaze of very small children: though we know them to be mechanical and inanimate, we simultaneously believe that puppets are alive, for they are infused with motion and voice'.

20 On the mimetic deceptiveness of the Platonic θαῦμα see Neer (2010b), 63–6; Hunzinger (2015), 434f.; Lightfoot (2021), ch. 7 and pp. 187–98. On the divine θαῦμα in Plato, see Nightingale (2001), 44–53, and ibid. (2004), 258–61.
21 See, e.g., *Republic* 520b or in *Apology* 23c, *Protagoras* 320a, 323c, *Alcibiades i* 118 c, *Meno* 92e and Naas (2018), ch. 2.
22 On θαῦμα in relation to technical automation: *Metaphysics* 983a14, θαυμάτων τα αὐτόματα; *Generation of Animals* 741b8f., ἐν τοῖς αὐτομάτοις θαύμασι, 734b10, τὰ αὐτόματα τῶν θαυμάτων. On technical automata and θαῦμα specifically in Aristotle, *Metaphysics*, see Spoerri (1985); Pugliara (2003), 62–75; Devecka (2013), 57; Primavesi (2018), cxiiif. Generally, on θαῦμα in Aristotle, see Nightingale (2004), 254, 261–5 and Carvalho (2015) with ample bibliography on the subject. Cf. further Meißner (1999), 58f. and Roby (2016), 147.
23 Henry (2005) argues that the νευροσπαστικόν refers to a mechanical automaton and not to a marionette. On the νευροσπαστικόν in Alexander, see also Fernandez and Mittelmann (2020), 278f. Cf. the use of the νευρόσπαστον in Simplicius, *On Aristotle Physics* 313 21–7, where, according to Henry (2005), all of its movements are the result of the action of an operator pulling a single cord.
24 Cf. ps.-Philoponus, *On Aristotle's: On the Generation of Animals* 77.14–29, and Michael of Ephesus, *On Aristotle's on the Generation of Animals* 14.3 77.14–23. However, Henry (2005), 38, suggests that Aristotle in *Generation of Animals* might be thinking of hypothetical automata 'whose internal motion is the actualisation of a single potential rather than a causal sequence passing through a series of mechanical gears'.
25 On how these automata might work, see, among others, Nussbaum (1976), 146–52, where she argues that the automata here refer to puppets which, when given an initial boost by the puppeteer and through a mechanism of cables, pegs or both, perform various motions without further direction. See also Nussbaum (1978), 43, where she corrects the κρουόντων ἀλλήλας τὰς στρέβλας (as in Bekker 1831), to κρουόντων ἄλλήλα τῶν ξύλων and translates 701b1f. as following: 'The movement of animals is like that of automatic puppets, which are set moving when a small motion occurs: the cables are released and the pegs strike against one another.' Nussbaum, however, does not define the type of automatic puppet. I agree with Henry (2005), 3f., who believes that the automatic wonders Aristotle talks about in the *Motion of Animals* could not resemble simple νευρόσπαστα, puppets 'whose limbs are moved independently of one another by a puppeteer manipulating strings attached directly to each limb'; instead, we must imagine them as mechanical puppets designed to move through the motion of one string controlled by an external agent and internal gears. See also Berryman (2002a; 2007a: 38f.; 2007b) and ibid. (2009), 71–5, 201–5. At p. 73, she argues that the

automaton which Aristotle refers to in *Motion of Animals* could be similar to the device Hero describes at *On Automata Making* 24. Primavesi (2018), cxv–cxxvi, believes that the automata in *Motion of Animals* must be like the stationary automata described in Hero's treatise on automata and he corrects the Bekker text to λυομένων τῶν στρεβλῶν καὶ κρουόντων πρὸς ἀλλήλας <εὐθὺς τῶν ζωιδίων τὰς μαχαίρας> in analogy to Hero's *On Automata Making* 22, where the stationary automata are described as sawing, working with axes, hammers, etc. He translates as follows: 'Wie aber die Automatentheater in Gang gesetzt werden, sobald nur eine kleine Bewegung stattgefunden hat- man lost die aufgezogenen Schnüre, und es schlagen <sofort die Figuren ihre Säbel> gegeneinander' (p. cxxv). Grillo (2019) suggests that the automaton's 'power source may have been the unwinding of cords (possibly of sinew) from a windlass' (p. lxxxv, see also 142–4); see, also, Grillo (2019), at II.6, where he maintains that Aristotle's automata 'cannot easily be made to correspond to any of the devices described by Hero' (p. 142).
26 In the Bekker (1831) text, the cart is ὅπερ ὀχούμενον αὐτὸ κινεῖ εἰς εὐθύ. Nussbaum (1978) accepts the emendation ὁ γὰρ ὀχούμενος. Primavesi (2018) corrects the text as follows: ὅπερ< ὁ> ὀχούμενος αὐτὸς κινεῖ εἰς εὐθύ.
27 Grillo (2019), lxxxv n. 159, argues that there is an implied contrast here between the initial impetus of motion associated with the automaton and the subsequent motion of a device, as in the case of the toy cart. De Groot (2014), in ch. 5, argues that the automaton here does not signify a succession of material movers in contact. Aristotle forms his δύναμις concept on the basis of the idea of mechanical potential which the lever principle displays.
28 On perception and self-motion see Nussbaum (1978), 256–69 and 380; Nussbaum and Puttman (1992); Furley (1994), 13f.; Freeland (1994), 53.
29 On *pneuma* in Aristotle, see Berryman (2002a) and Corcilius (2020).
30 See Aristotle, *Physics* 190b 3–11, on more specific processes by which things come into being: (1) μετασχηματισμός, change of shape (e.g. bronze statues), or (2) πρόσθεσις, as in things which grow, or (3) ἀφαίρεσις, as when a block of marble is chipped into a Hermes, or (4) σύνθεσις, as in building a house, or (5) ἀλλοίωσις, such modifications as those which affect the properties of the material itself (trans. by P. H. Wicksteed and F. M. Cornford).
31 Lennox (1982). But see Gotthelf (1989) and Lennox (2001b), 226, on spontaneous generation in Aristotle's biology and how this differs from spontaneity in *Physics*. On spontaneous generation in Aristotle, see also Dudley (2012), ch.5; Lehoux (2017), esp. ch.1; Wilson (2020); Kress (2020).
32 See further *On Automata Making* 1.3f.; 2.12; 4.4; 20.2, 4f.; 21.1f.; 22.1f., 4, 6; 24.1.
33 Grillo (2019), ixxxi, on 'mechanical and scenic flexibility' in Hero's *On Automata Making*. See also Grillo (2019), 114f.

34 See also Philo, *Belopoeica* 77.12–18 on the pneumatic devices of Ctesibius, and Schürmann (1991), 173–89, and Berryman (2009), 165–70.
35 See also Philo, *Belopoeica* 71.2–3, on the springiness of horn and certain wood. On the elasticity of air and its ability to spring back to its original situation, see Berryman (2009), 126f. – specifically on Philo's use of εὐτονία in his *Belopoeica* – pp. 169f. (here she also refers to how Hero's elasticity concept was influenced by Ctesibius's inventions which depend on compressed air), see further pp. 173, 193–7, and Roby (2016), 281, 282. Cf. Galen at *On the Natural Faculties* 1.7.17: in discussing how nutrition is necessary for growing things, Galen refers to children rubbing pig bladders and blowing air into them so that they expand. This artificial expansion makes the skin of the bladder thinner, since it cannot nourish in the same way that nature would have done. Cf. organs which are described as elastic, such as the lungs, ps.-Aristotle, *On Things Heard* 800b16, cited by Berryman (2009), 195.
36 Murphy (1995), 40 n. 3; Grillo (2019), 136.
37 Roby (forthcoming).
38 Drachmann (1948) 8; Meißner (1999), 162–5; and Roby (2016), 261–3 on the resilience of metals in Philo's *Belopoeica*.
39 The self-moving Archyta's dove is also made out of wood, probably due to a lightweight design concept (Aulus Gellius, *Attic Nights* 10. 12.8–10 (Loeb). On the properties of wood, see Aristotle, *Metereologica* 384b 16–20; 387b 27–9, on the inflamability and non-meltability of wood; 386a 27–9, on the non-plasticity of wood; 386b 1–24, on the non-malleability of wood; 386b 27, on the feasibility of wood; 387a 5–8, wood is cuttable; 387a 18–20, on the combustibility of wood. On wood constructions and properties, see also Biton, *Belopoeica* 44.5f., 52, Theophrastus, *History of Plants* 5.6; see further Oribasius, *Medical Collections* 49.3, on the springiness of oak, and Ulrich (2007, 2008). See also, among others, Lancaster and Ulrich (2013), and Lapatin (2014) with rich bibliographical references generally on materials in the Graeco-Roman world.
40 On material innovation, see among others, Wilson (2002); Schneider (2007), 159–62; Lancaster and Ulrich (2013), esp. 159f.; Flohr (2016).
41 Cf. Aristotle, *Physics* 199a15–17: arts improve nature or they can imitate nature. This is somehow different in Stoicism and Pliny where any kind of artificiality is often regarded as unnatural and related to *luxuria* (see e.g. Pliny 22.118, 24.4–5, 29.23). On that see Wallace-Hadrill (1990) and Newman (2004), 17–24. See further Galen, in *Natural Faculties* 2.82, where he insists that technology could not transform matter in the way nature does (e.g. turn wax into ivory or gold). On artificial versus natural materials, see e.g. Diodorus Siculus 3.45.7, on

αὐτοφυής and ἄπυρος, virgin and 'unfired' gold vs gold gained through mining and processing. Cf. further the Leiden and Stockholm papyri (Caley and Jensen 2008) which describe various technological processes through which artificial materials are produced in imitation of natural materials; on that see Newman (2004), 27.

42 See also Petronius, *Satyricon* 51; cf. Dio Cassius, *Roman History* 57.21 who has a different version of the story.

43 Especially on the screw see Drachmann (1958) and Oleson (1984), 291–4. Against the assumption that the screw is a Hellenistic invention, often ascribed to Archimedes, see Dalley and Oleson (2003).

44 On these simple machines see Schiefsky (2008); Laird (2015). On simple and complicated machines see Wilson (2008).

45 On the meaning of ὕσπληγξ at Hero, *On Automata Making* 2.6, see further Grillo (2019), 140–5, and Ruffell (forthcoming a). See also Drachmann (1963), 197.

46 See Ruffell (forthcoming a) on the technical reasons behind the limited use of anthropomorphic automata.

47 See also Hero, *On Automata Making* 13.9 and *Pneumatics* 1.7, 1.29, 1.32 and the term κρύπτω, hide – i.e. mechanisms/devices; cf. ps.-Aristotle, *Mechanics* 848a34–8, and Oribasius, *Medical Collections* 49.5.15. See, among others, Tybjerg (2003), 451, and Bosak-Schroeder (2016), 128, who argue that hiding mechanisms and techniques increases the feeling of wonderment. I argue that in Hero, wonderment lies mainly in the explanation of the mechanical spectacle; on that, see below. See also at Hero's *Pneumatics* 2.3, 2.7, 2.13f., where glass is used, allowing Hero to show, according to di Pasquale (2004), 66f., 'with clarity how the mechanical builder of complex machines, unlike what usually happens, does not want to conceal the marvellous effects visible in the transparency of this material through which its extraordinary efficacy can be seen'.

48 Von Staden briefly (1996), 86, draws on this when he refers to the relationship between Hellenistic medicine, especially Herophilus, and mechanics: 'The Kallimachean poetics of smallness, the miniaturization of mechanical technology by Ktesibios and others, and miniaturization in the decorative arts all belong to the "culture of smallness". So does a noteworthy feature of Herophilus's model of the body – what one might call his "miniaturization of anatomy".'

49 See *On Automata Making* 3.1 on the size of the base on which the mobile automaton is placed. The statue of Nysa, by contrast, which allegedly moves on its own accord, is quite big, 8 cubits high, probably in order for the operators to be able to hide within and in order for the statue itself to be seen from a distance (Athenaeus, *The Deipnosophists* 5.28.22).

50 See further on Hero's devices as safe constructions, without any dangers *On Automata Making* 1.7, 5.1f., 10.4, 21.1, 22.1; εὐκόπως, *On Automata Making* 11.11, 12.3, 19.2, *Pneumatics* 1.7.30f., 1.2842f., 1.38.39f.; cf. εὐλύτως, easily released, e.g. at *On Automata Making* 13.7, 16.3, 18.1,4, *Pneumatics* 1.11.17f., 1.16.29f., 1.34.6; εὐκυλίστως, easily rolled in *On Automata Making* 11.11; εὐκίνητος easily moved in 10.4.

51 Cf. Suetonius in *Claudius* 34: 'Emperor Claudius, if any automatic device (*automatum*) or mobile scenic structure (*pegma*) or anything else of the sort had not worked well, would force the carpenters or assistants to fight in the gladiatorial arena'.

52 Grillo (2019), cviiif. See also Tybjerg (2005), on novelty.

53 Gell (1992).

54 Simondon (2012). See also the Introduction of this book.

55 See Athenaeus Mechanicus, *On Machines* p. 31 W. = p. 58 W.-B. on Ctesibius' invention 'Γενναίου δὲ τοῦτο ἄξιον οὐθενός, ἀλλ' ἐκ θαυμάτων τὸ μηχάνημα συγκείμενον καὶ μάλιστα τὸν τεχνίτην τὸ θαυμάσαι.' This machine does not have any genuine value but is concocted from marvels and particularly (in order) to marvel at the technician.

56 On rhetorical display in Hero, see Tybjerg (2003), 453–6.

57 I agree with Cambiano (1994a), 617–21, Berryman (2009), 52f., Bosak-Schroeder (2016), 127f., Roby (2016), 5, 45f., 78, 266, Grillo (2019), at 1.1 (pp. 114–17), and Ruffell (forthcoming a) that the role of θαῦμα in Hero is acknowledged only for its effect on the audience; but it is not important for the discipline of mechanics itself as Tybjerg (2003) argues. On miracles and machines, see also Pugliara (2003), 5–11.

58 On the self-reflexivity of illusion in Hero's *On Automata Making*, see ní Mheallaigh (2014), 266–70 and on fiction as reality p. 274. See also Corso (1999) and Roby (2016), 146f. On theatrical automation, i.e. scenic machinery, generally in the imperial era and in the work of Hero in particular, see Johnson (2013); Beacham (2013). Cf. the reference to the automaton in Petronius, *Satyricon* 54.4 as part of other entertaining mechanical tricks (see further 34.8–10; 36.3f.; 60.1–3) and Grillo (2019), xc11–xcv with bibliography; see further Vitruvius, *On Architecture*, 10, proem 3; Seneca, *Epistles* 88.22, 90.15.

59 See also Diodorus, 16.74–5 and the wondrous war machine that even enemies were struck by its beauty and on one occasion asked Demetrius for a truce just to have a closer look at it; as cited by Cuomo (2018), 455.

60 On the concept of a technological history of art see, among others, Edelstein (1967), 78f. See also Mattusch (1988); Lapatin (2001) and (2014) on materials and techniques in art.

61 As described, for instance, by Quintilian, *Institutes of Oratory* 6.2.29, ps.-Longinus in *On the Sublime* 15.1 and Horace, *The Art of Poetry* 180-8. On that see Van Eck (2015), 45-68; Roby (2016), 91f. and ch. 3. Further on *phantasia* in ekphrastic context, among others, Webb (2009); Platt (2011), 230-4, 293-332; and Squire (2013).
62 Roby (2016). See also Beacham (2013).
63 See Roby (2016), 116f.; Bosak-Schroeder (2016), 127f.; and Grillo (2019), at 1.5.
64 On the aesthetics of naturalism in the classical period, see Pollitt (1965), 61-5, 154-5, 167; Métraux (1995); Spivey (1996), ch. 2; Neer (2010b), ch. 4; Squire (2011), ch. 2; Zanker (2015); on naturalism as artists' artistic objective, see the story told by Pliny the Elder in *Natural History* 35.65 on the painting contest between Zeuxis and Parrhasius; see further Brecoulaki (2015). Specifically, for lifelikeness as a Hellenistic motif, see, among others, the *andriantopoiika* of Posidippus and generally the ekphrastic epigrams; on that, see Manakidou (1993), 257-9; Männlein-Robert (2007a), esp. ch. 3, and Männlein-Robert (2007b); Squire (2010); Seidensticker (2015). For the naturalistic ideal especially in the Roman period, see Elsner (1995), 15-20, 28-39; Newman (2004), ch.1; Truit (2015), ch. 2.
65 On the cow of Myron (*Greek Anthology* 9.727), Squire (2010), 610f., also refers to talking statues. See also on the talking cow made by Myron (*Greek Anthology* 9.713-42, 793-8), Gross (1992), ch. 9.
66 See further on that *On Regimen* 21, Plato, *Cratylus* 432b 6-10, Xenophon, *Memorabilia* 3.10; Quintilian, *Institutes of Oratory* 2.13.13; and Galen, *Natural Faculties* 2.
67 See Berryman (2003), esp. 350-6, on the application of the mechanical analogy for explaining moving artefacts.
68 Translated by Barnish (1992).
69 On this type of *phantasia* see, among others, Watson (1988), ch. 4; Platt (2009); Squire (2013); Sheppard (2014), 80f.; and ibid.(2015).
70 Most of the depictions refer to statues; however, two items of his collection are paintings (Depictions 7 and 14). Unless otherwise stated, all translations of Callistratus' text are by Fairbanks (1931).
71 On the date of Callistratus' activity, see Nesselrath and Bäbler (2006), 3-5.
72 Lucian in *Gallus* 24 refers to a king reincarnated as a rooster who explains the nature of monarchy by depicting what lies inside beautiful statues (ἢν δὲ ὑποκύψας ἴδῃς τά γ' ἔνδον), which is: bars, struts, dowels, beams, wedges and pitch and clay and other ugly stuff such as mice and rats. Cf. further Lucian, *Tragic Zeus* 8 and Lapatin (2001), 71.

73 Cox Miller (2009), 3–7. On the 'material turn' in late antiquity, see further Caseau (1999); Harvey (2006), 57–9; Schibille (2014).
74 But Iamblichus, in some instances, condemns not only matter but also the makers of magical talismans and idols (see, e.g., *On the Mysteries* 3.13); see also Plotinus who thinks of matter as impairment, *Enneads* 1.8.8, 2.4. See Shaw (1995), 29, 37–44, for further cases where matter is disdained by theurgists (mostly in Iamblichus).
75 Emilsson (1988), 7f. On Neoplatonic ideas on art perception, see Mathew (1963), 12–22; Stern-Gillet (2002); Halfwassen (2007); Schibille (2014), ch. 6.
76 Betancourt (2018), ch. 6.
77 On Neoplatonic ideas of *phantasia*, see Sheppard (2014), ch. 3.
78 Consider the example of Phidias, who did not just imitate Zeus according to what he saw with his eyes, but through his mind, imagining what 'Zeus would look like if he wanted to make himself visible' (Plotinus, *Enneads* 5. 8. 38–40; see also Plotinus 5.8.1.10–26; but see *Enneads* 3.8.2; cf. 5.9 and Berryman (2003), 363; Proclus, *On Plato's Timaeus* I, 265.18–26).
79 On the Neoplatonic, theurgical tradition and manifestation of the divine in material form, where material σύμβολα were inserted into hollow cavities of a god's statue in order to animate it, see esp. Proclus, *On Plato's Timaeus* 1.330–1, 3. 155. 18–25, 3. 220, 22). In *On Plato's Cratylus* 51.33–6 Proclus states explicitly that statues can be turned into suitable receptacles for the gods through the use of the proper material. See further Porphyrius, *On Statues*; however, see Clement of Alexandria, *Exhortation to the Greeks* 4.48.1 (ed. Markovic). See Dodds (1947); Faraone (1992) and Steiner (2001), e.g. pp. 112–17, arguing for the existence of ritually animated statues as early as the archaic and classical period. See also Johnston (2008) and Deligiannakis (2015). Cf. Stewart (2003), ch. 6; Cox Miller (2009), 139; Uzdavinys (2009); Kindt (2016), ch. 6, on theurgy and animate statues. On the ritual materialism of the theurgists see Shaw (1995), ch. 1. See also the case of the Chaldaean Oracles: for instance, fr. 224 instructs a priest how to make an animate statue of Hekate in the open, under the moon, from wild rue and adorn it with animals which live around the house. Cf. Eunapius, *Lives of the Sophists* 475: he tells here the story of how Maximus of Ephesus made Hecate's statue laugh and caused the torches in her hand to light up automatically.
80 On technological advancements in late antiquity, see Roby (2016), 92–6, and Cuomo (2018), on the flourishing of technologies in general in late antiquity. See also Lavan (2007), on both technological innovation and stagnation in late antiquity, and Lewis (2007), on technological development in Byzantium. On Proclus see Berryman (2009), 59f. and ibid. (2020), 230.

81 On magic's relation to automatic art, see Kris and Kurz (1980), 89–99; Corso (1999); Bielfeldt (2014). In some cases, as reported in magical practices, magnets were placed inside figurines, seemingly to give them agency, see, e.g., *Greek Magical Papyri* (PGM) 4.1807–10, p. 3142. On that, see Lowe (2016), 3f. n. 5.

82 Vernant (1991b); Webb (2009); Platt (2011). Philostratus the Elder, in his *Imagines*, tries to explain to the audience how a painting could depict fire in the midst of water. He asks a young pupil whom he is guiding through a series of images: 'Did you recognise, my boy, that the painting here is based on Homer, or have you not yet recognised it, clearly thinking it as a wonder (*thauma*), wondering how on earth the fire could live in the midst of the water?' (1.1.1). As Philostratus puts it, the danger for the perceiver of art does not lie in the fact that she/he will mistake the painted fire in water for a real one, but rather that she/he will fail to respond to this situation with erudition. Philostratus explains extraordinary, paradoxical scenes in art, such as fire in the midst of the water, by creating similar mental images through literary *analoga* (see e.g. 1.8, 2.7).

83 Cf. similar use of *thauma* by the scholiasts; see Nünlist (2009), 145. Generally, on wonder as a constituent element of *ekphrasis*, see Pollitt (1974), 78, 189–91, 402–5; Becker (1995); Hunzinger (2015); Neer (2010), ch. 1.

84 See Cicero and his description of how the Roman audience reacted at first to the phenomenal sphere of Archimedes in *Republic* 1.21–2 (speciem ipsam non sum tanto opere admiratus).

85 The term relates to cunningly wrought animated figures. Cf. the δαίδαλα decorating, for instance, the crown of Pandora, an artefact by Hephaestus, which probably resembles automata, looking and talking like human beings (Hesiod, *Theogony* 581–4; cf. further in *Iliad* 18.591–2, *Odyssey* 19.227–9); on *daedaliques* see Delcourt (1957), 48–55; Faraone (1992), 101f. n. 44; Frontisi-Ducroux (1975), 83ff. and Morris (1992), esp. ch. 8; Männlein-Robert (2007a), 27–30.

86 Steiner (2001), 162, 176, 183. Cf. Callistratus' 7.3, where nature itself is spellbound by the art of music.

87 See also Narcissus in Philostratus, *Imagines* 1.23.3; on that see Newby (2009), 334, 338. Cf. the concept of *agalmatophilia*, see Corso (1999), 102–4; Steiner (2001), 186–207; Chaniotis (2014), 282–4. See also Gross (1992), 72–82, esp. Ovid's account of Pygmalion and Galatea (*Metamorphoses* 10. 243–97). See further Lucian, *Essays in Portaiture* 1 and Francis (2009b), 292.

88 Cf. Herophilus and Erasistratus on hidden δυνάμεις working in the body and Aristotle, *On the Soul* 414a 29–31; cf. von Staden (1996), 87f., cf. further pp. 92–8. See also Berryman (2007b), 363; ibid. (2009), 197–200; Schiefsky (2007); Roby (2016), 70.

89 Cf. the brief reference to the statue's wheels (Ἀεὶ τροχάω) in Posidippus' epigram, in *Greek Anthology* 16. 275. See also Kim (2017). For a 3D reconstruction of the Lysippan Kairos, see Kim (2015–16). For another Lysippean moving statue, see Pliny the Elder *Natural History* 34.38 on Zeus of Taras which 'can be moved by the hand' (mirum in eo quod manu). Cf. further Pliny, *Natural History* 34.65, who argues that the moving Lysippean statue could be related to the fact that Lysippus 'made them as they appeared to be' (a se quales viderentur esse). On Ausonius' Kairos statue, see *Epistles* 12 and Kim (forthcoming), arguing about the possibility that Kairos' statue might be considered a real automaton.

90 For circular motion as the basis of mechanical phenomena, cf. ps.-Aristotle, *Mechanics* 847b 15f., πάντων δὲ τῶν τοιούτων ἔχει τῆς αἰτίας τὴν ἀρχὴν ὁ κύκλος; furthermore, the circle is for the author 'the first principle of all marvels' (οὐδὲν ἄτοπον τὸ πάντων εἶναι τῶν θαυμάτων αὐτὸν ἀρχήν, 848a10–11, see also 19–37 and Schiefsky (2007). Similarly, Hero describes the motion of the theatrical automata animals as rotating around the axis (in *On Automata Making* 2.3 [. . .] τὰ δὲ ζῴδια περὶ ἄξονας χαλκοῦς ἐμβεβηκότας εἰς χοινικίδας χαλκᾶς συνεσμηρισμένας αὐτοῖς). Cf. also the rotating Dionysus in Hero, *On Automata Making* 13f. and Suetonius in the *Life of Nero* 31.2 on the dining table of Nero, which was round and rotated, imitating the motion of the globe.

91 Cf. the technical explanation of the Archimedes' sphere by Gallus in Cicero, *Republic* 1. 21–2.

92 In contrast, Julian Aegyptius at *Greek Anthology* 16.130 makes clear that if Niobe's statue appears to be lifeless, this should not lead us to blame the artist.

93 Morris (1992), 19–21; Berryman (2003), 352f. and (2009), 24–9; see also Männlein-Robert (2007a), 34, 96: 'Die ursprünglich magisch-religiös aufgefassten sprechenden Objekte sind zum Produkt eines menschlichen Künstlers geworden.'

94 Cited by Corso (1999), 104f. See also ibid., p. 106, on Praxiteles' art in connection to magic and divination.

95 Männlein-Robert (2007a), 110f.

96 A similar situation is described in *Greek Anthology* 16. 60 by the epigrammatist Simonides. According to him, the artist Scopas and not Bacchus is the one who made Bacchant's statue frenzied; likewise, regarding Praxiteles, see *Greek Anthology* 16.159, Τίς λίθον ἐψύχωσε; τίς ἐν χθονὶ Κύπριν ἐσεῖδεν;/ ἵμερον ἐν. πέτρῃ τίς τόσον εἰργάσατο;/ Πραξιτέλους χειρῶν ὅδε που πόνος, ἢ τάχ᾽ Ὄλυμπος/ χηρεύει Παφίης εἰς Κνίδον ἐρχομένης ('Who gave a soul to marble? Who saw Cypris on earth? Who wrought such love-longing in a stone? This must be the work of Praxiteles' hands, or else perchance Olympus is bereaved since Paphian has descended to Cnidus', tr. Paton).

97 3.5, ἐμοὶ μὲν δὴ θεασαμένῳ τὴν τέχνην ἐπῄει πιστεύειν, ὅτι καὶ χορὸν ἤσκησε κινούμενον Δαίδαλος καὶ χρυσῷ παρεῖχεν αἰσθήσεις, ὅπου καὶ Πραξιτέλης εἰς τὴν εἰκόνα τοῦ Ἔρωτος ἐνέθηκε μικροῦ καὶ νοήματα καὶ πτέρυγι τὸν ἀέρα τέμνειν ἐμηχανήσατο. 'As I gazed on this work of art, the belief came over me that Daedalus had indeed wrought a dancing group in motion and had bestowed sensation upon gold, while Praxiteles had all but put intelligence into his image of Eros and had so contrived that it should cleave the air with its wings.'

98 General on air as a vital force in Greek thought, see Solmsen (1957); Irby-Massie and Keyser (2002) 204–19. Cf. the role of *pneuma* in magical animation: an event described in a magical papyrus depicts a statue of Eros made of wax and plants. In front of this statue, seven birds are strangled in order for their *pneuma* to enter the statue and enliven it (*Greek Magical Papyri* 12.14–95). See also *Greek Magical Papyri* 5. 370–446, a hollow statue of Hermes is to be created and a papyrus is to be placed inside for the purpose of *empneumatosis*. However, Haluszka (2008), 484, 492f., argues that nothing here indicates animation. See further Dodds (1947), 63, who refers to the magical papyri offering recipes for constructing such images and animating them. See also the late Hermetic dialogue Asclepius, quoted by Dodds, p. 53, which refers to 'statuas animates sensu et spiritu plenas' which foretell the future (*Corpus Hermeticum* I, 338, 358). See also Ciraolo (1992) and Cox Miller (2009) 138.

99 See *Greek Anthology* 16. 244, on the pipe of the Satyr working, according to the text, of its own accord, αὐτομάτως. Cf. *Greek Anthology* 9.826, 12.57, 12.134, 16.225 for further pneumatic settings.

100 Cf. Christodorus Coptus' ekphrastic epigram for Demosthenes, where he is presented as wanting to 'endow his unbreathing statue (ἄπνοον τύπον) with voice, but art kept him tied with the seal of her brazen silence' (29–31: ἀλλά ἑ τέχνη χαλκείης ἐπέδησεν ὑπὸ σφρηγῖδα σιωπῆς); in this case, materials do not become animated, i.e. they cannot express emotions or intentions probably as a response to the pagan animation of statues. See Bassett (1996) and Kaldellis (2007) on Christodorus' *ekphrasis*.

101 The idea that air can be pressed is grounded in the debatable notion of the materiality of air; see Empedocles fr. 100, Aristotle, *Problems* 939a37–b4; Philo, *Belopoeica* 77. 12–27; Hero, *Pneumatics* 1 proem 108–90.

102 Hero describes a similar phenomenon in his *Pneumatics* where an organ is constructed in such a way so as to produce the sound of a flute when a windmill operates, powered by the wind (1.43, ὀργάνου κατασκευή, ὥστε ἀνέμου συρίζοντος ἦχον ἀποτελεῖσθαι αὐλοῦ).

103 On the art of giving voice to a mute art object in *ekphrasis*, see Männlein-Robert (2007a), 15, 18, 33–5, 268–9, and ibid. (2007b), 94f. On silent statues, see Steiner

(2001), 136–45. On statues talking via inscribed words, see Gross (1992), 142f.; Cox Miller (2009), 137f.; Hersey (2009), 14; Stähli (2014), 214, and e.g. Plutarch, *Camillus* 6, on Juno's talking statue.

104 [...] αἱ δὲ Αἰθιόπων χεῖρες πόρους τῶν ἀμηχάνων ἐξεῦρον καὶ τὴν ἀφθογγίαν ἐξενίκησαν τοῦ λίθου. 'Yet the hands of Ethiopians discovered means to accomplish the impossible, and they overcame the inability of stone to speak.'

105 Aristotle's *On the Soul* 1 406b15–22 reports that Daedalus made a statue of Aphrodite move by merely filling it with quicksilver. On Daedalus' animated statues, see further Chapters 1 and 2 in this book.

106 On Memnon's statue, see Bowersock (1984); Duffey (2007); Platt (2009), 136–44. On the techniques behind/in the statue see Pettorino (1999); Bur (2016), 182–4.

107 See further the singing birds of Hero in *Pneumatics* 1.15–16, 2.4, made to whistle by flowing water; also Ctesibius' singing birds known from Vitruvius 10.7.4. Philo of Byzantium, *Pneumatics* 58, 60 (Prager 1974) also refers to singing birds.

108 Cf. the sonic animation of the Memnon statue, one of the sacred images moving with the help of light studied by Pentcheva (2009, 2010, 2011). Specifically, see her experimental work on the icon of the Archangel at San Marco, where she discusses (through film) how candlelight animates the metal relief image. These points are also succinctly made by Pentcheva (2009). On sonic/light animation and Hagia Sophia see Schibille (2014) and later in this chapter.

109 The material's mimetic flexibility is akin to the genre of pantomime, where the dancer readjusts to each occasion (cf. Lucian, *On Dancing* 77, [...] ὡςλυγίζεσθαί τε ὅπῃ καιρὸς καὶ συνεστάναι καρτερῶς, εἰ τούτου δέοι) in order to efficiently present *ethos* and *pathos*, for instance Athamas in a state of frenzy and Ino in terror in Lucian *On Dancing* 67; see Lada-Richards (2003).

110 On bronze and liveness, see further the 'new' Posiddipus poems, 63–5, 68, 95 (ed. Austin and Bastianini) and Mattusch (forthcoming).

111 Regarding touching and the response of matter, see *Greek Anthology* 9.738.3. According to Julian the Aegyptius, art seems to surpass nature when one looks at it, but, when one touches it, nature is only nature.

112 See 9.2, where the material appears to respond to sound. Cf. Hero, *Pneumatics* 1.15 and Roby (2016), 117f.

113 τῶν ὀμωτῆς τέχνης μὴ πειθομένης τῆς ὕλης, ἀλλὰ νοούσης ὅτι σχηματίζει θεὸν καὶ δεῖ δυναστεύειν, 'the material not rendering obedience to the law of art, but realising that it represents a god and that he must work his own will'. Cf. *Greek Anthology* 16.160; the material, in this case iron, does not obey the sculptor and only with the intrusion of Ares Cnidea is Aphrodite's statue completed. See on that Corso (2004), 258.

114 On cultic statues being truly possessed by what they represent, see, e.g., Dio Chrysostom, *Oration* 12: on the statue of Zeus of Phidias, he asks himself how religious ideas are portrayed and transformed into something visible and tangible. See further on that Faraone (1992); Corso (1999) 101; Scheer (2000); Steiner (2001), 101f.; Platt (2011), 221f. Cf. also Chaniotis (2014), 267f., on how the god's or goddess's *epiphaneia* was directed to his/her cultic statue, as well as Bremmer (2013) and Platt (2011), 224–35. The matter is, of course, of great importance to *iconophilia* but this discussion is beyond the scope of this chapter.
115 On Triphiodorus, dating ranging from the third to the fifth century CE, see, Miguélez-Cavero (2013), 4–6.
116 On the building of the Trojan Horse, see further Oppian 1.173-95, Virgil's 2nd book 13–39 and Miguélez-Cavero (2013), 156–66. Cf. Faraone (1992), 101, and Francis (2009a) on the relationship between the automaton Pandora in Hesiod and the Trojan Horse.
117 The anonymous *Narratio de S. Sophia*, dating from the eighth or ninth century, describes a cistern, the Leontarion, on which animals with water flowing from their throats were carved by means of a mechanism (26, ed. Mango).
118 See, e.g., Nicetas Choniates, *Designis* 4, p. 856f.; on that, Mango (1972), 44f.
119 On late antique clocks, see Lewis (2000).
120 On Byzantine ekphrasis see, among others, Webb (1999); Nelson (2000). Generally, on the Byzantine concept of the living artefact and animation, see Belting (1994), 261–96; Cormack (2003); Barber (2006); Pentcheva (2009); ibid. (2010), esp. pp. 191–8; ibid. (2011); Peers (2012); Schibille (2014); Chatterjee (2014), esp. her introduction which focuses on the metaphor of the 'living icon', as well as the particularly useful bibliography. Cf. Papaioannou (2006), who discusses the issue of animation and aesthetics in Psellos and offers helpful bibliography on the subject.
121 Diels (1917), 5. See also Ruffell (forthcoming a).
122 Hunzinger (2005, 2015, 2018).
123 On that, see Gerolemou (2018a).
124 Webb (1999), 69.
125 Schibille (2009a, 2014).
126 On this *ekphrasis*, see Macrides and Magdalino (1988); James and Webb (1991); Webb (1999), 68f.; Pentcheva (2011); Schibille (2014), 20–6.
127 Pont (2005), 82; Schibille (2009a-b). On the scientific nature of Hagia Sophia, see further, among others, Downey (1946–8); Meek (1952); Hoffmann and Theocharis (2002); Svenshon and Stichel (2006).
128 See Mango (1972), 90 n. 168.

129 Cf. a passage in Photius' *ekphrasis* of the Pharos palatine chapel in Constantinople where a similar spectacle is being described (Homily X. 5, ed. Laourdas) and see Pentcheva (2010), 141–3, and (2016) 225; Betancourt (2018), ch. 7.
130 Roberts (1989), 74.
131 Translated by Mango (1972).
132 On further cases of technological animation in antiquity, see Bur, Gerolemou and Ruffell (forthcoming).

Conclusions

1 Gell (1992); Simondon (2012).

Bibliography

Adam, C. and P. Tannery (eds) (1904), *Oeuvres de Descartes*, Volume 7, *Meditationes de prima philosophia*, Paris.

Adams, E. (2018), 'The Psychology of Prostheses: Substitution Strategies and Notions of Normality Prostheses in Antiquity', in J. Draycott (ed.), *Prostheses in Antiquity, Medicine and the Body in Antiquity*, 180–208, Abingdon.

Adams, S. M. (1931), 'The Burial of Polyneices', *Classical Review*, 45: 110–11.

Adams, S. M. (1955), 'The *Antigone* of Sophocles', *Phoenix*, 9: 47–62.

Adkins, A. W. H. (1966), 'Basic Greek Values in Euripides', *Hecuba* and *Hercules Furens*', *Classical Quarterly*, 60: 218–19.

Alesse, F. (2009), 'Neurospastia: la problematica di anima e corpo in Marco Aurelio', in W. Lapini, L. Malusa and L. Mauro (eds), *Gli Antichi e Noi. Studi in Onore di Antonio Mario Battegazzore*, 255–67, Genova.

Alexandridis, A. (2017), 'Tod eines Roboters. Talos und der "ganz besondere Saft"', in M. Busch, S. Kroll and M. A. Maksymiak (eds), *Hippokratische Grenzgänge – Ausflüge in kultur- und medizingeschichtliche Wissensfelder. Festschrift für Hans-Uwe Lammel zum 65. Geburtstag*, 11–27, Hamburg.

Amato, E. (ed.) (2010), *Rose di Gaza: gli scritti retorico-sofistici e le Epistole di Procopio di Gaza*, Hellenica. Testi e strumenti di letteratura greca antica, medievale e umanistica, 35, Alessandria.

Amato, E. and P. Maréchaux (ed.) (2014), *Procope de Gaza: Discours et fragments; texte établi, introduit et commenté par Eugenio Amato; avec la collaboration de Aldo Corcella et Gianluca Ventrella; traduit [en français] par P. Maréchaux*, Paris.

Arendt, H. (1998), *The Human Condition*, 2nd edn, Chicago, IL.

Arnott, P. D. (1989), *Public and Performance in the Greek Theatre*, London and New York.

Arrowsmith, W. (1954), *The Conversion of Herakles: An Essay in Euripidean Tragic Structure*, Princeton, NJ.

Arthur, M. B. (1982), 'Cultural Strategies in Hesiod's *Theogony*: Law, Family, and Society', *Arethusa*, 15: 63–82.

Arthur, M. B. (1983), 'The Dream of a World Without Women: Poetics and Circles of Order in the *Theogony* Prooemium', *Arethusa*, 16: 97–116.

Asper, M. (2015), 'Explicit Knowledge', in M. Hose and D. Schenker (eds), *A Companion to Greek Literature*, Blackwell Companions to the Ancient World, 401–14, Malden, MA, and London.

Auslander, Ph. (1999), *Liveness: Performance in a Mediatized Culture*, Abington and New York.

Austin, C. and C. Bastianini (eds) (2002), *Posidippi Pallaei quae supersunt omnia*, Milan.

Austin, C. and S. D. Olson (eds) (2004), *Aristophanes: Thesmophoriazusae*, edited with introduction and commentary, Oxford.

Badmington, N. (2011), 'Posthumanism', in M. K. Booker and M. Ryan (eds), *The Encyclopedia of Literary and Cultural Theory, Vol. 3: Cultural Theory*, 1212–16, Oxford.

Balme, D. M. (1962), 'Development of Biology in Aristotle and Theophrastus: Theory of Spontaneous Generation', *Phronesis*, 7: 91–104.

Balsamo, A. (1996), *Technologies of the Gendered Body: Reading Cyborg Women*, Durham.

Balsamo, A. (2000), 'Reading Cyborgs Writing Feminism', in G. Kirkup (ed.), *The Gendered Cyborg: A Reader*, 148–58, London and New York.

Barad, K. (2012), *Agentieller Realismus: Über die Bedeutung materiell-diskursiver Praktiken*, Berlin.

Barber, Ch. (2006), 'Living Painting, or the Limits of Pointing? Glancing at Icons with Michael Psellos', in Ch. Barber and D. Jenkins (eds), *Reading Michael Psellos (The Medieval Mediterranean: Peoples, Economies and Cultures, 400–1500*, vol. 61, 117–30, Leiden.

Barnish, S. J. B. (1992), *Cassiodorus: Variae*, Translated Texts for Historians, 12, Liverpool.

Barrett, W. S. (1964), *Euripides: Hippolytos*, ed. with introduction and commentary, Oxford.

Bartoš, H. (2014), 'The Concept of *Mimesis* in the Hippocratic *De Victu*', *Classical Quarterly*, 64: 542–57.

Bassett, G. S. (1996), '*Historiae custos*: Sculpture and Tradition in the Baths of Zeuxippos', *American Journal of Archaeology*, 100: 491–506.

Bassi, K. (1998), *Acting Like Men: Gender, Drama, and Nostalgia in Ancient Greece*, Ann Arbor, MI.

Baudrillard, J. (1993), *Symbolic Exchange and Death*, translated by I. H. Grant with an introduction by M. Gane, published in association with Theory, Culture & Society, London.

Beacham, R. (2013), 'Heron of Alexandria's "Toy Theatre" Automaton: Reality, Allusion and Illusion', in K. Reilly (ed.), *Theatre, Performance and Analogue Technology: Historical Interfaces and Intermedialities*, 15–39, New York.

Becker, A. S. (1995), *The Shield of Achilles and the Poetics of Ekphrasis*, Lanham, MD.

Becker, O. (1937), *Das Bild des Weges und verwandte Vorstellungen im frühgriechischen Denken*, vol. 4, Berlin.

Bekker, I. (1831), *Aristoteles Graece: Aristotelis Opera*, Berlin Academy, I and II, Berlin.

Belfiore, E. S. (1986), 'Wine and *Catharsis* of the Emotions in Plato's *Laws*', *Classical Quarterly*, 36: 421–37.

Belting, H. (1994), *Likeness and Presence: A History of the Image Before the Era of Art*, translated by E. Jephcott, Chicago, IL.

Benjamin, W. (1935), *Das Kunstwerk im Zeitalter seiner technischen Reproduzierbarkeit: Drei Studien zur Kunstsoziologie*, Frankfurt am Main.

Benjamin, W. (1986), 'On the Mimetic Faculty', in P. Demetz (ed.), *Reflections: Essays, Aphorisms, Autobiographical Writings*, 333–6, New York.

Benjamin, W. (2010), 'The Work of Art in the Age of Its Technological Reproducibility [First Version]', translated by M. Jennings *Grey Room*, 39: 11–38.

Bennett, J. (2010), *Vibrant Matter: A Political Ecology of Things*, Durham.

Bensaude-Vincent, B. and W. R. Newman (eds) (2007), 'Introduction: The Artificial and the Natural: State of the Problem', in B. Bensaude-Vincent and W. R. Newman (eds), *The Artificial and the Natural: An Evolving Polarit*, 1–19, Cambridge.

Benveniste, É. (1948), *Noms d'agent et noms d'action en indo-européen*, Paris.

Bergson, H. ([1900] 1914), *Laughter: An Essay on the Meaning of the Comic*, translated by C. Brereton and F. Rothwell, New York.

Bernard, W. (1993), *Shame and Necessity*, Sather Classical Lectures, vol. 57, Berkeley, CA.

Berryman, S. (2002a), 'Aristotle on πνεῦμα and Animal Self-motion', *Oxford Studies in Ancient Philosophy*, 23: 85–97.

Berryman, S. (2002b), 'Galen and the Mechanical Philosophy Sylvia Berryman', *Apeiron*, 35 (3): 235–53.

Berryman, S. (2003), 'Ancient Automata and Mechanical Explanation', *Phronesis*, 48: 34–69.

Berryman, S. (2007a), 'The Imitation of Life in Ancient Greek Philosophy', in J. Riskin (ed.), *Genesis Redux: Essays in the History and Philosophy of Artificial Life*, 3–45, Chicago, IL.

Berryman, S. (2007b), 'Teleology without Tears: Aristotle and the Role of Mechanistic Conceptions of Organisms', *Canadian Journal of Philosophy*, 37: 351–70.

Berryman, S. (2009), *The Mechanical Hypothesis in Ancient Greek Natural Philosophy*, Cambridge.

Berryman, S. (2020), 'Ancient Greek Mechanics and the Mechanical Hypothesis', in L. Taub (ed.), *The Cambridge Companion to Ancient Greek and Roman Science*, 229–47, Cambridge.

Betancourt, R. (2018), *Sight, Touch, and Imagination in Byzantium*, Cambridge.

Bianchi, E. (2006), 'Material Vicissitudes and Technical Wonders: The Ambiguous Figure of Automaton in Aristotle's Metaphysics of Sexual Difference', *Epoché*, 11: 109–39.

Bianchi, E. (2014), *The Feminine Symptom: Aleatory Matter in the Aristotelian Cosmos*, New York.

Bianchi, E., S. Brill and B. Holmes (eds) (2019), *Antiquities Beyond Humanism*, Oxford.

Bielfeldt, R. (2014), 'Gegenwart und Vergegenwärtigung: dynamische Dinge im Ausgang von Homer', in R. Bielfeldt (ed.), *Ding und Mensch in der Antike*, 15–48, Heidelberg.

Bliquez, L.J. (1983), 'Classical Prosthetics', *Archaeology*, 36 (5): 25–9.

Blume, H. D. (1984), *Einführung in das antike Theaterwesen*, 2, durchgesehene Auflage, Darmstadt.

Blumenberg, H. (2000), 'Imitation of Nature: Toward a Prehistory of the Idea of the Creative Being', *Qui parle?*, 12: 17–54.

Bodensteiner, E. (1893), 'Szenische Fragen über den Ort des Auftretens und Abgehens von Schauspielern und Chor im griechischen Drama', *Jahrbuch für klassische Philologie*, Supplementband 19: 637–808.

Boisa, É. (1923), *Dictionnaire étymologique de la langue Grecque*, Heidelberg.

Bosak-Schroeder, C. (2016), 'The Religious Life of Greek Automata', *Archiv für Religionsgeschichte*, 17: 123–36.

Bostrom, N. (2005), 'In Defence of Posthuman Dignity', *Bioethics*, 19: 202–14.

Bowersock, W. G. (1984), 'The Miracle of Memnon', *Bulletin of the American Society of Papyrologists*, 21: 21–32.

Bowie, A. M. (1997), 'Thinking with Drinking: Wine and the Symposium in Aristophanes', *Journal of Hellenic Studies*, 117: 1–21.

Boy-Stones, G. R. (2007), 'Physiognomy in Ancient Philosophy', in S. Swain and G. R. Boys-Stones (eds), *Polemon's Physiognomy from Classical Antiquity to Medieval Islam*, 19–124, Oxford.

Braidotti, R. (2013), *The Posthuman*, Cambridge.

Braidotti, R. (2015), 'The Posthuman in Feminist Theory', in L. Disch and M. Hawkesworth (eds), *Oxford Handbook of Feminist Theory*, 673–98, Oxford.

Braidotti, R. (2017), 'Four Theses on Posthuman Feminism', in R. Grusin (ed.), *Anthropocene Feminism*, 21–48, Minneapolis, MN.

Brecoulaki, H. (2015), 'Greek Painting and the Challenge of *Mimēsis*', in P. Destrée and P. Murray (eds), *A Companion to Ancient Aesthetics*, Blackwell Companions to the Ancient World, 218–36, Malden, MA, and Oxford, Chichester.

Bremmer, J. N. (1991), 'Walking, Standing and Sitting in Ancient Greek Culture', in J. N. Bremmer and H. Roodenburg (eds), *A Cultural History of Gesture: From Antiquity to the Present Day*, 15–35, Cambridge.

Bremmer, J. N. (2008), *Greek Religion and Culture, the Bible and the Ancient Near East*, Jerusalem Studies in Religion and Culture, Vol. 8, Leiden.

Bremmer, J. N. (2013), 'The Agency of Greek and Roman Statues: From Homer to Constantine', *Opuscula*, 6: 7–21.

Brioso Sánchez, M. (2006), 'Sobre la maquinaria teatral en la Atenas clásica: el ἐκκύκλημα', *HABIS*, 37: 67–85.

Brockliss, W. (2019), *Homeric Imagery and the Natural Environment*, Hellenic Studies Series, 82, Washington, DC: Center for Hellenic Studies. Available online: http://nrs.harvard.edu/urn-3:hul.ebook:CHS_BrocklissW.Homeric_Imagery_and_the_Natural_Environment.2019 (accessed 3 September 2021).

Brückner, B. (2007), *Delirium und Wahn: Geschichte, Selbstzeugnisse und Theorien von der Antike bis 1900, Bd. I: Vom Altertum bis zur Aufklärung*, Hürtgenwald.

Brumbaugh, R. S. (1966), *Ancient Greek Gadgets and Machines*, New York.

Bublitz, M., R. Marek, C. L. Steinmann and H. Winkler (2010), 'Einleitung', in H. Bublitz, R. Marek, Ch. L. Steinmann and H. Winkler (eds), *Automatismen*, 5–16, München.

Bur, T. (2016), 'Mechanical Miracles: Automata in Ancient Greek Religion', MA thesis, University of Sydney. Available online: http://hdl.handle.net/2123/15398 (accessed 15 March 2022).

Bur, T. (2020), 'Mirrors and the Manufacture of Religious Aura in the Graeco-Roman World', in M. Gerolemou and L. Diamantopoulou (eds), *Mirrors and Mirroring from Antiquity to the Early Modern Period*, London.

Bur, T., M. Gerolemou and I. A. Ruffell (eds) (forthcoming), *Technological Animation in Greco-Roman Antiquity*, Oxford.

Burford, A. (1972), *Craftsmen in Greek and Roman Society*, Aspects of Greek and Roman Life, Ithaca, NY.

Burgess, S. A. (2000), 'How to Build a Human Body: An Idealist's Guide', in A. M. Wright and A. Barker (eds), *Reason and Necessity: Essays on Plato's Timaeus*, 43–58, London, Oakville, CA, and Swansea.

Burkert, W. (2004), *Babylon, Memphis, Persepolis: Eastern Contexts of Greek Culture*, Cambridge, MA, and London.

Bussels, S. (2012), *The Animated Image: Roman Theory on Naturalism, Vividness and Divine Power*, Berlin.

Butler, Sh. (2015), *The Ancient Phonograph*, New York.

Buxton, R. (2016), 'Weapons and Day's White Horses: The Language of Ajax', in I. J. F. de Jong and A. Rijksbaron (eds), *Sophocles and the Greek Language*, 11–23, Leiden.

Cairns, D. (2014), 'Ψυχή, Θυμός, and Metaphor in Homer and Plato', *Les Études Platoniciennes*, 11. Available online: http://etudesplatoniciennes.revues.org/566 (accessed 10 March 2022).

Cairns, D. (2019), s.v. Thymos in *Oxford Classical Dictionary* (OCD). Available online: http://oxfordre.com/classics/view/10.1093/acrefore/9780199381135.001.0001/acrefore-9780199381135-e-8180 (accessed 10 March 2022).

Caley, R. E. and B. W. Jensen (2008), *The Leyden and Stockholm Papyri: Greco-Egyptian Chemical Documents from the Early 4th Century* AD (an English Translation with Brief Notes by E. Radcliffe Caley, edited, with a new general introduction, a note on techniques, and a materials index by W. B. Jensen), Cincinnati, OH.

Cambiano, G. (1994a), 'Automaton', *StudStor*, 35: 613–33.

Cambiano, G. (1994b), 'Mensch werden', in J.-P. Vernant (ed.), *Der Mensch der griechischen Antike*, 98–139, Frankfurt and New York.

Campa, R. (ed.) (2015), *Humans and Automata: A Social Study of Robotics (Beyond Humanism: Trans- and Posthumanism/Jenseits des Humanismus: Trans- und Posthumanismus)*, Frankfurt am Main.

Caneva, S. G. (2014), 'Ruler Cults in Practice: Sacrifices and Libations for Arsinoe Philadelphos, from Alexandria and Beyond', in T. Gnoli and F. Muccioli (eds), *Divinizzazione, culto del sovrano e apoteosi. Tra Antichità e Medioevo*, 85–116, Bologna.

Canevaro, L. G. (2018), *Women of Substance in Homeric Epic: Objects, Gender Agency*, Oxford.

Canevaro, L. G. (2019), 'Materiality and Classics: (Re) Turning to the Material', *Journal of Hellenic Studies*, 139: 222–32.

Carvalho, M. J. P. de A. (2015), 'Experience, Cause and Wonder', in A. M. Martins (ed.), *Cause, Knowledge and Responsibility*, Philosophy in International Context/Philosophie im internationalen Kontext, Bd. 8, 141–71, Berlin, Münster and Wien.

Caseau, B. (1999), 'Christian Bodies: The Senses and Early Byzantine Christianity', in L. James (ed.), *Desire and Denial in Byzantium: Papers from the Thirty-First Spring Symposium of Byzantine Studies, Brighton, March 1997*, Society for the Promotion of Byzantine Studies Publications 6, 101–9, Aldershot.

Catoni, M. L. (2011), 'Mimesis and Motion in Classical Antiquity', in S. Leyssen and P. Rathgeber (eds), *Bilder animierter Bewegung. Images of Animate Movement*, 199–220, Basel.

Catoni, M. L. (2012), 'From Motion to Emotion. An Ancient Greek Iconography between Literal and Symbolic Interpretations', in H. Bredekamp, M. Lauschke and A. Arteaga (eds), *Bodies in Action and Symbolic Forms. Zwei Seiten der Verkörperungtheorie*, 99–120, Berlin.

Cavarero, A. (2019), 'The Human Reconceived', in E. Bianchi, S. Brill and B. Holmes (eds), *Antiquities Beyond Humanism*, 31–46, Oxford.

Ceccarelli, P. (1996), 'L'Athènes de Périclès: Un "Pays de cocagne"? L' Idéologie démocratique et le thème de l'automatos bios dans la comédie ancienne', *Quaderni Urbinati di Cultura Classica N.S.*, 54 (3): 109–59.

Chalk, H. H. O. (1962), 'Bia and Arete in Euripides' *Heracles*', *Journal of Hellenic Studies*, 82: 7–18.

Chaniotis, A. (2014), 'The Life of Statues [Η ζωή τῶν ἀγαλμάτων]', *Proceedings of the Academy of Athens*, 89: 246–97.

Chantraine, P. (1968), *Dictionnaire étymologique de la langue Grecque*, Paris.

Chapuis, A. and E. Droz (1958), *Automata: A Historical and Technological Study*, New York.

Chaston, C. (2009), *Tragic Props and Cognitive Function: Aspects of the Function of Images in Thinking*, Mnemosyne Supplements 317, Leiden.

Chatterjee, P. (2014), *The Living Icon in Byzantium and Italy: The Vita Image, Eleventh to Thirteenth Centuries*, Cambridge.

Chesi, G.-M. and G. Sclavi (2020), 'Pandora and Robotic Technology Today', in G. M. Chesi and F. Spiegel (eds), *Classical Literature and Posthumanism*, 301–8, London.

Chesi, G. M. and F. Spiegel (eds) (2020), *Classical Literature and Posthumanism*, London.

Chondros, G. Th., K. Milidonis, G. Vitzilaios and J. Vaitsis (2013), '"Deus-Ex-Machina": Reconstruction in the Athens Theater of Dionysus', *Mechanism and Machine Theory*, 67: 172–91.

Ciraolo, L. J. (1992), 'The Warmth and Breath of Life: Animating Physical Object πάρεδροι in the Greek Magical Papyri', *Society of Biblical Literature*: 240–54.

Clay, J. S. (2003), *Hesiod's Cosmos*, Cambridge and New York.

Clements, A. (2014), *Aristophanes' Thesmophoriazusae: Philosophizing Theatre and the Politics of Perception*, Cambridge.

Cohen, B. (1994), 'From Bowman to Clubman: Herakles and Olympia', *Art Bulletin*, 76: 696–715.

Coleman, K. M. (1996), 'Ptolemy Philadelphus and the Roman Amphitheatre', in W. J. Slater (ed.), *Roman Theater and Society: E. Togo Salmon Papers I*, 49–68, Ann Arbor, MI.

Compton-Engle, G. (2003), 'Control of Costume in Three Plays of Aristophanes', *American Journal of Philology*, 124: 507–35.

Conacher, D. J. (1967), *Euripidean Drama: Myth, Theme and Structure*, Toronto.

Cooper, S. D. (2016), 'Aristophanes, Posthumanism, and the Roots of Science Fiction', PhD diss., Princeton University, Princeton, NJ. Available online: http://arks.princeton.edu/ark:/88435/dsp017p88ck02j (accessed 15 March 2022).

Corcilius, K. (2020), 'Resuming Discussion of the Common Cause of Animal Self-Motion: How does the Soul Move the Body?', in C. Rapp and O. Primavesi (eds), *Aristotle's De motu animalium 6: Symposium Aristotelicum*, 299–344, Oxford.

Cormack, R. (2003), 'Living Painting', in E. Jeffreys (ed.), *Rhetoric in Byzantium*, 235–53, Aldershot.

Corso, A. (1999), 'Ancient Greek Sculptors as Magicians', *Numismatica e Antichita' Classiche*, 28: 97–111.

Corso, A. (2004), *The Art of Praxiteles: The Development of Praxiteles' Workshop and Its Cultural Tradition until the Sculptor's Acme (364–1 BC)*, Rome.

Cox Miller, P. (2009), *The Corporeal Imagination: Signifying the Holy in Late Ancient Christianity*, Divinations: Rereading Late Ancient Religion, Philadelphia, PA.

Craik, E. M. (2001), 'Medical Reference in Euripides', *Bulletin of the Institute of Classical Studies*, 45: 81–95.

Csapo, E. (1999–2000), 'Later Euripidean Music', in M. Cropp, K. Lee and D. Sansone (eds), *Euripides and Tragic Theatre in the Late Fifth Century*, Illinois Classical Studies, vols 24/25, 399–426, Champaign.

Csapo, E. (2002), 'Kallipides on the Floor-Sweepings: The Limits of Realism in Classical Acting and Performance Styles', in P. Easterling and E. Hall (eds), *Greek and Roman Actors: Aspects of an Ancient Profession*, 127–47, Cambridge and New York.

Csapo, E. (2010), *Actors and Icons of the Ancient Theater*, Malden, MA, and Oxford.

Csapo, E. (2013), *The Dionysian Parade and the Poetics of Plenitud*, University College London Houseman Lecture, Department of Greek and Latin, London.

Cullhed, E. (2014), 'Movement and Sound on the Shield of Achilles in Ancient Exegesis', *Greek, Roman and Byzantine Studies*, 54: 192–219.

Cuomo, S. (2000), *Pappus of Alexandria and the Mathematics of Late Antiquity*, Cambridge Classical Studies, Cambridge.

Cuomo, S. (2007), *Technology and Culture in Greek and Roman Antiquity*, Cambridge.

Cuomo, S. (2018), 'Greek Mechanics' in A. Jones and L. Taub (eds), *The Cambridge History of Science*, Part 3: *Greek and Greco-Roman*, 449–67, Cambridge.

D'Amato, R. (2016), 'Arms and Weapons', in G. L. Irby (ed.), *A Companion to Science, Technology, and Medicine in Ancient Greece and Rome*, 2 vols, 801–16, Chichester.

Dalley, St. and J. P. Oleson (2003), 'Sennacherib, Archimedes, and the Water Screw: The Context of Invention in the Ancient World', *Technology and Culture*, 44: 1–26.

De Groot, J. (2008), 'Dunamis and the Science of Mechanics: Aristotle on Animal Motion', *Journal of the History of Philosophy*, 46: 43–68.

De Groot, J. (2014), *Aristotle's Empiricism: Experience and Mechanics in the Fourth Century BC*, Las Vegas, NV, Zurich and Athens.

De Groot, J. (2016), 'Motion and Energy', in G. L. Irby-Massie (ed.), *A Companion to Science, Technology, and Medicine in Ancient Greece and Rome*, 43–59, Chichester.

De Jong, I. F. (2011), 'The Shield of Achilles: From Metalepsis to Mise En Abyme', *Ramus*, 40: 1–14.

De Lacy, Ph. (1978), *On the Doctrines of Hippocrates and Plato*, vol. 5, pt 4, fasc. 1–2, Berlin.

De Solla Price, D. J. (1964), 'Automata and the Origins of Mechanism and Mechanistic Philosophy', *Technology and Culture*, 5: 9–23.

Decker, J. E. (2018), 'Manufacturing the Mother: Technical Appropriations of Birth in Ancient Greek Thought', in A. Einion and J. Rinaldi (eds), *Bearing the Weight of the World: Exploring Maternal Embodiment*, 83–98, Bradford.

Delatte, A. (1934), *Les Conceptions de l'enthousiasme chez les philosophes présocratiques*, Paris.

Delcourt, M. (1957), *Héphaistos: Ou, la légende du magicien*, vol. 8, fasc. 146, Paris.

Deleuze, G. and F. Guattari (2004), *Anti-Oedipus: Capitalism and Schizophrenia*, translated by R. Hurley, M. Seem, and H. R. Lane, London and New York.

Deligiannakis, G. (2015), 'Religious Viewing of Sculptural Images of Gods in the World of Late Antiquity: From Dio Chrysostom to Damaskios', *Journal of Late Antiquity*, 8: 168–94.

Denniston, J. D. (1927), 'Technical Terms in Aristophanes', *Classical Quarterly*, 21: 113–21.

Descartes, R. (1988), *Selected Philosophical Writings and The Philosophical Writings of Descartes*, trans. John Cottingham, Robert Stoothoff and Dugall Murdoch, vol. 2, Cambridge.

Detienne, M. (1989), *Dionysus at Large*, translated by A. Goldhammer, Cambridge, MA.

Devecka, M. (2013), 'Did the Greeks Believe in their Robots?', *Cambridge Classical Journal*, 59: 52–69.

Devereux, G. (1970), 'The Psychotherapy Scene in Euripides' *Bacchae*', *Journal of Hellenic Studies*, 90: 35–48.

Devereux, G. (1971), 'The Psychosomatic Miracle of Iolaos: A Hypothesis', *La Parola del Passato*, 26: 167–95.

Di Pasquale, G. (2004), 'Scientific and Technological Use of Glass in Graeco-Roman Antiquity', in M. Beretta (ed.), *When Glass Matters: Studies in the History of Science and Art from Graeco-Roman Antiquity to Early Modern Era*, 31–76, Olschki.

DiPietro, J. (2016), *IT Disaster Recovery, Cloud Computing and Information Security News: To Err is Human, to Automate, Divine*, available online: https://www.continuitycentral.com/index.php/news/technology/1269-to-err-is-human-to-automate-divine (accessed 15 December 2021).

Diels, H. (1917), *Über die von Prokop beschriebene Kunstuhr von Gaza. Mit einem Anhang enhaltend Text und Übersetzung der* Εκφρασις ωρολογιου *des Prokopios von Gaza*, Abhandlungen der Preussischen Akademie der Wissenschaften, Philosophisch-historische Klasse, 7, Berlin.

Diels, H. (1924), *Antike Technik: Sechs Vorträge*, Leipzig.
Dobrov, G. W. (2001), *Figures of Play: Greek Drama and Metafictional Poetics*, 2001.
Dodds, E. R. (1947), 'Theurgy and Its Relationship to Neoplatonism', *Journal of Roman Studies*, 37: 55–69.
Dodds, E. R. (1951), *The Greeks and the Irrational*, Berkeley, Los Angeles, CA.
Dodds, E. R. (1960), *Euripides' Bacchae*, edited with introduction and commentary, 2nd edn, Oxford.
Dodds, E. R. (1973), *The Ancient Concept of Progress and other Essays on Greek Literature and Belief*, Oxford.
Dodds, E. R. (1974), 'Die Rolle des Ethischen und des Politischen in der ‚Oresteia'', in H. Hommel (ed.), *Wege zu Aischylos, Bd. 2: Die einzelnen Dramen*, 149–72, Darmstadt.
Dolansky, F. (2012), 'Playing with Gender: Girls, Dolls, and Adult Ideals in the Roman World', *Classical Antiquity*, 31: 256–92.
Dover, K. (1993), *Aristophanes: Frogs. Edited with Introduction*, Oxford.
Downey, G. (1946–8), 'Byzantine Architects: Their Training and Methods', *Byzantion*, 18: 99–118.
Drachmann, A. G. (1948), *Ktesibios, Philon and Heron: A Study in Ancient Pneumatics*, Copenhagen.
Drachmann, A. G. (1958), 'The Screw of Archimedes', *Actes du VIIIe Congrès International d'Histoire des Sciences*, 3: 940–3.
Drachmann, A. G. D. (1963), *The Mechanical Technology of Greek and Roman Antiquity*, Copenhagen.
Draycott, J. (2018), *Prostheses in Antiquity*, Medicine and the Body in Antiquity, Abingdon.
DuBois, P. (1988), *Sowing the Body: Psychoanalysis and Ancient Representations of Women*, Women in Culture and Society, Chicago, IL.
DuBois, P. (1992), 'Eros and the Woman', *Ramus*, 21: 97–116.
Dudley, J. (2012), *Aristotle's Concept of Chance: Accidents, Cause, Necessity, and Determinism*, New York.
Duffey, M. R. (2007), 'The Vocal Memnon and Solar Thermal Automata', *Leonardo Music Journal*, 17: 51–4.
Duncan, A. (2006), *Performance and Identity in the Classical World*, Cambridge.
Dunn, F. M. (1996), *Tragedy's End: Closure and Innovation in Euripidean Drama*, Oxford.
Dutsch, D. (2002), 'Towards A Roman Theory of Theatrical Gesture', in G. M. Harrison and V. Liapis (eds), *Performance in Greek and Roman Theatre*, Mnemosyne Supplements 353, 409–32, Leiden.

Easterling, P. A. (1999), 'Actors and Voices: Reading Between the Lines in Aeschines and Demosthenes', in S. Goldhill and R. Osborne (eds), *Performance Culture and Athenian Democracy*, 154–65, Cambridge and New York.

Eco, U. (1986), *Travels in Hyperrreality*, translated by W. Weaver, New York.

Edelstein, L. (1967a), *Ancient Medicine: Selected Papers of Ludwig Edelstein*, edited by O. Temkin and C. Lilian Temkin, translated by C. L. Temkin, Baltimore, MD.

Edelstein, L. (1967b), *The Idea of Progress in Classical Antiquity*, Baltimore, MD.

Edwards, M. W. (1991), *The Iliad: A Commentary: Vol. 5, Books 17–20*, Cambridge.

Effe, B. (2000), 'Tragischer Wahnsinn: Ein Motiv der attischen Tragödie und seine Funktionalisierung', in B. Effe and R. F. Glei (eds), *Genie und Wahnsinn. Konzepte Psychischer 'Normalität' und 'Abnormalität' im Altertum*, Bochumer Altertumswissenschaftliches Colloquium 46, 45–62, Trier.

Einion, A. and J. Rinaldi (eds) (2018), *Bearing the Weight of the World: Exploring Maternal Embodiment*, Bradford.

Elbert Decker, J. (2018), 'Hail Hera, Mother of Monsters! Monstrosity as Emblem of Sexual Sovereignty', *Women's Studies*, 45: 743–57.

Elderkin, K. McK. (1930), 'Jointed Dolls in Antiquity', *American Journal of Archaeology*, 34: 455–79.

Else, G. F. (1958), '"Imitation" in the Fifth Century', *Classical Philology*, 53: 73–90.

Elsner, J. (1995), *Art and the Roman Viewer: The Transformation of Art from the Pagan World to Christianity*, Cambridge.

Elsner, J. (1996), 'Naturalism and the Erotics of the Gaze: Intimations of Narcissus', in N. Boymel Kampen, B. Bergmann, A. Cohen, P. duBois, B. Kellum and E. Stehle (eds), *Sexuality in Ancient Art: Near East, Egypt, Greece, and Italy*, 247–61, Cambridge and New York.

Elsner, J. (1998), *Imperial Rome and Christian Triumph: The Art of the Roman Empire AD 100–450*, Oxford.

Elsner, J. (2004), 'Late Antique Art: The Problem of the Concept and the Cumulative Aesthetic', in S. Swain and M. J. Edwards (eds), *Approaching Late Antiquity: The Transformation from Early to Late Empire*, 271–309, Oxford and New York.

Emilsson, E. K. (1988), *Plotinus on Sense-Perception: A Philosophical Study*, Cambridge.

Fairbanks, A. (ed. and trans.) (1931), *Philostratus the Elder, Imagines. Philostratus the Younger, Imagines. Callistratus, Descriptions*, Loeb Classical Library 256, Cambridge, MA.

Falkner, Th. M. (1999), 'Madness Visible: Tragic Ideology and Poetic Authority in Sophocles' Art', in Th. M. Falkner, N. Felson and D. Konstan (eds), *Contextualizing Classics: Ideology, Performance, Dialogue: Essays in Honor of John J. Peradott*, 173–201, Lanham, MD.

Fantham, E. (2002), 'Orator and/et Actor', in P. Easterling and E. Hall (eds), *Greek and Roman Actors: Aspects of an Ancient Profession*, 362–76, Cambridge.

Faraone, Ch. A. (1987), 'Hephaestus the Magician and Near Eastern Parallels for Alcinous' Watchdogs', *Greek, Roman and Byzantine Studiees*, 28: 257–80.

Faraone, Ch. A. (1991a), 'The Agonistic Context of Early Greek Binding Spells', in Ch. A. Faraone and D. Obbink (eds), *Magika Hiera: Ancient Greek Magic and Religion*, 3–32, New York.

Faraone, Ch. A. (1991b), 'Binding and Burying the Forces of Evil: The Defensive Use of "Voodoo Dolls" in Ancient Greece', *Classical Antiquity*, 10: 165–205.

Faraone, Ch. A. (1992), *Talismans and Trojan Horses: Guardian Statues in Ancient Greek Myth and Ritual*, New York.

Farioli, M. (2001), *Mundus alter. Utopie e distopie nella commedia greca antica*, Milano.

Fernandez, P. A. and J. Mittelmann (2020), 'When Life Imitates Art: Vital Locomotion and Aristotle's Craft Analogy', in H. Bartoš and C. G. King (eds), *Heat, Pneuma, and Soul in Ancient Philosophy and Science*, 260–87, Cambridge.

Finkelberg, M. (1998), *The Birth of Literary Fiction in Ancient Greece*, Oxford.

Finley, M. I. (1959), 'Essays in Bibliography and Criticism XL: Technology in the Ancient World', *Economic History Review*, 12: 120–5.

Finley, M. I. (1965), 'Technical Innovation and Economic Progress in the Ancient World', *Economic History Review*, 18: 29–45.

Fletcher, J. (2013), 'Weapons of Friendship: Props in Sophocles' *Philoctetes* and *Ajax*', in G. W. M. Harrison and V. Liapis (eds), *Performance in Greek and Roman Theater*, 199–215, Leiden.

Flickinger, R. C. (1922), *The Greek Theater and Its Drama*, Chicago, IL.

Flickinger, R. C. (1939), 'Off-Stage Speech in Greek Tragedy', *Classical Journal*, 34: 355–60.

Flohr, M. (2016), 'Innovation and Society in the Roman World', in *Oxford Handbooks Online*. Available online: https://www.oxfordhandbooks.com/view/10.1093/oxfordhb/9780199935390.001.0001/oxfordhb-9780199935390-e-85?print=pdf (accessed 10 August 2021).

Foley, H. (2000), 'The Comic Body in Greek Art and Drama', in B. Cohen (ed.), *Not the Classical Ideal: Athens and the Construction of the Other in Greek Art*, 275–311, Leiden.

Foley, H. P. (2001), *Female Acts in Greek Tragedy*, Princeton, NJ, and Oxford.

Ford, A. L. (2002), *The Origins of Criticism: Literary Culture and Poetic Theory in Classical Greece*, Princeton, NJ.

Förg, M. (2019), 'Manus medici. Die Bedeutung der Hand bei der ärztlichen Diagnose und Therapie in Antike und Früher Neuzeit', in R. Jütte and R. Schmitz-Esser, *Handgebrauch Geschichten von der Hand aus dem Mittelalter und der Frühen Neuzeit*, 159–72, Leiden.

Foucault, M. (1977), *Discipline and Punish: The Birth of the Prison*, translated by A. Sheridan, New York.
Fowler, H. N. (1921), *Plato in Twelve Volumes*, vol. 12, translation, Cambridge, MA.
Fraenkel, E. (1950), *Aeschylus' Agamemnon*, Oxford.
Fraenkel, H. (1962), *Dichtung und Philosophie des frühen Griechentums. Eine Geschichte der griechischen Epik, Lyrik und Prosa bis zur Mitte des fünften Jahrhunderts*, 2nd edn., Munich.
Fragaki, H. (2012), 'Automates et statues merveilleuses dans l'Alexandrie antique', *Journal des Savants*, 1: 29–67.
Francis, J. A. (2003), 'Living Icons: Tracing a Motif in Verbal and Visual Representation from the Second to Fourth Centuries C.E.', *American Journal of Philology*, 124: 575–600.
Francis, J. A. (2009a), 'Metal Maidens, Achilles' Shield, and Pandora: The Beginnings of "Ekphrasis"', *American Journal of Philology*, 130: 1–23.
Francis, J. A. (2009b), 'Visual and Verbal Representation: Image, Text, Person, and Power', in Ph. Rousseau (ed.), *A Companion to Late Antiquity*, Blackwell Companions to the Ancient World, 285–305, Oxford.
Fraser, L. G. (2011), 'A Woman of Consequence: Pandora in Hesiod's *Works and Days*', *Cambridge Classical Journal*, 57: 9–28.
Fraser, P. M. (1972), *Ptolemaic Alexandria*, vols 1–3, Oxford.
Frazer, J. G. (1922/1991), *The Golden Bough: A Study of Magic and Religion*, London.
Freeland, C. A. (1994), 'Aristotle on Perception', in J. G. Lennox and M. L. Gill (eds), *Self-Motion: From Aristotle to Newton*, 35–63, Princeton, NJ.
Freeland, C. A. (2017), 'Aristotle on Perception, Appetition, and Self-Motion', in J. G. Lennox and M. L. Gill (eds), *Self-Motion: From Aristotle to Newton*, 35–64, Princeton, NJ.
Freud, S. (1919), 'Das Unheimliche', *Imago*, 5: 297–324.
Freud, S. (1930), *Das Unbehagen in der Kultur*, Wien.
Fried, M. (1967), 'Art and Objecthood', *ArtForum*, 5: 12–23.
Frisk, H. (1960), *Griechisches etymologisches Worterbuch*, Band I, Heidelberg.
Fritz, G. (1972), 'Heron von Alexandria', in K. Fassmann et. al. (eds), *Die Großen der Weltgeschichte*, volume 2, 332–79, Zürich.
Frontisi-Ducroux, Fr. (1975), *Dédale: Mythologie de l'artisan en Grèce ancienne*, Paris.
Fulton, E. (1996), 'On the Eve of Destruction: Technology, Nostalgia, and the Fetishized Maternal Body', *Critical Matrix*, 10: 90–9.
Furley, D. J. (1955), '[Aristotle] On the Cosmos', in E. S. Forster, D. J. Furley (trans.), *Aristotle. On Sophistical Refutations; On Coming-to-Be and Passing-Away; On the Cosmos*, 333–409, Cambridge, MA.

Furley, D. J. (1994), 'Self-Movers', in J. G. Lennox and M. L. Gill (eds), *Self-Motion: From Aristotle to Newton*, 3–14, Princeton, NJ.

Garland, R. (1995), *The Eye of the Beholder: Deformity and Disability in the Graeco-Roman World*, Ithaca, NY.

Gavrylenko, V. (2012), 'The Body without Skin in the Homeric Poems', in M. Horstmanshoff, H. King and C. Zittel (eds), *Blood, Sweat, and Tears: The Changing Concepts of Physiology from Antiquity into Early Modern Europe*, 479–502, Leiden.

Gell, A. (1988), 'Technology and Magic', *Anthropology Today*, 4 (2): 6–9.

Gell, A. (1992), 'The Technology of Enchantment and the Enchantment of Technology', in J. Coote and A. Shelton (eds), *Anthropology, Art, and Aesthetics*, 40–63, Oxford.

Gerolemou, M. (2011), *Bad Women, Mad Women: Gender und Wahnsinn in der griechischen Tragödie*, Classica Monacensia, vol. 40, Tübingen.

Gerolemou, M. (2016), 'Homeric and Tragic Madness', in H. Perdicoyianni-Paléologou (ed.), *The Concept of Madness from Homer to Byzantium: Manifestations and Aspects of Mental Illness and Disorder*, 1–34, Amsterdam.

Gerolemou, M. (2018a), 'Wonder-ful Memories in Herodotus' Histories'. in M. Gerolemou (ed), *Recognizing Miracles in Antiquity and Beyond*, 133–51, Berlin.

Gerolemou, M. (2018b), 'Zur Auffasung des Wunders in der griechischen Tragödie', *Mnemosyne* 71: 750–76.

Gerolemou, M. (2018c), 'Staging Artificial Intelligence: the case of Greek drama', in Meineck P., W.-M. Short (eds) *The Routledge Handbook of Classics and Cognitive Theory*, 345–55, London.

Gerolemou, M. (2019a), 'Some Thoughts on the Mechanical Features of Pantomime Dancers', *Araucaria. Revista Iberoamericana de Filosofía, Política, Humanidades y Relaciones Internacionales*, 21 (41): 273–87.

Gerolemou, M. (2019b), 'Technological Wonder in Herodotus' *Histories*', in G. Kazantzidis (ed.), *Medicine and Paradoxography in the Ancient World*, Trends in Classics, 41–52, Berlin and Boston, MA.

Gerolemou, M. (2019c) 'Why can't I have wings? Aristophanes' *Birds*', in G. M. Chesi and F. Spiegel (eds), *Classical Literature and Posthumanism*, 175–81, 373–5, New York and London.

Gerolemou, M. (2020a), 'Laughing Against the Machine', in P. Swallow and E. Hall (eds), *Aristophanic Humour Theory and Practice*, 145–52, London.

Gerolemou, M. (2020b), 'Plane and Curved Mirrors in Classical Antiquity', in M. Gerolemou and L. Diamantopoulou (eds), *Mirrors and Mirroring from Antiquity to the Early Modern Period*, 157–64, London.

Gerolemou, M. (forthcoming a), 'From Hand-Bows to Torsion Artillery Devices', in M. Flohr, St. Mols and T. Tieleman (eds), *Anchoring Technology*, Leiden.

Gerolemou, M. (forthcoming b), 'Technical Physicians and Medical Machines in the Hippocratic Corpus', in M. Gerolemou and G. Kazantzidis (eds), *Body and Machine in Classical Antiquity*, Cambridge.

Gerolemou, M. and Kazantzidis, G. (eds) (forthcoming), *Body and Machine in Classical Antiquity*, Cambridge.

Gill, Ch. (1980), 'Bow, Oracle, and Epiphany in Sophocles' "Philoctetes"', *Greece & Rome*, 27: 137–46.

Gill, Ch. (1990), 'The Character–Personality Distinction', in C. B. R. Pelling (ed.), *Characterization and Individuality in Greek Literature*, 1–31, Oxford.

Gill, Ch. (1996), *Personality in Greek Epic, Tragedy, and Philosophy: The Self in Dialogue*, Oxford.

Gill, M.L. (2017), 'Aristotle on Self-Motion', in J. G. Lennox and M. L. Gill (eds), *Self-Motion: From Aristotle to Newton*, 15–34, Princeton, NJ.

Gödde, S. (2011), *Euphemia. Die gute Rede in Kult und Literatur der griechischen Antike*, Heidelberg.

Goldhill, S. (1986), *Reading Greek Tragedy*, Cambridge.

Goldhill, S. (1994), 'The Naive and Knowing Eye: Ecphrasis and the Culture of Viewing in the Hellenistic World', in S. Goldhill and R. Osborne (eds), *Art and Text in Ancient Greek Culture*, 197–223, Cambridge.

González, J. (2000), 'Envisioning Cyborg Bodies: Notes from Current Research', in D. Bell and B. M. Kennedy (eds), *The Cybercultures Reader*, 540–51, London.

González, J. M. (2013), *The Epic Rhapsode and His Craft: Homeric Performance in a Diachronic Perspective*, Hellenic Studies Series, 47, Washington, DC.

Gotthelf, A. (1989), 'Teleology and Spontaneous Generation in Aristotle: A Discussion', in T. Penner and R. Kraut (eds), *Nature, Knowledge and Virtue: Essays in Memory of Joan Kung, Apeiron Series*, 23 (4): 181–93.

Graf, F. (1991), 'Gesture and Conventions: The Gestures of Roman Actors and Orators', in J. N. Bremmer and H. Roodenburg (eds), *A Cultural History of Gesture: From Antiquity to the Present Day*, 15–35, Cambridge.

Graf, F. (1995), 'Ekphrasis: die Entstehung der Gattung in der Antike', in G. Boehm and H. Pfotenhauer (eds), *Beschreibungskunst, Kunstbeschreibung: Ekphrasis von der Antike bis zur Gegenwart*, 143–55, Munich.

Graf, F. (1997), *Magic in the Ancient World*, translated by F. Philip, Revealing Antiquity 10, Cambridge.

Green, R. (2002), 'Towards a Reconstruction of Performance Style', in P. Easterling and E. Hall (eds), *Greek and Roman Actors: Aspects of an Ancient Profession*, 93–126, Cambridge and New York.

Greenberg, C. (1939), 'Avant-Garde and Kitsch', *Partisan Review* 6: 3–49.
Greenberg, C. (1940), 'Towards a New Laocoön', *Partisan Review* 7: 296–310
Greene, K. (2000), 'Technological Innovation and Economic Progress in the Ancient World: M. I. Finley Reconsidered', *Economic History Review*, 53: 29–59.
Greene, K. (2008), 'Historiographical and Theoretical Approaches', in J. P. Oleson (ed.), *Handbook of Engineering and Technology in the Classical World*, 62–90, New York and Oxford.
Gregory, J. (1977), 'Euripides' Heracles', *Yale Classical Studies*, 25: 259–75.
Grethlein, J. (2008), 'Memory and Material Objects in the Iliad and Odyssey', *Journal of Hellenic Studies*, 128: 27–51.
Grillo, Fr. (2019), 'Hero of Alexandria's Automata: A Critical Edition and Translation, Including a Commentary on Book One', PhD diss., Glasgow University.
Gross, K. (1992), *The Dream of the Moving Statue*, London.
Günther, Z. (1955), *The Political Plays of Euripides*, Manchester.
Guthrie, W. K. C. (1981), *A History of Greek Philosophy, Vol. 6: Aristotle: An Encounter*, Cambridge.
Gutzwiller, K. J. (2004), 'Seeing Thought: Timomachus' Medea and Ecphrastic Epigram', *American Journal of Philology*, 125: 339–86.
Hadrill, W. A. (1990), 'Pliny the Elder and Man's Unnatural History', *Greece & Rome*, 37: 80–96.
Halberstam, J. M. and I. I. Livingston (eds) (1995), *Posthuman Bodies*, Bloomington, IN.
Halfwassen, J. (2007), 'Schönheit und Bild im Neuplatonismus', in V. Olejniczak Lobsien and C. Olk (eds), *Neuplatonismus und Ästhetik. Zur Transformationsgeschichte des Schönen*, Transformationen der Antike Band 2, 43–58, Berlin and New York.
Hall, E. (2002), 'The Singing Actors of Antiquity', in P. Easterling and E. Hall (eds), *Greek and Roman Actors: Aspects of an Ancient Profession*, 3–38, Cambridge and New York.
Hall, E. (2006), *The Theatrical Cast of Athens. Interactions between Ancient Greek Drama and Society*, Oxford.
Hall, E. (2010), 'Towards a Theory of Performance Reception', in E. Hall and S. Harrop (eds), *Theorizing Performance: Greek Drama, Cultural History, and Critical Practice*, 10–28, London.
Hall, E. (2018a), 'Hephaestus the Hobbling Humorist: The Club-Footed God in the History of Early Greek Comedy', *Illinois Classical Studies*, 43: 366–87.
Hall, E. (2018b), 'Materialisms Old and New', in M. Telò and M. Mueller (eds), *The Materialities of Greek Tragedy: Objects and Affect in Aeschylus, Sophocles, and Euripides*, 203–17, London.

Hallett, C. H. (1986), 'The Origins of the Classical Style in Sculpture', *Journal of Hellenic Studies*, 106: 71–84.
Halliwell, S. (1986), *Aristotle's Poetics*, London.
Halliwell, S. (2002), *The Aesthetics of Mimesis: Ancient Texts and Modern Problems*, Princeton, NJ, and Oxford.
Haluszka, A. (2008), 'Sacred Signified: The Semiotics of Statues in the Greek Magical Papyri', *Arethusa*, 41: 479–94.
Hamilton, R. (1985), 'Slings and Arrows: The Debate with Lycus in the *Heracles*', *Transactions of the American Philological Association*, 115: 19–25.
Hammond, E. (2018), 'Alex Garland's Ex Machina or The Modern Epimetheus', in J. Weiner, B. Eldon Stevens and B. M. Rogers (eds), *Frankenstein and Its Classics: The Modern Prometheus from Antiquity to Science Fiction*, 190–205, London.
Hammond, N. G. L. (1972), 'Personal Freedom and Its Limitations in the Oresteia', in M. H. McCall, Jr. (ed.), *Aeschylus: A Collection of Critical Essays*, 90–105, Hoboken, NJ.
Hanink, J. (2017), 'Archives, Repertoires, Bodies, and Bones: Thoughts on Reperformance for Classicists', in R. Hunter and A. Uhlig (eds), *Imagining Reperformance in Ancient Culture: Studies in the Traditions of Drama and Lyric*, 21–41, Cambridge Classical Studies, Cambridge.
Hanson, V. D. (1995), *The Other Greeks: The Family Farm and the Agrarian Roots of Western Civilization*, New York.
Hanson, V. D. (1996), 'Hoplites into Democrats: The Changing Ideology of Athenian Infantry', in J. Ober and C. Hedrick (eds), *Demokratia. A Conversation on Democracies, Ancient and Modern*, 289–312, Princeton, NJ.
Haraway, D. J. (1991), 'A Cyborg Manifesto: Science, Technology, and Socialist-Feminism in the Late Twentieth Century', in D. J. Haraway (ed.), *Simians, Cyborgs and Women: The Reinvention of Nature*, 149–81, New York.
Harrison, J. E. (1903), *Prolegomena to the Study of Greek Religion*, Cambridge.
Hartigan, K. (1987), 'Euripidean Madness: Herakles and Orestes', *Greece & Rome*, 34: 126–35.
Harvey, S. A. (2006), *Scenting Salvation: Ancient Christianity and the Olfactory Imagination*, Berekeley and Los Angeles, CA, and London.
Hawes, G. (2014), *Rationalizing Myth in Antiquity*, Oxford.
Hawhee, D. (2005), *Bodily Arts: Rhetoric and Athletics in Ancient Greece*, Austin, TX.
Hayles, K. N. (1999), *How We became Posthuman: Virtual Bodies in Cybernetics, Literature, and Informatics*, Chicago, IL.
Hedreen, G. (2016), *The Image of the Artist in Archaic and Classical Greece: Art, Poetry, and Subjectivity*, New York.

Heidegger, M. (1977), *The Question Concerning Technology and Other Essays*, translated and with an introduction by W. Lovitt, New York and London.

Heidel, A. (1951), *The Babylonian Genesis*, 2nd edn, Chicago, IL.

Heinimann, F. (1945), *Nomos und Physis: Herkunft und Bedeutung einer Antithese im griechischen Denken des 5. Jahrhunderts*, Basel.

Heinimann, F. (1961), 'Eine vorplatonische Theorie der τέχνη', *Museum Helveticum*, 18 (3): 105–30.

Held, G. F. (1983), 'Antigone's Dual Motivation for the Double Burial', *Hermes*, 111: 190–201.

Henrichs, A. (1996), 'Dancing in Athens, Dancing on Delos: Some Patterns of Choral Projection in Euripides', *Philologus*, 140: 48–62.

Henry, D. (2003), 'Themistius and Spontaneous Generation in Aristotle's Metaphysics', *Oxford Studies in Ancient Philosophy*, 24: 183–208.

Henry, D. (2005), 'Embryological Models in Ancient Philosophy', *Phronesis*, 50: 1–42.

Hersey, G. L. (2009), *Falling in Love with Statues: Artificial Humans from Pygmalion to the Present*, Chicago, IL.

Herzog-Hauser, G. (1936), 'Neurospasta', *Realencyclopädie der classischen Altertumswissenschaft*, 17 (1): 161–3.

Heubeck, A. and A. Hoekstra (1989), *A Commentary on Homer's Odyssey, Vol. II: Books IX–XVI*, Oxford.

Heynen, C. and R. Krumeich (1999), 'Inachos', in R. Krumeich, N. Pechstein and B. Seidensticker (eds), *Das Griechische Satyrspie*, 313–43, Darmstadt.

Hickman, R. M. (1938), *The Ghostly Etiquette on the Classical Stage*, Iowa Studies in Classical Philology, 7, Iowa.

Hieronymus, F. (1970), 'ΜΕΛΕΤΗ: Übung, Lernen und angrenzende Begriffe', 2 vols, PhD diss., Basel University.

Hoffmann, E. T. A. (1816), *The Sandman*, Berlin.

Hoffmann, V. and N. Theocharis (2002), 'Der geometrische Entwurf der Hagia Sophia in Istanbul. Erster Teil', *Istanbuler Mitteilungen*, 52: 393–428.

Hofmann, J. B. (1949), *Etymologisches Wörterbuch des Griechischen*, München.

Holmes, B. (2008), 'Euripides' Heracles in the Flesh', *Classical Antiquity*, 27: 231–81.

Holmes, B. (2010a), 'Medical Knowledge and Technology', in D. H. Garrison (ed.), *A Cultural History of the Human Body, Vol. 1: In Antiquity*, 83–105, Oxford.

Holmes, B. (2010b), *The Symptom and the Subject: The Emergence of the Physical Body in Ancient Greece*, Princeton, NJ.

Holmes, B. (2012), *Gender: Antiquity and Its Legacy*, Ancients and Moderns, Oxford and New York.

Holmes, B. (2013), 'Causality, Agency, and the Limits of Medicine', *Apeiron*, 46: 302–26.

Holmes, B. (2017), 'The Body of Western Embodiment: The Early History of a Problem', in J. E. H. Smith (ed.), *Embodiment*, 17–47, New York.
Hose, M. (1990–1), *Studien zum Chor bei Euripides*, vol. 2, Stuttgart.
Hourmouziades, N. C. (1965), *Production and Imagination in Euripides: Form and Function of the Scenic Space*, Athens.
Huffman, A. C. (2005), *Archytas of Tarentum: Pytagorean, Philosopher and Mathematician King*, New York.
Hultsch, F. O. (1876), *Pappi Alexandrini collectionis quae supersunt*, 3 vols, Berlin.
Humphrey, J. W., J. P. Oleson and A. N. Sherwood (1998), *Greek and Roman Technology: An Annotated Translation of Greek and Latin Texts and Documents*, London.
Hunter, R. L. (1989), *Apollonius of Rhodes: Argonautica Book III*, Cambridge.
Hunzinger, Ch. (2005), 'La Perception du merveilleux: thaumazô et theêomai', in L. Villard (ed.), *Études sur la vision dans l'Antiquité Classique*, 29–38, Rouen.
Hunzinger, Ch. (2010), 'Entre séduction et déception: l'ambiguïté de la beauté du merveilleux dans l'épopée grecque archaïque', in A. Gaillard, J.-R. Valette and B. Vouilloux (eds), *La Beauté du merveilleux*, 21–41, Bordeaux.
Hunzinger, Ch. (2015), 'Wonder', in P. Destrée and P. Murray (eds), *A Companion to Ancient Aesthetics*, Blackwell Companions to the Ancient World. 422–37 Malden, MA, Oxford and Chichester.
Hunzinger, Ch. (2018), 'Perceiving thauma in Archaic Greek Epic', in M. Gerolemou (ed.), *Recognizing Miracles in Antiquity and Beyond*, 25–73, Berlin.
Huxley, T. H. (1874), 'On the Hypothesis that Animals are Automata, and Its History', *Fortnightly Review*, 22: 555–80. Reprinted in *Collected Essays: Vol. I, Method and Results*, 195–250, London.
Hyde, W. W. (1917), 'The Prosecution of Lifeless Things and Animals in Greek Law: Part II', *American Journal of Philology*, 38: 285–303.
Ihde, D. (1990), *Technology and the Lifeworld: From Garden to Earth*, Bloomington, IN.
Irby-Massie, G. L and P. T. Keyser (2002), *Greek Science of the Hellenistic Era: A Sourcebook*, London and New York.
Iles Johnson, S. (2008), 'Animating Statues: A Case Study in Ritual', *Arethusa*, 41 (3): 445–78.
Jain, S. S. (1999), 'The Prosthetic Imagination: Enabling and Disabling the Prosthesis Trope', *Science, Technology and Human Values*, 24: 31–54.
James, L. and R. Webb (1991), 'To Understand Ultimate Things and Enter Secret Places: Ekphrasis and Art in Byzantium', *Art History*, 14: 1–17.
Janet, P. (1889), *L'automatisme psychologique. Essai de psychologie expérimentale sur les formes inférieures de l'activité humaine. Première partie: Automatisme total*, Paris.

Jentsch, E. (1906), 'Zur Psychologie des Unheimlichen', *Psychiatrisch-Neurologische Wochenschrift*, 8, no. 22 (25 August): 195–8 and 8, no. 23 (1 September): 203–5.

Johansen, T. K. (2021), *Productive Knowledge in Ancient Philosophy: The Concept of 'Technê'*, Cambridge.

Johnson, M. R. (2009), 'Spontaneity, Democritean Causality and Freedom', *Elenchos* 30: 5–52.

Johnson, M. R. (2015), 'Luck in Aristotle's Physics and Ethics', in D. Henry and K. M. Nielsen (eds), *Bridging the Gap between Aristotle's Science and Ethics*, 254–75, Cambridge.

Johnson, O. (2013), 'Manufacturing Elephants: Technologies of Knowledge in Theatre History', in K. Reilly (ed.), *Theatre, Performance and Analogue Technology: Historical Interfaces and Intermedialities*, 40–53, New York.

Johnston, S. I. (2008), 'Animating Statues: A Case Study in Ritual', *Arethusa*, 41: 445–77.

Jones, A. (2017), *A Portable Cosmos: Revealing the Antikythera Mechanism, Scientific Wonder of the Ancient World*, New York.

Jones, W. H. S. (ed. and trans.) (1931), *Hippocrates VI: Nature of Man, Regimen in Health, Humours, Aphorisms, Regimen 1–3, Dreams, Heracleitus: On the Universe*, Loeb Classical Library 150, Cambridge, MA.

Jouanna, J. (1987), 'Médecine hippocratique et tragédie grecque', *Cahiers du Gita*, 3: 109–31.

Kagan, D. and G. F. Viggiano (2013), *Men of Bronze: Hoplite Warfare in Ancient Greece*, Princeton, NJ, and Oxford.

Kahn, A. D. (1970), 'Every Art Possessed by Man Comes from Prometheus: The Greek Tragedians and Science and Technology', *Technology and Culture*, 11: 133–62.

Kahn, Ch. H. (1979), *The Art and Thought of Heraclitus: An Edition of the Fragments with Translation and Commentary*, Cambridge.

Kakoudaki, D. (2014), *Anatomy of a Robot, Literature, Cinema, and the Cultural Work of Artificial People*, New Brunswick, NJ.

Kaldellis, A. (2007), 'Christodoros on the Statues of the Zeuxippos Baths: A New Reading of the *Ekphrasis*', *Greek, Roman and Byzantine Studies*, 47: 361–83.

Kalligeropoulos, D. and S. Vasileiadou (2008), 'The Homeric Automata and Their Implementation', in S. A. Paipetis (ed.), *Science and Technology in Homeric Epics*, History of Mechanism and Machine Science, vol. 6, 77–84, Dordrecht.

Kang, M. (2011), *Sublime Dreams of Living Machines: The Automaton in the European Imagination*, Cambridge.

Kannicht, R. (1969), *Euripides' Helena*, 2 vols, Heidelberg.

Karageorghis, V. (1992), 'Soldiers and Other Toys in the Coroplastic Art of Cyprus', in A. P. Jonsered (ed.), *Acta Cypria, Part 2*, 171–83, Stockholm.

Kassel, R. (1983), 'Dialogue mil Statuen', *Zeitschrift für Papyrologie und Epigraphik*, 51: 1–12.
Kassel, R., Austin, C. (eds) (1983), *Poetae Comici Graeci, IV: Aristophon- Crobylus*, Berlin.
Kenaan, V. L. (2008), *Pandora's Senses: The Feminine Character of the Ancient Text*, Madison, WI.
Kim, S. (2015–16), 'Kairotopia'. Available online: https://palgoo.wixsite.com/kairotopia/about (accessed 20 March 2022).
Kim, S. (2017), 'Toward a Phenomenology of Time in Ancient Greek Art', in L. Doering and J. Ben-Dov (eds), *The Construction of Time in Antiquity*, 142–72, Cambridge.
Kim, S. (forthcoming), 'Visualising Time: The Lysippan Kairos in the Scientific Landscape of the Fourth Century BCE', in T. Bur, M. Gerolemou and I. A. Ruffell (eds), *Technological Animation in Greco-Roman Antiquity*, Oxford.
Kindt, J. (2012), *Rethinking Greek Religion*, Cambridge.
Kindt, J. (2016), *Revisiting Delphi: Religion and Storytelling in Ancient Greece*, Cambridge Classical Studies, Cambridge.
King, L. W. (1902), *The Seven Tablets of Creation*, London.
Kirkpatrick, J. and F. M. Dunn (2002), 'Heracles, Cercopes, and Paracomedy', *Transactions of the American Philological Association*, 132: 29–61.
Knappett, C. (2005), *Thinking through Material Culture: An Interdisciplinary Perspective*, Philadelphia, PA.
Koetsier, T. and H. Kerle (2016), 'The Automaton Nysa: Mechanism Design in Alexandria in the 3d Century BC', in F. Sorge and G. Genchi (eds), *Essays on the History of Mechanical Engineering*, History of Mechanism and Machine Science, 31, 347–66, Switzerland.
Kokolakis, M. (1980), 'Homeric Animism', *Museum Philologum Londiniens*, 4: 89–113.
Koller, H. (1954), *Die Mimesis in der Antike. Nachahmung, Darstellung, Ausdruck*, Berne.
Konstan, D. (2010), 'Socrates in Aristophanes' *Clouds*', in D. R. Morrison (ed.), *The Cambridge Companion to Socrates*, Cambridge Companions to Philosophy, 75–90, Cambridge.
Konstan, D. (2012), 'A World without Slaves: Crates' Thêria', in C. W. Marshall and George Kovacs (eds), *No Laughing Matter: New Studies in Athenian Comedy*, 13–18, London.
Konstan, D. (2013), 'Propping up Greek Tragedy: The Right Use of Opsis', in G. W. M. Harrison and V. Liapis (eds), *Performance in Greek and Roman Theatre*, Mnemosyne Supplements, 353, 63–75, Leiden.
Konstan, D. (2015), 'Implicit Knowledge', in M. Hose and D. Schenker (eds), *A Companion to Greek Literature*, Blackwell Companions to the Ancient World, 415–26, Malden, MA, and London.
Kosak, J. C. (2004), *Heroic Measures: Hippocratic Medicine in the Making of Euripidean Tragedy*, Leiden.

Kovacs, D. (1994), *Euripidea*, Mnemosyne Supplements 132, Leiden.

Kovacs, D. (ed. and trans.) (2002), *Euripides: Bacchae, Iphigenia at Aulis, Rhesus*, Loeb Classical Library 495, Cambridge, MA.

Kovacs (ed. and trans.) (1998), *Euripides III: Euripides, Suppliant Women; Electra; Heracles*, Cambridge, MA.

Krafft, F. (1967), 'Die Anfänge der theoretischen Mechanik und die Wandlung ihrer Stellung zur Wissenschaft von der Natur', in W. Baron (ed.), *Beiträge zur Methodik der Wissenschaftsgeschichte*, Beiträge zur Geschichte der Wissenschaft und der Technik, Heft, 9, 12–33, Wiesbaden.

Krafft, F. (1970), *Dynamische und Statische Betrachtungsweise in der Antike Mechanik*, Wiesbaden.

Krafft, F. (1971), 'Die Stellung der Technik zur Naturwissenschaft in Antike und Neuzeit', *Humanismus und Technik*, 15: 33–50.

Krafft, F. (1972), 'Heron von Alexandria', in K. Fassmann u.a. (Hgg.), *Die Großen der Weltgeschichte*, Band 2, 332–79, Zürich.

Kranz, W. (1924), 'Das Verhältnis des Schöpfers zu seinem Werk in der althellenischen Literatur', *Neue Jahrbücher für das klassische Altertum, Geschichte und deutsche Literatur*, 27: 65–86.

Kranz, W. (1938), 'Gleichnis und Vergleich in der Frühgriechischen Philosophie', *Hermes*, 73: 99–122.

Kraus, C. S. (1998), 'Dangerous Supplements: Etymology and Genealogy in Euripides' Heracles', *Proceedings of the Cambridge Philological Society*, 44: 137–57.

Kress, E. (2020), 'Aristotle on Spontaneous Generation, Spontaneity, and Natural Processes', *Oxford Studies in Ancient Philosophy*, 58: 157–204.

Kris, E. and O. Kurz (1980), *Die Legende vom Künstler: Ein geschichtlicher Versuch*, Frankfurt am Main.

Kube, J. (1969), *TEXNH und APETH: sopistisches und platonisches Tugendwissen*, Quellen und Studien zur Geschichte der Philosophie, vol. 12, Berlin.

Kurke, L. (2013), 'Imagining Chorality: Wonder, Plato's Puppets, and Moving Statues', in A. E. Peponi (ed.), *Performance and Culture in Plato's Laws*, 123–70, Cambridge.

Lada-Richards, I. (1999), *Initiating Dionysus: Ritual and Theatre in Aristophanes' Frogs*, Oxford.

Lada-Richards, I. (2002), 'The Subjectivity of Greek Performance', in E. Hall and P. E. Easterling (eds), *Greek and Roman Actors: Aspects of an Ancient Profession*, 395–418, Cambridge.

Lada-Richards, I. (2003), 'Mobile Statuary: Refractions of Pantomime Dancing from Callistratus to Emma Hamilton and Andrew Ducrow', *International Journal of Classical Tradition*, 10: 3–37.

Laird, W. R. (2015), 'Heron of Alexandria and the Principles of Mechanics', in B. Holmes and K.-D. Fischer (eds), *The Frontiers of Ancient Science: Essays in Honor of Heinrich von Staden*, Beiträge zur Altertumskunde 338, 289–306, Berlin.

Lambert, W. G. (2007), 'Mesopotamian Creation Stories', in M. J. Geller and M. Schipper (eds), *Imagining Creation*, IJS Studies in Judaica, 5, 15–59, Leiden.

Lanata, G. (ed.) (1963), *Poetica Pre-Platonica: Testimonianze e frammenti*, vol. 43, Filosofia antica, Firenze.

Lancaster, L. C. and R. B. Ulrich (2013), 'Materials and Techniques', in B. R. Ulrich and C. K. Quenemoen (eds), *A Companion to Roman Architecture*, Blackwell Companions to the Ancient World, 157–92, Malden, MA, Oxford and Chichester.

Langslow, D. R. (1999), 'The Language of Poetry and the Language of Science: The Latin Poets and Medical Latin', in J. N. Adams and R. G. Mayer (eds), *Aspects of the Language of Latin Poetry*, 97–133, Oxford.

Lapatin, K. D. C. (2001), *Chryselephantine Statuary in the Ancient Mediterranean World*, Oxford.

Lapatin, K. (2014), 'The Materials and Techniques of Greek and Roman Art', in C. Marconi (ed.), *The Oxford Handbook of Greek and Roman Art and Architecture*, 203–40, Oxford.

Lateiner, D. (2013), 'Gestures & Body Language', in H. M. Roisman (ed.), *The Encyclopedia of Greek Tragedy*, 3 vols, Chichester, Malden, MA, Oxford.

Lather, A. (2018), 'The Extended Mind of Hephaestus: Automata and Artificial Intelligence in Early Greek Hexameter', in P. Meineck, W. M. Short and J. Devereaux (eds), *The Routledge Companion to Classics and Cognitive Theory*, 331–44, London.

Latour, B. (1993), *We Have Never Been Modern*, translated by C. Porter. Cambridge, MA.

Latour, B. (1996), 'On Interobjectivity', *Mind, Culture and Activity*, 3: 228–45.

Latour, B. (1999), *Pandora's Hope: Essays on the Reality of Science Studies*, Cambridge, MA.

Latour, B. (2004), 'How to Talk about the Body? The Normative Dimension of Science Studies', in M. Akrich and M. Berg (eds), 'Bodies on Trial', *Body and Society*, 10 (2/3): 205–29.

Latour, B. (2005), *Reassembling the Social: An Introduction to Actor-Network-Theory*, Clarendon Lectures in Management Studies, New York.

Lavan, L. (2007), 'Explaining Technological Change: Innovation, Stagnation, Recession and Replacement', in L. Lavan, E. Zanini and A. C. Sarantis (eds), *Technology in transition: A.D. 300–650*, xv–xl, Leiden.

Lawtoo, N. (2015), 'The Matrix E-Motion: Simulation, Mimesis, Hypermimesis', in S. Cowdell, C. Fleming and J. Hodge (eds), *Mimesis, Movies and Media: Violence, Desire, and the Sacred*, 89–104, London.

Lawtoo, N. (2019), '"This is No Simulation!": Hypermimesis from Being John Malkovich to Her', *Quarterly Review of Film and Videos*, 37 (2): 116–44.

Lee, M. M. (2015), *Body, Dress, and Identity in Ancient Greece*, Cambridge.

Lehoux, D. (2017), *Creatures Born of Mud and Slime: The Wonder and Complexity of Spontaneous Generation*, Baltimore, MD.

Lendle, O. (1957), *Die 'Pandorasage' bei Hesiod*, Würzburg.

Lennox, J. G. (1982), 'Teleology, Chance, and Aristotle's Theory of Spontaneous Generation', *Journal of History of Philososphy*, 20: 219–38.

Lennox, J. G. (2001a), *Aristotle's Philosophy of Biology: Studies in the Origins of Life Science*, Cambridge.

Lennox, J. G. (2001b), 'Teleology, Chance, and Aristotle's Theory of Spontaneous Generation', in J. G. Lennox, *Aristotle's Philosophy of Biology: Studies in the Origins of Life Science*, 229–49, Cambridge.

Lesky, A. (1961), *Göttliche und menschliche Motivation im homerischen Epos*, Heidelberg.

Lewis, M. J. T. (2000), 'Theoretical Hydraulics, Automata, and Water Clocks', in Ö. Wikander (ed.), *Handbook of Ancient Water Technology*, 343–69, Leiden.

Lewis, M. J. T. (2007), 'Antique Engineering in the Byzantine World', in L. Lavan, E. Zanini and A. C. Sarantis (eds), *Technology in Transition: A.D. 300–650*, 367–78, Leiden.

Ley, G. (2005), 'The Nameless and the Named: Techne and Technology in Ancient Athenian Performance', *Performance Research*, 10: 97–104.

Liapis, V. J. (2006), 'Intertextuality as Irony: Heracles in Epic and in Sophocles', *Greeece & Rome*, 53: 48–59.

Lightfoot, J. (2018), *Wonder and the Marvellous from Homer to the Hellenistic World*, Cambridge.

Lissarrague, F. (1990), *L'Autre guerrier: Archers, peltastes, cavaliers dans l'imagerie attique*, Images à l' appui 3, Paris and Rome.

Lissarrague, F. (2001), 'La Fabrique de Pandora: naissance d'images', in J.-C. Schmitt (ed.), *Eve et Pandora: la création de la premierefemme*, 39–67, Paris.

Lissarrague, F. (2008), 'Corps et armes: figures grecques du Guerrier', in V. Dasen et J. Wilgaux (éds), *Langages et métaphores du corps dans le monde antique*, 15–27, Rennes.

Liveley, G. (2006), 'Science Fictions and Cyber Myths: Or, Do Cyborgs Dream of Dolly the Sheep?', in V. Zajko and M. Leonard (eds), *Laughing with Medusa*, 275–94, Oxford.

Liveley, G. and S. Thomas (2020), 'Homer's Intelligent Machines: AI in Antiquity', in S. Cave, K. Dihal and S. Dillon (eds), *AI Narratives: A History of Imaginative Thinking about Intelligent Machines*, 25–48, Oxford.

Lloyd, A. B. (1975–6), *Herodotus: Book II, Introduction* (I) and *Commentary* (II), Leiden.
Lloyd, G. E. R. (1966), *Polarity and Analogy: Two Types of Argumentation in Early Greek Thought*, Cambridge.
Lloyd, G. E. R. (1979), *Magic, Reason and Experience: Studies in the Origins and Development of Greek Science*, Cambridge.
Lloyd-Jones, H. (1957), 'A New Text of Fr.50', in H. W. Smyth and H. Lloyd-Jones (trans.) *Aeschylus II*, 541–56, London.
Lloyd-Jones, H. (1962), 'The Guilt of Agamemnon', *Classical Quarterly*, 12: 187–99.
Lloyd-Jones, H. (1994), *Sophocles*, Cambridge, MA.
Löbl, R. (1997), *Technē: Untersuchung zur Bedeutung dieses Wortes in der Zeit von Homer bis Aristoteles/1: Von Homer bis zu den Sophisten*, Würzburg.
Löbl, R. (2003), *Technē: Untersuchung zur Bedeutung dieses Wortes in der Zeit von Homer bis Aristoteles/2: Von den Sophisten bis zu Aristoteles*, Würzburg.
Löbl, R. (2008), *Technē: Untersuchung zur Bedeutung dieses Wortes in der Zeit von Homer bis Aristoteles/3: Die Zeit des Hellenismus*, Würzburg.
Lodge, R. C. (1953), *Plato's Theory of Art*, International Library of Psychology, Philosophy, and Scientific Method, New York.
Long, A. A. (2015), *Greek Models of Mind and Self*, Cambridge, MA.
Longo, O. (1996), 'Le Héros, l'armure, le corps', *Dialogues d'histoire ancienne*, 22 (2): 25–51.
Lonie, I. M. (1981), 'Hippocrates the Iatromechanist', *Medical History*, 25: 11–50.
Loraux, N. (1978), 'Sur la race des femmes et quelques-unes de ses tribus', *Arethusa*, 11: 4–89.
Loraux, N. (1981), 'Le Lit, la guerre', *L' Homme*, 21: 37–67.
Loraux, N. (2000), *Born of the Earth: Myth and Politics in Athens*, translated by S. Stewart, Ithaca, NY.
Lorimer W. L. (ed.) (1933), *Aristotelis qui fertur libellus de mundo*, Paris.
Lowe, D. M. (2016), 'Suspending Disbelief: Magnetic and Miraculous Levitation from Antiquity to the Middle Ages', *Classical Antiquity*, 35: 247–78.
Lucarini, C. M. (2016), 'L' ekkyklema nel teatro greco dell' età classica', *Hermes*, 144: 138–56.
Lucas, D. W. (1968), *Aristotle. Poetics*, Oxford.
Luschnat, O. (1961–2), 'Autodidaktos: Eine Begriffsgeschichte', *Theologia Viatorum*, 8: 157–72.
Lutz, L. (ed.) (2014), *Aristophanes: Wespen*, Berlin.
Macrides, R. and P. Magdalino (1988), 'The Architecture of Ekphrasis: Construction and Context of Paul the Silentiary's Poem on Hagia Sophia', *Byzantine and Modern Greek Studies*, 12: 47–82.

Malafouris, L. (2008), 'Is it "Me" or is it "Mine"? The Mycenaean Sword as a Bodypart', in J. Robb and D. Boric (eds), *Past Bodies: Body-Centered Research in Archaeology*, 115–23, Oxford.

Malafouris, L. (2014), 'Third Hand Prosthesis (comment for Bruner & Lozano)', *Journal of Anthropological Sciences*, 92: 281–3.

Malafouris, L. (2019), 'Mind and Material Engagement', *Phenomenology and the Cognitive Sciences*, 18: 1–17.

Malinowski, B. (1948), *Magic, Science and Religion and Other Essays Selected, and with an Introduction by Robert Redfield*, Boston, MA, and Glenco.

Manakidou, F. P. (1993), *Beschreibung von Kunstwerken in der hellenistischen Dichtung. Ein Beitrag zur hellenistischen Poetik*, Beiträge zur Altertumskunde. vol. 36, Stuttgart.

Mango, C. (1972), *The Art of the Byzantine Empire 312–1453: Sources and Documents*, Toronto, Buffalo, NY, and London.

Männlein-Robert, I. (2007a), *Stimme, Schrift und Bild. Zum Verhältnis der Künste in der hellenistischen Dichtung*, Bibliothek der klassischen Altertumswissenschaften, Heidelberg.

Männlein-Robert, I. (2007b), 'Epigrams on Art: Voice and Voicelessness in Hellenistic Epigram', in P. Bing and J. Steffen Bruss (eds), *Brill's Companion to Hellenistic Epigram*, Brill's Companions in Classical Studies, 251–71, Leiden.

Mansfield, E. C. (1997), *Too Beautiful to Picture: Zeuxis, Myth, and Mimesis*, Minneapolis, MN.

Manson, M. (1992), 'Les Poupées Antiques', *Jeux et Jouets dans l'Antiquité et au Moyen Age*, *Dossiers de l'Archéologie*, 168: 48–57.

March, J. (1989), 'Euripides' *Bakchai*: A Reconsideration in the Light of Vase-Paintings', *Bulletin of the Institute of Classical Studies*, 36: 33–65.

Marcinkowski, A. and J. Wilgaux (2004), 'Automates et créatures artificielles en Grèce ancienne: Entre science et fiction', *Techniques et Culture*, 43–4: 167–90.

Marder, E. (2012), *The Mother in the Age of Mechanical Reproduction: Psychoanalysis, Photography, Deconstruction*, New York.

Marder, E. (2014), 'Pandora's Fireworks; or, Questions Concerning Femininity, Technology, and the Limits of the Human', *Philosophy & Rhetoric*, 47: 386–99.

Margon, J. S. (1969), 'The First Burial of Polyneices', *Classical Journal*, 64: 289–95.

Marquardt, P. A. (1982), 'Hesiod's Ambiguous View of Woman', *Classical Philology*, 77: 283–91.

Marshall, C. W. (1999), 'Some Fifth-Century Masking Conventions', *Greece & Rome*, 46: 188–202.

Marshall, C. W. (2014), *The Structure and Performance of Euripides' Helen*, Cambridge.

Mastronarde, D. J. (1990), 'Actors on High: The Skene Roof, the Crane, and the Gods in Attic Drama', *Classical Antiquity*, 9: 247–94.

Mastronarde, D. J. (2010), *The Art of Euripides: Dramatic Technique and Social Context*, Cambridge.

Mathew, G. (1963), *Byzantine Aesthetics*, London.

Mattes, J. (1970), *Der Wahnsinn im griechischen Mythos und in der Dichtung bis zum Drama des fünften Jahrhunderts*, Heidelberg.

Mattusch, C. C. (1988), *Greek Bronze Statuary: From the Beginnings Through the Fifth Century B.C.*, Ithaca, NY, and London.

Mattusch, C. C. (forthcoming), 'Dead or Alive? Giving Life to Bronze', in T. Bur, M. Gerolemou and I. A. Ruffell (eds), *Technological Animation in Greco-Roman Antiquity*, Oxford.

Mauss, M. (1935), 'Les Techniques du corps', *Journal de psychologie normal et patholigique*, 32: 271–93.

Mayor, A. (2018), *Gods and Robots: Myths, Machines, and Ancient Dreams of Technology*, Princeton, NJ.

McCall, M. (1972), 'Divine and Human Action', *Yale Classical Studies*, 22: 10–17.

Meek, A. (1952), 'The Architect and His Profession in Byzantium', *Journal of the Royal Institute of British Architects*, 59: 216–20.

Meiklejohn, K. W. (1932), 'The Burial of Polynices', *Classical Review*, 46: 4–5.

Meißner, B. (1999), *Die technologische Fachliteratur der antike. Struktur, Überlieferung und Wirkung technischen Wissens in der Antike (ca. 400 v. Chr.–ca. 500 n. Chr)*, Berlin.

Melchinger, S. (1974), *Das theater der Tragödie: Aischylos, Sophokles, Euripides auf der Bühne ihrer Zeit*, München.

Merry, W. W. and J. Riddell (eds) (1886), *Homer's Odyssey*, Oxford.

Messemer, E. J. (1942), 'The Double Burial of Polyneices', *Classical Journal*, 37: 515–26.

Métraux, G. P. R. (1995), *Sculptors and Physicians in Fifth-century Greece: A Preliminary Study*, Montreal.

Michelini, A. M. (1987), *Euripides and the Tragic Tradition*, Wisconsin.

Miguélez-Cavero, L. (2013), *Triphiodorus: The Sack of Troy. A General Introduction and Commentary*, Texte und Kommentare, 45, Berlin.

Millett, P. (2001), 'Productive to Some Purpose? The Problem of Ancient Economic Growth', in D. J. Mattingly and J. Salmon (eds), *Economies Beyond Agriculture in the Classical World*, 17–48, New York.

Mistretta, R. M. (2017), 'Hermes the Craftsman: The Invention of the Lyre', *Gaia* 20: 5–22.

Montiglio, S. (2000), *Silence in the Land of Logos*, Princeton, NJ.

Montiglio, S. (2005), *Wandering in Ancient Greek Culture*, Chicago, IL.

Montserrat, D. (1998a), 'Introduction', in D. Montserrat (ed.), *Changing Bodies, Changing Meanings: Studies on the Human Body in Antiquity*, 1–19, London and New York.

Montserrat, D. (1998b), 'Unidentified Human Remains: Mummies and the Erotics of Biography', in D. Montserrat (ed.), *Changing Bodies, Changing Meanings. Studies on the Human Body in Antiquity*, 162–97, London and New York.

Mora, F. (1989), 'Religious Silence in Herodotus and the Athenian Theatre', in C. M. Grazia (ed.), *The Regions of Silence: Studies in the Difficulty of Communicating, Amsterdam*, vol. 17, 41–65, Amsterdam.

Morris, S. P. (1992), *Daidalos and the Origins of Greek Art*, Princeton, NJ.

Most, G. W. (ed. and trans.) (2006), *Hesiod. Theogony, Works and Days, Testimonia*, Cambridge, MA.

Most, W. G. (ed. and trans.) (2006), *Hesiod: Theogony, Works and Days, Testimonia*, Loeb Classical Library 57, Cambridge, MA.

Most, G. W. (ed. and trans.) (2007), *Hesiod: The Shield, Catalogue of Women, Other Fragments*, Loeb Classical Library, Cambridge, MA.

Muecke, F. (1982), 'A Portrait of the Artist as a Young Woman', *Classical Quarterly*, 32: 41–55.

Mueller, M. (2016), *Objects as Actors: Props and the Poetics of Performance in Greek Tragedy*, Chicago, IL.

Müller, A. (1886), *Lehrbuch der griechischen Bühnenaltertümer*, Freiburg.

Mulvey, L. (1992), 'Pandora: Topographies of the Mask and Curiosity', in B. Colomina and J. Bloomer (eds), *Sexuality & Space*, 53–71, New York.

Mulvey, L. (1996), *Fetishism and Curiosity*, London.

Muratov, M. B. (2005), 'From the Mediterranean to the Bosporos: Terracotta Figurines with Articulated Limbs', PhD diss., New York University.

Murnaghan, S. (1988), 'Body and Voice in Greek Tragedy', *Yale Journal of Criticism*, 2: 23–43.

Murphy, S. (1995), 'Heron of Alexandria's on Automaton-Making', *History of Technology*, 17: 1–46.

Murray, P. (1981), 'Poetic Inspiration in Early Greece', *Journal of Hellenic Studies*, 101: 87–100.

Murray, P. (1989), 'Poetic Genius and Its Classical Origins', in P. Murray (ed.), *Genius: The History of an Idea*, 9–41, Oxford.

Musäus, I. (2004), *Der Pandoramythos bei Hesiod und seine Rezeption bis Erasmus von Rotterdam*, Hypomnemata, Band, 15, Göttingen.

Naas, M. (2018), *Plato and the Invention of Life*, Fordham.

Naddaf, G. (2005), *The Greek Concept of Nature*, New York.

Naddaf, G. (2010), 'Spontaneous Generation and Creationism in Presocratic Monism in Light of Aristotle's Analysis in the *Physics*', *Anais De Filosofia Clássica*, 5 (8): 23–40.

Nagy, G. (1979), *The Best of the Achaeans: Concepts of the Hero in Archaic Greek Poetry* Baltimore, MD.

Neckel, O. (1889) *Das ekkyklema*, Friedland.

Neer, R. T. (2010a), 'Jean-Pierre Vernant and the History of the Image', *Arethusa*, 43: 181–95.

Neer, R. T. (2010b), *The Emergence of the Classical Style in Greek Sculpture*, Chicago, IL.

Neils, J. (2005), 'The Girl in the *Pithos*. Hesiod's *Elpis*', in J. M. Barringer and J. M. Hurwit (eds), *Periklean Athens and Its Legacy: Problems and Perspectives*, 37–45, Austin, TX.

Nelson, R. S. (2000), 'To Say and to See: Ekphrasis and Vision in Byzantium', in R. S. Nelson (ed.), *Visuality Before and Beyond the Renaissance: Seeing as Others Saw*, Cambridge.

Nesselrath, H.-G. and B. Bäbler (2006), *Ars et Verba. Die Kunstbeschreibungen des Kallistratos. Einführung, Text, Übersetzung, Anmerkungen, archäologischer Kommentar*, Munich.

Nestle, W. (1938), 'Hippocratica', *Hermes*, 73: 1–38.

Neuberger, A. (1919), *Die Technik des Altertums*, Leipzig.

Newby, Z. (2009), 'Absorption and Erudition in Philostratus' *Imagines*', in E. Bowie and J. Elsner (eds), *Philostratus: Greek Culture in the Roman World*, 322–42, Cambridge.

Newiger, H.-J. (1996), *Drama und Theater. Ausgewählte Schriften zum griechischen Drama*, Stuttgart.

Newman, R. W. (2004), *Promethean Ambitions: Alchemy and the Quest to Perfect Nature*, Chicago, IL.

Newmyer, S. T. (2017), *The Animal and the Human in Ancient and Modern Thought: The 'Man Alone of Animals' Concept*, Routledge Monographs in Classical Studies, New York.

Ní Mheallaigh, K. (2014), *Reading Fiction with Lucian: Fakes, Freaks and Hyperreality*, Cambridge.

Nightingale, A. W. (2001), 'On Wandering and Wondering: Theôria in Greek Philosophy and Culture', *Arion*, 9: 23–58.

Nightingale, A. W. (2004), *Spectacles of Truth in Classical Greek Philosophy: Theoria in its Cultural Context*, Cambridge.

Noel, J. A.-S. (2018), 'Prosthetic Imagination in Greek Literature', in J. Draycott (ed.), *Prostheses in Antiquity*, Medicine and the Body in Antiquity, 159–79, Abingdon.

Nünlist, R. (2009), *The Ancient Critic at Work: Terms and Concepts of Literary Criticism in Greek Scholia*, Cambridge.

Nussbaum, M. C. (1976), 'The Text of Aristotle's De Motu Animalium', *Harvard Studies in Classical Philology*, 80: 111–59.

Nussbaum, M. C. (1978), *Aristotle's De Motu Animalium: Text with Translation, Commentary, and Interpretive Essays*, Princeton, NJ.

Nussbaum, M. C. and H. Putnam (1992), 'Changing Aristotle's Mind', in M. C. Nussbaum and A. O. Rorty (eds), *Essays on Aristotle's De Anima*, 27–56, Oxford.

O'Bryhim, S. D. (2015), 'The Economics of Agalmatophilia', *Classical Journal*, 110 (4): 419–29.

O'Higgins, D. (1993), 'Above Rubies: Admetus' Perfect Wife', *Arethusa*, 26: 77–97.

Olejniczak L. V. and V. Olk (eds) (2007), *Neuplatonismus und Ästhetik. Zur Transformationsgeschichte des Schönen*, Transformationen der Antike Band 2, Berlin and New York.

Oleson, J. P. (1984), *Greek and Roman Mechanical Water-Lifting Devices: The History of a Technology*, Toronto, Buffalo, NY, and London.

Oleson, J. P. (2008), *The Oxford Handbook of Engineering and Technology in the Classical World*, Oxford.

Olson, S. D. (2002), *Aristophanes' Acharnians*, Oxford.

Olson, S. D. and Sens, A. (1999), *Matro of Pitane and the Tradition of Epic Parody in the Fourth Century BCE: Text, Translation, and Commentary*, American Philological Association, Atlanta, GA.

Osborne, R. (2010), *The History Written on the Classical Body*, Cambridge.

Padel, R. (1981), 'Madness in Fifth-Century Athenian Tragedy', in P. Heelas and A. Lock (eds), *Indigenous Psychologies: The Anthropology of the Self*, 105–31, London.

Padel, R. (1992), *In and Out of the Mind: Greek Images of the Tragic Self*, Princeton, NJ.

Padel, R. (1995), *Whom Gods Destroy: Elements of Greek and Tragic Madness*, Princeton, NJ.

Padilla, M. (1992), 'The Gorgonic Archer: Danger of Sight in Euripides' *Heracles*', *Classical World*, 86: 1–12.

Papadopoulou, Th. (2005), *Heracles and Euripidean Tragedy*, Cambridge.

Papaioannou, Str. (2006), 'Animated Statues: Aesthetics and Movement', in Ch. Barber and D. Jenkins (eds), *Reading Michael Psellos, The Medieval Mediterranean: Peoples, Economies and Cultures, 400–1500*, vol. 61, 95–116, Leiden.

Papastamati-von Moock, Ch. (2014), 'The Theatre of Dionysus Eleuthereus in Athens: New Data and Observations on its "Lycurgan" Phase', in E. Csapo, H. R. Goette, J. R. Green and P. Wilson (eds), *Greek Theatre in the Fourth Century B.C.*, 15–76, Berlin and Boston, MA.

Papastamati-von Moock, Ch. (2015), 'The Wooden Theatre of Dionysos Eleuthereus in Athens: Old Issues, New Research', in R. Frederiksen, E. R. Gebhard and- A. Sokolicek (eds), *The Architecture of the Ancient Greek Theatre*, Acts of an International Conference at the Danish Institute at Athens 27–30 January 2012, 39–79, Aarhus.

Paton, W. R. (ed. and trans.) (1918), *The Greek Anthology, Volume V: Book 13: Epigrams in Various Metres. Book 14: Arithmetical Problems, Riddles, Oracles. Book 15: Miscellanea. Book 16: Epigrams of the Planudean Anthology not in the Palatine Manuscript*, Loeb Classical Library 86. Cambridge, MA.

Payne, M. (2016), 'Teknomajikality and the Humanimal in Aristophanes' *Wasps*', in Ph. Walsh (ed.), *The Brill Companion to the Reception of Aristophanes*, vol. 8, 129–47, Leiden.

Peers, G. (2012), 'Real Living Painting: Quasi-Objects and Dividuation in the Byzantine World', *Religion and the Arts*, 16: 433–60.

Pelliccia, H. (1995), *Mind, Body, and Speech in Homer and Pindar*, Hypomnemata, Göttingen.

Pentcheva, B. V. (2009), 'Moving Eyes: Surface and Shadow in the Byzantine Mixed-Media Relief Icon', *Res: Anthropology and Aesthetics*, 53: 223–34.

Pentcheva, B. V. (2010), *The Sensual Icon: Space, Ritual, and the Senses in Byzantium*, University Park, PA.

Pentcheva, B. V. (2011), 'Hagia Sophia and Multisensory Aesthetics', *Gesta*, 50: 9–111.

Pentcheva, B. V. (2016), 'Glittering Eyes: Animation in the Byzantine Eikōn and the Western Imago', *Codex Aqvilarensis*, 32: 20–36.

Pettorino, M. (1999), 'Memnon, the Vocal Statue', in J. Ohala, Y. Hasegawa, M. Ohala, D. Granveille and A. Bailey Ohala (eds), *Proceedings of the 14th International Congress of Phonetic Sciences*, vol. 2, 1321–4, Berkeley, CA.

Pfeifer, R. (1968), *History of Classical Scholarship: From the Beginnings to the End of the Hellenistic Age*, Oxford.

Phelan, P. (1993), *Unmarked: The Politics of Performance*, London and New York.

Philipp, H. (1968), *Tektonon Daidala. Der bildende Künstler und sein Werk im vorplatonischen Schrifttum*, Berlin.

Pickard-Cambridge, A. W. (1946), *The Theatre of Dionysus in Athens*, Oxford.

Pickard-Cambridge, A. W. (1988), *The Dramatic Festivals of Athens*, rev. with a new supplement by J. Gould and D. M. Lewis, Oxford.

Pickering, A. (1995), *The Mangle of Practice: Time, Agency, and Science*, Chicago, IL.

Platt, V. J. (2002), 'Viewing, Desiring, Believing: Confronting the Divine in a Pompeian House', *Art History*, 25: 87–112.

Platt, V. J. (2009), 'Virtual Visions: Phantasia and the Perception of the Divine in Philostratus' Life of Apollonius of Tyana', in E. L. Bowie and J. Elsner (eds), *Philostratus*, 131–54, Cambridge.

Platt, V. J. (2011), *Facing the Gods: Epiphany and Representation in Graeco-Roman Art, Literature and Religion*, Cambridge.

Platt, V. J. (2016), 'The Artist as Anecdote: Creating Creators in Ancient Texts and Modern Art History', in R. Fletcher and J. Hanink (eds), *Creative Lives in Classical Antiquity: Poets, Artists and Biography*, 274–304, Cambridge.

Platt, V. J. and M. Gaifman (2018), 'Introduction: From Grecian Urn to Embodied Object', in V. Platt, M. Gaifman and M. Squire (eds), *The Embodied Object in Greek and Roman Art*, Special Issue, *Art History*, 41 (3): 402–19.

Pollitt, J. J. (1965), *The Art of Greece, 1400–31 BC: Sources and Documents*, Englewood Cliffs, NJ.

Pollitt, J. J. (1974), *The Ancient View of Greek Art: Criticism, History, and Terminology*, New Haven, CT.

Pont, G. (2005), 'The Education of the Classical Architect from Plato to Vitruvius', *Nexus Network Journal*, 7: 76–85.

Porter, J. I. (2006), 'Introduction: What is 'Classical' about Classical Antiquity?', in J. I. Porter (ed.), *Classical Pasts: The Classical Traditions of Greece and Rome*, 1–65, Princeton, NJ, and Oxford.

Porter, J. I. (2010), *The Origins of Aesthetic Thought in Ancient Greece: Matter, Sensation, and Experience*, Cambridge.

Power, T. (2010), *The Culture of Kitharoidia*, Hellenic Studies Series, 15, Washington, DC.

Prager, F. D. (1974), *Philo of Byzantium: Pneumatica*, Göttingen.

Primavesi, O. (2018), *Aristotles: De motu animalium / Über die Bewegung der Lebewesen*, translated by K. Corcilius, Philosophische Bibliothek, 636, Hamburg.

Pucci, P. (1977), *Hesiod and the Language of Poetry*, Baltimore, MD.

Pugliara, M. (2002), *Il mirabile e l'artificio: Creature animate e semoventi nel mito e nella tecnica degli antichi*, vol. 5, Roma.

Purves, A. C. (2004), 'Topographies of Time in Hesiod', in R. M. Rosen (ed.), *Time and Temporality in the Ancient World*, 147–68, Philadelphia, PA.

Purves, A. C. (2015), 'Ajax and Other Objects: Homer's Vibrant Materialism', in S. Lindheim and H. Morales (eds), *New Essays in Homer: Language, Violence, and Agency*, Ramus Special Issue, 75–94, Cambridge.

Purves, A. C. (2019), *Homer and the Poetics of Gesture*, Oxford and New York.

Rabinowitz, N.-S. (1993), *Anxiety Veiled: Euripides and the Traffic in Women*, Ithaca, NY.

Radke, G. (2003), *Tragik und Metatragik: Euripides' Bakchen und die moderne Literaturwissenschaft*, Berlin.

Ranisch, R. and S. L. Sorgner (eds) (2014), *Post- and Transhumanism: An Introduction*, New York.

Rashed, M. (2007), 'The Structure of the Eye and Its Cosmological Function in Empedocles: Reconstruction of Fragment 84 D.-K', in S. Stern-Gillet and K. Corrigan (eds), *Reading Ancient Texts, Volume I: Presocratics and Plato*, 21–39, Leiden.

Rau, P. (1967), *Paratragodia: Untersuchung einer komischen Form des Aristophanes*, Zetemata, 45, Munich.

Reale, G. and Bos A. P. (trans. and ed.) (1995), *Il trattato Sul cosmo per Alessandro attribuito ad Aristotele*. 2nd edn. Centro di ricerche di metafisica. Collana Temi metafisici e problemi del pensiero antico. Studi e testi, 42, Milano.

Rechenauer, G. (2009), 'Demokrits Seelenmodell und die Prinzipien der atomistischen Physik', in D. Frede and B. Reis (eds), *Body and Soul in Ancient Philosophy*, 111–42, Berlin.

Rehm, A. (1937), 'Antike Automobile', *Philologus*, 92: 317–30.

Rehm, R. (1994), *Marriage to Death: The Conflation of Wedding and Funeral Rituals in Greek Tragedy*, Princeton, NJ.

Rehm, R. (2002), *The Play of Space: Spatial Transformation in Greek Tragedy*, Princeton, NJ.

Reilly, K. (2011), *Automata and Mimesis on the Stage of Theatre History*, Basingstoke.

Revermann, M. (2006), *Comic Business: Theatricality, Dramatic Technique, and Performance Contexts of Aristophanic Comedy*, Oxford.

Rice, E. E. (1983), *The Grand Procession of Ptolemy Philadelphus*, Oxford.

Richard, G. (2002), 'Towards a Reconstruction of Performance Style', in P. Easterling and E. Hall (eds), *Greek and Roman Actors: Aspects of an Ancient Profession*, 93–126, Cambridge.

Ridley, G. (2016), 'Making the Perfect Woman: Female Automata from Pandora to Belinda', in D. W. Nichol (ed.), *Anniversary Essays on Alexander Pope's 'The Rape of the Lock'*, 5–69, Toronto, Buffalo, NY, London.

Riley, K. (2008), *The Reception and Performance of Euripides' Herakles: Reasoning Madness*, Oxford Classical Monographs, New York.

Ringer, M. (1998), *Electra and the Empty Urn: Metatheater and Role Playing in Sophocles*, Chapel Hill, NC.

Robbins, E. (1993), 'The Education of Achilles', *Quaderni Urbinati Di Cultura Classica*, 45 (3): 7–20.

Roberts, M. (1989), *The Jeweled Style: Poetry and Poetics in Late Antiquity*, Ithaca, NY, and London.

Robinson, D. N. (2013), 'The Insanity Defense as a History of Mental Disorder', in K. W. M. Fulford, M. Davies, R. G. T. Gipps, G. Graham, J. Z. Sadler, G. Stanghellini and T. Thornton (eds), *The Oxford Handbook of Philosophy and Psychiatry*, 18–36, Oxford.

Roby, C. (2016), *Technical Ekphrasis in Greek and Roman Science and Literature: The Written Machine between Alexandria and Rome*, Cambridge.

Roby, C. (forthcoming), 'Strange Loops: Experiment and Program in Hero of Alexandria's Automata', in T. Bur, M. Gerolemou and I. A. Ruffell (eds), *Technological Animation in Greco-Roman Antiquity*, Oxford.

Rolfe, J. C. (ed. and trans.) (1927), *Gellius. Attic Nights, Volume II: Books 6-13*, Loeb Classical Library 200, Cambridge, MA.

Rosenmeyer, P. A. (2001), *Ancient Epistolary Fictions: The Letter in Greek Literature*, Cambridge.

Rothaus, R. M. (1990), 'The Single Burial of Polyneices', *Classical Journal*, 85: 209–17.

Rouse, H. D. (1911), 'The Two Burials in the *Antigone*', *Classical Review*, 25: 40–2.

Royle, N. (2003), *The Uncanny*. Manchester and New York.

Ruffell, I. (2000), 'The World Turned Upside Down: Utopia and Utopianism in the Fragments of Old Comedy', in F. D. Harvey and J. Wilkins (eds), *The Rivals of Aristophanes: Studies in Athenian Old Comedy*, 473–506, London.

Ruffell, I. A. (2011), *Politics and Anti-Realism in Athenian Old Comedy: The Art of the Impossible*, Oxford.

Ruffell, I. A. (forthcoming a), 'Not Yet the Cyborg: The Limits of Wonder in Ancient Automata', in M. Gerolemou and G. Kazantzidis (eds), *Body and Machine in Classical Antiquity*, Cambridge.

Ruffell, I. A. (forthcoming b), 'Trains and Boats and Planes: Animating the Ship in Greek Culture', in T. Bur, M. Gerolemou and I. A. Ruffell (eds), *Technological Animation in Greco-Roman Antiquity*, Oxford.

Russo, J. (2012), 'Re-Thinking Homeric Psychology: Snell, Dodds and their Critics', *Quaderni Urbinati di Cultura Classica*, 101 (2): 11–28.

Saintillan, D. (1996), 'Du festin à l'échange: les grâces de Pandore: Dossier sur le statut de Pandora chez Hésiod', in F. Biaise, P. Judet de La Combe and Ph. Rousseau (eds), *Le Métier du mythe: Lectures d'Hésiode*, 316–48, Paris.

Sarton, G. (1959), *A History of Science: Hellenistic Science and Culture in the Last Three Centuries B.C.*, Cambridge, MA, and London.

Sarton, G. (1993), *Hellenistic Science and Culture in the Last Three Centuries B.C.*, New York.

Scheer, T. S. (2000), *Die Gottheit und ihr Bild. Untersuchungen zur Funktion griechischer Kultbilder in Religion und Politik*, Zetemata, Munich.

Schibille, N. (2009a), 'Astronomical and Optical Principles in the Architecture of Hagia Sophia in Constantinople', *Science in Context*, 22: 27–46.

Schibille, N. (2009b), 'The Profession of the Architect in Late Antique Byzantium', *Byzantion*, 79: 360–79.

Schibille, N. (2014), *Hagia Sophia and the Byzantine Aesthetic Experience*, Ashgate.

Schiefsky, M. J. (2005), *Hippocrates On Ancient Medicine: Translated with Introduction and Commentary*, Leiden.

Schiefsky, M. J. (2007), 'Art and Nature in Ancient Medicine', in B. Bensaude-Vincent and W. R. Newman (eds), *The Artificial and the Natural: An Evolving Polarity*, 67–108, Cambridge.

Schiefsky, M. J. (2008), 'Theory and Practice in Heron's Mechanics', in W. R. Laird and S. Roux (eds), *Mechanics and Natural Philosophy before the Scientific Revolution*, Boston Studies in the Philosophy of Science, 254, 15–49, Dordrecht and London.

Schlesier, R. (1985), 'Der Stachel der Götter: Zum Problem des Wahnsinns in der euripideischen Tragödie', *Poetica*, 17: 1–45.

Schlesier, R. (2004), 'Künstlerische Kreation und Religiöse Erfahrung, Verwendungsgeshichtliche Anmerkungen zum Begriff der Inspiration', in G. Mattenklott (ed.), *Ästhetische Erfahrung im Zeichen der Entgrenzung der Künste, Epistemische, ästhetische und religiöse Formen von Erfahrung im Vergleich*, 177–94, Hamburg.

Schmidt, J. (1989), 'Der Triumph des Dionysos. Aufklärung und neureligiöser Irrationalismus in den "Bakchen" des Euripides', in J. Schmidt (ed.), *Aufklärung und Gegenaufklärung in der europäischen Literatur, Philosophie und Politik von der Antike bis zur Gegenwart*, 56–71, Darmstadt.

Schmidt, W. (1904), 'Aus der antiken Mechanik', *Neue Jahrbücher für das Klassische Altertum, Geschichte und Deutsche Literatur, und für Pädagogik*, 13: 329–51.

Schmitt, A. (1990), *Selbständigkeit und Abhängigkeit menschlichen Handelns bei Homer: Hermeneutische Untersuchungen zur Psychologie Homers*, Stuttgart.

Schnapp, A. (1994), 'Are Images Animated? The Psychology of Statues in Ancient Greece', in C. Renfrew and E. B. W. Zubrow (eds), *The Ancient Mind: Elements of Cognitive Archaeology*, 40–4, Cambridge.

Schneider, H. (1986), *Das griechische Technikverständnis: Von den Epen Homers bis zu den Anfängen der technologischen Fachliteratur*, Impulse der Forschung, Darmstadt.

Schneider, H. (2007), 'Technology', in W. Scheidel, I. Morris, R. P. Saller (eds), *The Cambridge Economic History of the Greco-Roman World*, 144–72, Cambridge.

Schrade, H. (1950), 'Der homerische Hephaestus', *Gymnasium*, 57: 38–55, 94–112.

Schraube, E. and E. Sørensen (2013), 'Exploring Sociomaterial Mediations of Human Subjectivity', *Subjectivity*, 6: 1–11.

Schröder, H. O. (1983), 'Marionetten: Ein Beitrag zur Polemik des Karneades', *Rheinisches Museum für Philologie*, 126: 1–24.

Schürmann, A. (1991), *Griechische Mechanik und antike Gesellschaft: Studien zur staatlichen Förderung einer technischen Wissenschaft*, Stuttgart.

Schürmann, A. (2002), 'Pneumatics on Stage in Pompeii: Ancient Automatic Devices and their Social Context', in G. Castagnetti, A. Ciarallo, J. Renn (eds), *Homo Faber:*

Studies on Nature, Technology, and Science at the Time of Pompeii. Presented at a Conference at the Deutsches Museum, Munich, 21–22 March, Studi della Soprintendenza Archeologica di Pompei, 6, 35–56, Rome.

Schwinge, E.-R. (2014), 'Aristophanes' *Thesmophoriazusen* – eine Hommage an Euripides', *Würzburger Jahrbücher für die Altertumswissenschaft*, 38: 65–100.

Scodel, R. (1984), 'Epic Doublets and Polynices' Two Burials', *Transactions of the American Philological Association*, 114: 49–58.

Scott, W. C. (1975), 'Two Suns over Thebes: Imagery and Stage Effects in the *Bacchae*', *Transactions of the American Philological Association*, 105: 333–46.

Scott, W. C. (2009), *The Artistry of the Homeric Simile*, Hanover and London.

Seaford, R. (1981), 'Dionysiac Drama and the Dionysiac Mysteries', *Classical Quarterly*, 31: 252–75.

Seaford, R. (1996), *Euripides: Bacchae*, Warminster.

Sedley, D. (2007), *Creationism and Its Critics in Antiquity*, Sather Classical Lectures, 66. Berkeley, CA.

Segal, Ch. (1986), *Interpreting Greek Tragedy, Myth, Poetry, Text*, Ithaca, NY.

Segal, Ch. (1993), *Euripides and the Poetics of Sorrow: Art, Gender, and Commemoration in Alcestis, Hippolytus, and Hecuba*, Durham and London.

Segal, Ch. (1997), *Dionysiac Poetics and Euripides' Bacchae. Expanded Edition, with a New Afterword by the Author*, Princeton, NJ.

Seidensticker, B. (1982), *Palintonos Harmonia: Studien zu komischen Elementen in der griechischen Tragödie*, Hypomnemata, Göttingen.

Seidensticker, B. (2012), 'The Satyr Plays of Sophocles', in A. Markantonatos (ed.), *Brill's Companion to Sophocles*, 211–44, Leiden.

Seidensticker, B. (2015), 'Andriantopoiika', in B. Seidensticker, A. Stähli and A. Wessels (eds), *Der Neue Poseidipp. Text – Übersetzung – Kommentar*, Wissenschaftliche Buchgesellschaft, 247–81, Darmstadt.

Sekunda, N. (2000), *Greek Hoplite: 480–323 BC*, Oxford.

SeungJung, K. (2014), 'Concepts of Time and Temporality in the Visual Tradition of Late Archaic and Classical Greece', PhD diss., Columbia University, New York.

Sharon, T. (2014), *Human Nature in an Age of Biotechnology: The Case for Mediated Posthumanism*, Philosophy of Engineering and Technology, 14, Dordrecht.

Sharples, R. W. (1983), '"But Why has My Spirit Spoken with Me Thus?": Homeric Decision-Making', *Greece & Rome*, 30: 1–7.

Shaw, G. (1995), *Theurgy and the Soul: The Neoplatonism of Iamblichus*, University Park, PA.

Sheppard, A. (2014), *The Poetics of Phantasia: Imagination in Ancient Aesthetics*, London.

Sherwood, A. N., M. Nikolic, J. W. Humphrey and J. P. Oleson (1998), *Greek and Roman Technology: A Sourcebook: Annotated Translations of Greek and Latin Texts and Documents*, London and New York.

Sifakis, G. M. (2013), 'The Misunderstanding of Opsis in Aristotle's Poetics', in G. W. M. Harrison and V. Liapis (eds), *Performance in Greek and Roman Theatre*, Mnemosyne Supplements, 353, 45–62, Leiden.

Simon, B. (1978), *Mind and Madness in Ancient Greece: The Classical Roots of Modern Psychiatry*, Ithaca, NY.

Simondon, G. (2012), 'On technoaesthetics', *Parrhesia*, 14 (1): 1–8.

Simondon, G. (2017), 'The Genesis of Technicity', *E-flux Journal*, 82, 1–15.

Sissa, G. (1990), *Greek Virginity*, translation by Arthur Goldhammer, Cambridge, MA.

Skinner, J. (2006), 'The Uses of Bow Imagery in a Greek Context: The Enemy Within', in J. Day (ed.), *SOMA 2004: Symposium on Mediterranean Archaeology: Proceedings of the Eighth Annual Meeting of Postgraduate Researchers*, 167–72, Oxford.

Slater, N. W. (1990), 'The Idea of the Actor', in J. J. Winkler and F. I. Zeitlin (eds), *Nothing to Do with Dionysos? Athenian Drama in Its Social Context*, 385–95, Princeton, NJ.

Sluiter, I. and R. M. Rosen (2003), 'General Introduction', in R. M. Rosen and I. Sluiter (eds), *Andreia: Studies in Manliness and Courage in Classical Antiquity*, 1–24, Leiden.

Smith, W. D. (1967), 'Disease in Euripide's *Orestes*', *Hermes*, 95: 291–307.

Smyth, H. W. (ed., trans.) (1992), *Aeschylus II, with Appendix and Addendum by Hugh Lloyd-Jones*, Cambridge.

Snell, B. (1924), *Die Ausdrücke für den Begriff des Wissens in der vorplatonischen Philosophie (σοφία, γνώμη, σύνεσις, ἱστορία, μάθημα, ἐπιστήμη)*, Philologische Untersuchungen, 29, Berlin.

Snell, B. (1975), *Die Entdeckung des Geistes: Studien zur Entstehung des europäischen Denkens bei den Griechen*, Göttingen.

Snodgrass, A. M. (1965), 'The Hoplite Reform and History', *Journal of Hellenic Studies*, 85: 110–22.

Snodgrass, A. M. (1967), *Arms and Armor of the Greeks*, Ithaca, NY.

Sobchack, V. (2006), 'A Leg to Stand on: Prosthetics, Metaphor, and Materiality', in M. Smith and J. Morra (eds), *The Prosthetic Impulse: From a Posthuman Present to a Biocultural Future*, 17–41, Cambridge.

Solmsen, F. (1957), 'The Vital Heat, the Inborn Pneuma and the Aether', *Journal of Hellenic Studies*, 77: 119–23.

Solmsen, F. (1963), 'Nature as Craftsman in Greek Thought', *Journal of the History of Ideas*, 24 (4): 473–96.

Solmsen, F. (ed., trans.) (1975), *Intellectual Experiments of the Greek Enlightenment*, Princeton, NJ.

Sommerstein, A. H. (1994), *Thesmophoriazusae: The Comedies of Aristophanes*, vol. 8, Warminster.

Sommerstein, A. H. (ed. and trans.) (2008), *Aeschylus I: Persians, Seven against Thebes, Suppliants, Prometheus Bound*, Loeb Classical Library 145, Cambridge, MA.

Sorabji, R. (1988), *Matter, Space and Motion: Theories in Antiquity and Their Sequel*, London.

Sörbom, G. (1966), *Mimesis and Art: Studies in the Origin and Early Development of an Aesthetic Vocabulary*, Stockholm.

Spira, A. (1960), *Deus Ex Machina: Untersuchungen zum Deus ex machina bei Sophokles und Euripides*, Kallmünz.

Spivey, N. J. (1996), *Understanding Greek Sculpture: Ancient Meanings, Modern Readings*, New York.

Spoerri, W. (1985), 'Inkommensurabilität, Automaten und philosophisches Staune in Alpha der Metaphysik', in J. Wiesner (ed.), *Aristoteles, Werk und Wirkung: Paul Moraux gewidmet*, 239–72, New York.

Squire, M. (2009), *Image and Text in Graeco-Roman Antiquity*, Cambridge.

Squire, M. (2010), 'Making Myron's Cow Moo? Ecphrastic Epigram and the Poetics of Simulation', *American Journal of Philology*, 131: 589–634.

Squire, M. (2011), *The Art of the Body: Antiquity and its Legacy*, London.

Squire, M. (2013), 'Apparitions Apparent: Ekphrasis and the Parameters of Vision in the Elder Philostratus' Imagines', *Helios*, 40: 97–114.

Stähli, A. (2010), 'Mimesis als Aufführung und Darstellung', in M. Vöhler, Chr. Voss and G. Koch (eds), *Die Mimesis und ihre Künste*, 43–67, München.

Stähli, A. (2014), 'Sprechende Gegenstände', in R. Bielfeldt (ed.), *Ding und Mensch in der Antike*, 113–42, Heidelberg.

Stehle, E. (2002), 'The Body and Its Representations in Aristophanes' *Thesmophoriazousai*: Where does the Costume End?', *American Journal of Philology*, 123: 369–406.

Steiner, D. T. (1994), *The Tyrant's Writ: Myths and Images of Writing in Ancient Greece*, Princeton, NJ.

Steiner, D. T. (1995), 'Eyeless in Argos: The Kolossoi in Aeschylus' Agamemnon', *Journal of Hellenic Studies*, 115: 175–82.

Steiner, D. T. (1998), 'Moving Images: Fifth-Century Victory Monuments and the Athlete's Allure', *Classical Antiquity*, 17: 123–50.

Steiner, D. T. (2001), *Images in Mind: Statues in Archaic and Classical Greek Literature and Thought*, Princeton, NJ.

Steiner, D. T. (2013), 'The Priority of Pots: Pandora's Pithos re-viewed', in Éditions de l'École des hautes études en sciences sociales, Daedalus (ed.), *Mères et maternités en Grèce ancienne*, 211–38, Paris and Athens.

Steiner, D. (forthcoming), 'Affecting Artefacts: Interacting with Objects in Archaic and Early Classical Greece, in T. Bur, M. Gerolemou and I. A. Ruffell (eds), *Technological Animation in Greco-Roman Antiquity*, Oxford.

Stern, J. (trans.) (1996), *Palaephatus: On Unbelievable Tales*, Wauconda.

Stern-Gillet, S. (2002), 'Neoplatonist Aesthetics', in P. Smith and C. Wilde (eds), *A Companion to Art Theory*, 40–8, Oxford and New Malden.

Stewart, D. J. (1968), 'Nous in Aristophanes', *Classical Journal*, 63: 253–5.

Stewart, E. (2016), 'Professionalism and the Poetic Persona in Archaic Greece', *Cambridge Classical Journal*, 1: 1–24.

Stewart, P. (2003), *Statues in Roman Society: Representation and Response*, Oxford.

Stieber, M. (1994), 'Aeschylus' *Theoroi* and Realism in Greek Art', *Transactions of the American Philological Association*, 124: 85–119.

Stieber, M. (2011), *Euripides and the Language of Craft*, Mnemosyne Supplements, 327, Leiden.

Stiepel, G. R. (1968), *Die Bühne des Euripides. Theaterwissenschaftliche Studien zu den Problemen des altgriechischen Bühnenwesens*, Köln-Lindenthal.

Stohn, G. (1993), 'Zur Agathonszene in den "Thesmophoriazusen" des Aristophanes', *Hermes*, 121: 196–205.

Sussman, L. (1978), 'Workers and Drones: Labor, Idleness and Gender Definition in Hesiod's Beehive', *Arethusa*, 11: 27–41.

Svenbro, J. (1976), *La Parole et le marbre. Aux origines de la poétique grecque*, Klassiska Institutionen, Lund.

Svenshon, H. and R. H. W. Stichel (2006), '"Systems of Monads" as Design Principle in the Hagia Sophia: Neo-Platonic Mathematics in the Architecture of Late Antiquity', *Nexus VI, Architecture and Mathematics*, 6: 111–20.

Taplin, O. (1977), *The Stagecraft of Aeschylus: The Dramatic Use of Exits and Entrances in Greek Tragedy*, Oxford.

Taplin, O. (1978), *Greek Tragedy in Action*, Berkeley, CA.

Tassios, T. P. (2008), 'Mycenean Technology', in S. A. Paipetis (ed.), *Science and Technology in Homeric epics*, 3–34, Dordrecht.

Taub, L. (2012), 'Physiological Analogies and Metaphors in Explanations of the Earth and the Cosmos', in M. Horstmanshoff, H. King and C. Zittel (eds), *Blood, Sweat and Tears: The Changing Concepts of Physiology from Antiquity into Early Modern Europe*, Intersections, 25, 41–63, Leiden.

Telò, M. and M. Mueller (2018), *The Materialities of Greek Tragedy Objects and Affect in Aeschylus, Sophocles, and Euripides*, London.

Thalmann, W. G. (1984), *Conventions of Form and Thought in Early Greek Epic Poetry*, Baltimore, MD, London.
Theodorou, Z. (1993), 'Subject to Emotion: Exploring Madness in Orestes', *Classical Quarterly*, 43: 32–46.
Thom, J. C. (ed.) (2014), *Cosmic Order and Divine Power: Pseudo-Aristotle, On the Cosmos*, Darmstadt.
Tigerstedt, E. (1970), 'Furor Poeticus: Poetic Inspiration in Greek Literature before Democritus and Plato', *Journal of the History of Ideas*, 31: 163–78.
Torrance, I. (2010), 'Writing and Self-Conscious Mythopoesis in Euripides', *Cambridge Classical Journal*, 56: 213–58.
Totelin, L. (2018), 'Animal and Plant Generation in Classical Antiquity', in N. Hopwood, R. Flemming and L. Kassell (eds), *Reproduction: Antiquity to the Present*, 53–66, Cambridge.
Trammell, E. P. (1941), 'The Mute Alcestis', *Classical Journal*, 37: 144–50.
Truit, E. (2015), *Medieval Robots: Mechanism, Magic, Nature, and Art*, Philadelphia.
Tsitsirides, S. (2001), 'Euripideische Kosmogonie bei Aristophanes (*Thesm.* 14–18)', Ἑλληνικά, 51: 43–67.
Tybjerg, K. (2003), 'Wonder-Making and Philosophical Wonder in Hero of Alexandria', *Studies in History and Philosophy of Science*, 34: 443–66.
Tybjerg, K. (2005), 'Hero of Alexandria's Mechanical Treatises: Between Theory and Practice', in A. Schürmann (ed.), *Geschichte der Mathematik und Naturwissenschaften 3: Physik / Mechanik: BD*, 3, 204–26, Stuttgart.
Uhlig, A. (2020), 'Birth by Hammer: Pandora and the Construction of Bodies', in J. Dyer and A. Surtees (eds), *Exploring Gender Diversity in the Ancient World*, 54–66. Edinburgh.
Ulrich, B. R. (2007), *Roman Woodworking*, New Haven, CT, and London.
Ulrich, B. R. (2008), 'Woodworking', in J. P. Oleson (ed.), *The Oxford Handbook of Engineering and Technology in the Classical World*, 439–64, Oxford.
Uzdavinys, A. (2009), 'Animation of Statues in Ancient Civilizations and Neoplatonism', in P. Vassilopoulou and S. R. L. Clark (eds), *Other Ways to Truth: Late Antique Epistemology*, 118–40, Basingstoke.
Valakas, K. (2002), 'The Use of the Body by Actors in Tragedy and Satyr-Play', in P. Easterling and E. Hall (eds), *Greek and Roman Actors: Aspects of an Ancient Profession*, 69–92, Cambridge.
Van Eck, C. (2015), *Art, Agency, and Living Presence: From Animated Image to Excessive Object*, Leiden.
Van Wees, H. (1992), *Status Warriors: War, Violence and Society in Homer and History*, Amsterdam.

Van Wees, H. (1994), 'The Homeric Way of War: The "Iliad" and the Hoplite Phalanx (I)', *Greece & Rome*, 41: 1–18.

Van Wees, H. (1997), 'Homeric Warfare', in I. Morris and B. Powell (eds), *A New Companion to Homer*, Mnemosyne, bibliotheca classica Batava. Suplementum, 163, 668–93, Leiden.

Van Wees, H. (2001), 'The Myth of the Middle-Class Army: Military and Social Status in Ancient Athens', in T. Bekker-Nielsen and L. Hannestad (eds), *War as a Cultural and Social force. Essays on Warfare in Antiquity*, Historisk-filosofiske Skrifter, 22, 45–71, Copenhagen.

Verbeek, P.-P. (2005), *What Things Do: Philosophical Reflections on Technology, Agency, and Design*, University Park PA.

Verdenius, W. J. (1985), *A Commentary on Hesiod 'Works and Days' vv. 1–382*, Mnemosyne, Suppl., 86, Leiden.

Vernant, J.-P. (1983), *Myth and Thought among the Greeks*, translated by J. Lloyd and J. Fort, London and Boston, MA.

Vernant, J.-P. (1989), 'Dim Body, Dazzling Body', in M. Feher, R. Naddaff and N. Tazi (eds), *Fragments for a History of the Human Body*, vols 3–4, 19–47, Cambridge, MA.

Vernant, J.-P. (1990a), *Myth and Society in Ancient Greece*, translated by J. Lloyd, New York.

Vernant, J.-P. (1990b), 'One … Two … Three: Eros', in D. M. Halperin, J. J. Winkler and F. I. Zeitlin (eds), *Before Sexuality: The Construction of Erotic Experience in the Ancient Greek World*, 465–78, Princeton, NJ.

Vernant, J.-P. (1991a), 'A "Beautiful Death" and the Disfigured Corpse in Homeric Epic', in J.-P. Vernant, edited by F. Zeitlin, *Mortals and Immortals: Collected Essays*, 50–74, Princeton, NJ.

Vernant, J.-P. (1991b), 'The Birth of Images', in J.-P. Vernant, edited by by F. Zeitlin, *Mortals and Immortals: Collected Essays*, 164–86, Princeton, NJ.

Vernant, J.-P. (1991c), 'From the "Presentification" of the Invisible to the Imitation of Appearance', in J.-P. Vernant, edited by F. Zeitlin, *Mortals and Immortals: Collected Essays*, 151–63, Princeton, NJ.

Vernant, J.-P. (1991d), 'Mortals and Immortals: The Body of the Divine', in J.-P. Vernant, edited by F. Zeitlin, *Mortals and Immortals: Collected Essays*, 27–49, Princeton, NJ.

Vernant, J.-P. (1991e), 'Psyche: Simulacrum of the Body or Image of the Divine?', in J.-P. Vernant, edited by F. Zeitlin, *Mortals and Immortals: Collected Essays*, 186–92, Princeton, NJ.

Vernant, J.-P. (2011), 'Semblances of Pandora: Imitation and Identity', translated by F. Zeitlin, *Critical Inquiry*, 37: 404–18.

Vicaire, P. (1963), 'Les Grecs et le mystère de l'inspiration poétique', *Bulletin de l'Association Guillaume Budé*, 1: 68–85.

Vivante, P. (1955), 'Sulla designazione del corpo in Omero', *Archivio glottologico italiano*, 40: 39–50.

Vivante, P. (1966), 'On the Representation of Nature and Reality in Homer', *Arion: A Journal of Humanities and the Classics*, 5: 149–90.

Vogt-Spira, G. (2011), 'Prae sensibus. Das Ideal der Lebensechtheit in römischer Rhetorik und Dichtungstheorie', in G. Radke-Uhlmann and A. Schmitt (eds), *Anschaulichkeit in Kunst und Literatur. Wege bildlicher Visualisierung in der europäischen Geschichte*, vol. 11, 13–34, New York.

Von Hesberg, H. (1987), 'Mechanische Kunstwerke und ihre Bedeutung für die höfische Kunst des frühen Hellenismus', *Marburger Winckelmann-Programm*, 47–72, Marburg.

Von Möllendorff, P. (2017), 'Technologies of Performance: Machines, Props, Dramaturgy (translated by M. Revermann)', in M. Revermann (ed.), *A Cultural History of Theatre in Antiquity*, vol. 1, 163–79, London and New York.

Von Staden, H. (1996), 'Body and Machine: Interactions Between Medicine, Mechanics and Philosophy in Early Alexandria', in K. Hamma (ed.), *Alexandria and Alexandrianism*, 85–106, Malibu, CA.

Von Staden, H. (2007), 'Physis and Technē in Greek Medicine', in B. Bensaude-Vincent and W. R. Newman (eds), *The Artificial and the Natural: An Evolving Polarity*, 67–108, Cambridge, MA.

Wallace-Hadrill, A. (1990), 'Pliny the Elder and Man's Unnatural History', *Greece & Rome*, 37: 80–96.

Wardy, R. (1996), *The Birth of Rhetoric: Gorgias, Plato and Their Successors*, London and New York.

Warner, M. (1985), *Monuments and Maidens: The Allegory of the Female Form*, Berkeley, Los Angeles, CA.

Watson, G. (1988), *Phantasia in Classical Thought*, Galway.

Webb, R. (1999), 'The Aesthetics of Sacred Space: Narrative, Metaphor and Motion in Ekphraseis of Church Buildings', *Dumbarton Oaks Papers*, 53: 59–74.

Webb, R. (2009), *Ekphrasis, Imagination and Persuasion in Ancient Rhetorical Theory and Practice*, Farnham and Burlington.

Webster, C. (2014), 'Technology and/as Theory: Material Thinking in Ancient Science and Medicine', PhD diss., Columbia University, New York.

Webster, C. (forthcoming), *Organa and the Organism*, Chicago, IL.

Webster, T. B. L. (1967), *The Tragedies of Euripides*, London.

Weiberg, E. (2018), 'Weapons as Friends and Foes in Sophocles' *Ajax* and Euripides' *Heracles*', in M. Telò and M. Mueller (eds), *The Materialities of Greek Tragedy Objects and Affect in Aeschylus, Sophocles, and Euripides*, 63–78, London.

Weinreich, O. (1929), 'Türöffnung in Wunder, Prodigien- und Zauberglauben der Antike, des Judentums und Christentums', *Tübinger Beiträge zur Altertumswissenschaft*, 5: 200–464.

Wessels, A. (2014), 'Zwischen Illusion und Distanz. Zur Wirkungsästhetik lebensechter Gegenstände', in R. Bielfeldt (ed.), *Ding und Mensch in der Antike*, 275–301, Heidelberg.

Wessels, A. (forthcoming), 'Animated Doors', in T. Bur, M. Gerolemou and I. A. Ruffell (eds), *Technological Animation in Greco-Roman Antiquity*, Oxford.

Wessels, A. and R. Krumeich (1999), 'Isthmiastai oder Theoroi', in R. Krumeich, N. Pechstein and B. Seidensticker (eds), *Das griechische Satyrspiel*, 131–48, Darmstadt.

West, M. L. (1978), *Hesiod: Works and Days*, edited with prolegomena and commentary, Oxford.

West, M. L. (1997), *The East Face of Helicon: West Asiatic Elements in Greek Poetry and Myt*, Oxford.

White, K. D. (1984), *Greek and Roman Technology*, Aspects of Greek and Roman Life, London.

Wickkiser, B. L. (2010), 'Hesiod and the Fabricated Woman: Poetry and Visual Art in the *Theogony*', *Mnemosyne*, 63: 557–76.

Wicksteed, P. H. and F. M. Cornford (ed. and trans.) (1934), *Aristotle. Physics, Volume II: Books 5–8*, Loeb Classical Library 255, Cambridge, MA.

Wicksteed, P. H. and F. M. Cornford (ed. and trans.) (1957), *Aristotle. Physics, Volume I: Books 1–4*, Loeb Classical Library 228, Cambridge, MA.

Wiesing, U. (2008), 'The History of Medical Enhancement: From Restitutio ad Integrum to Transformatio ad Optimum?', in B. Gordijn and R. Chadwick (eds), *Medical Enhancement and Posthumanity*, 9–24, Netherlands.

Wilamowitz-Moellendorff, U. von (ed. and trans.) (1895), *Euripides Herakles*, 2 vols, Berlin.

Wilamowitz-Moellendorff, U. von (ed.) (1928), *Hesiodos Erga*, Berlin.

Wiles, D. (1991), *The Masks of Menander: Sign and Meaning in Greek and Roman Performance*, Cambridge.

Wiles, D. (2020), *The Players' Advice to Hamlet: The Rhetorical Acting Method from the Renaissance to the Enlightenment*, Cambridge.

Wilgaux, J. and A. Marcinkowski (2004), 'Automates et créatures artificielles d' Héphaïstos: entre science et fiction', *Techniques and Culture*: 43–4.

Wilhelm Nitzsch, G. (1831), *Erklärende Anmerkungen zu Homer's Odyssee*, vol. 2, Hannover.

William, H. (1651), *Exercitationes de generatione animalium. Quibus accedunt quaedam de partu, de membranis ac humoribus uteri, et de conceptione*, London.

Williams, B. (1993), *Shame and Necessity*, Berkeley, Los Angeles, CA, and Oxford.

Wilson, A. (2002), 'Machines, Power and the Ancient Economy', *Journal of Roman Studies*, 92: 1–32.

Wilson, A. I. (2008), 'Machines in Greek and Roman Technology', in J. P. Oleson (ed.), *The Oxford Handbook of Engineering and Technology in the Classical World*, 337–66, Oxford.

Wilson, M. (2000), *Aristotle's Theory of the Unity of Science*, Toronto.

Wilson, M. (2020), 'Heat, Meteorology and Spontaneous Generation', in H. Bartoš (ed.), *Heat, Pneuma and the Soul in Ancient Philosophy and Science*, 159–81, Cambridge.

Wohl, V. (1998), *Intimate Commerce: Exchange, Gender, and Subjectivity in Greek Tragedy*, Austin, TX.

Wolkow, B. M. (2007), 'The Mind of a Bitch: Pandora's Motive and Intent in the Erga', *Hermes*, 135: 247–62.

Woman, N. (2012), 'Cutting to the Bone: Recalcitrant Bodies in Sophocles', in K. Ormand (ed.), *A Companion to Sophocles*, 349–66, Malden, MA, Oxford and Chichester.

Wood, G. (2002), *Living Dolls: A Magical History of the Quest for Mechanical Life*, London.

Woodring, B. (2006), 'Trajectories of Things: Spears, Arrows, and Agency in Ancient Greek Epic Poetry', Senior thesis, Brandeis University, Waltham/Boston, MA. Available online: https://chs.harvard.edu/CHS/article/displayPdf/371 (accessed 10 March 2022).

Worman, N. (1997), 'The Body as Argument: Helen in Four Greek Texts', *Classical Antiquity*, 16: 151–203.

Worman, N. (2012), 'Cutting to the Bone: Recalcitrant Bodies in Sophocles', in K. Ormand (ed.), *The Blackwell Companion to Sophocles*, 351–66, Malden, MA, and Oxford.

Worman, N. (2018), 'Electra, Orestes, and the Sibling Hand', in M. Telò and M. Mueller (eds), *The Materialities of Greek Tragedy: Objects and Affect in Aeschylus, Sophocles, and Euripides*, 185–202, London.

Worman, N. (2021), *Tragic Bodies Edges of the Human in Greek Drama*, London.

Wosk, J. (2015), *My Fair Ladies: Female Robots, Androids, and Other Artificial Eves*, New Brunswick, NJ.

Wright, M. (2005), *Euripides' Escape-Tragedies: A Study of Helen, Andromeda, and Iphigenia Among the Taurians*, Oxford.

Wright, M. (2012), *The Comedian as Critic: Greek Old Comedy and Poetics*, London and New York.

Wright, M. (2016), *The Lost Plays of Greek Tragedy, Volume 1: Neglected Authors*, London.

Wyles, R. (2011), *Costume in Greek Tragedy*, London and New York.

Yunis, H. (1988), *A New Creed: Fundamental Religious Beliefs in the Athenian Polis and Euripidean Drama*, Hypomnemata, 91, Göttingen.

Zanker, A. T. (2019), *Metaphor in Homer: Time, Speech, and Thought*, Cambridge.

Zanker, G. (2015), 'The Contexts and Experience of Poetry and Art in the Hellenistic World', in P. Destrée and P. Murray (eds), *A Companion to Ancient Aesthetics*, Blackwell Companions to the Ancient World, 47–67, Malden, MA, Oxford and Chichester.

Zeitlin, F. I. (1985), 'The Power of Aphrodite: Eros and the Boundaries of the Self in the "Hippolytus"', in P. Burian (ed.), *Directions in Euripidean Criticism: A Collection of Essays*, 52–111, Durham, NC.

Zeitlin, F. I. (1994), 'The Artful Eye: Vision, Ekphrasis, and Spectacle in Euripidean Drama', in S. Goldhill and R. Osborne (eds), *Art and Text in Ancient Greek Culture*, 138–96, Cambridge.

Zeitlin, F. I. (1995a), 'The Economics of Hesiod's Pandora', in E. D. Reeder (ed.), *Pandora: Women in Classical Greece*, 49–56, Baltimore, MD, and Princeton NJ.

Zeitlin, F. I. (1995b), 'Signifying Difference: The Myth of Pandora', in R. Hawley and B. Levick (eds), *Women in Antiquity: New Assessments*, 58–74, London and New York.

Zeitlin, F. I. (1996), *Playing the Other: Gender and Society in Classical Greek Literature*, Chicago, IL.

Zhmud, L. (2006), *The Origin of the History of Science in Classical Antiquity*, translated by A. Chernoglazov, Peripatoi, Band 19, Berlin and New York.

Zielinski, S. and P. Weibel (eds), *Allah's Automata: Artifacts of the Arab–Islamic Renaissance (800–1200)*, translated by J. Gaines and S. Gore, Ostfildern.

Zohny, H. (2016), 'Enhancement, Disability and the Riddle of the Relevant Circumstances', *Journal of Medical Ethics*, 42: 605–10.

Zuntz, G. (1955), *The Political Plays of Euripides*, Manchester.

Index

Acharnians (Euripides) 39
Achilles 14, 20, 49
acting/actors 35–6, 37
Admetus 28–9
adornment scene with regard to
  Pandora 28
Aeschylus
  Agamemnon 22, 28, 61
  Prometheus Bound 51
  Suppliant Women, The 50–1
  Theoroi or *Isthmiastai* 43
aesthesis 84
Aesthetics of Mimesis, The (Halliwell,
  Stephen) 14
Agamemnon 61
Agamemnon (Aeschylus) 22, 28, 61
Agaue 64–5
Agesilaus (Plutarch) 36
air 87–8
Ajax 61
Ajax (Sophocles) 54, 61
Alcestis (Euripides) 28–9, 43–4
Alcidamas 46
  *On the Writers of Written Speeches, or,
    On Sophists* 46
Alexander of Aphrodisias
  Mantissa 73
Amphitryon 51–2
Ancient Medicine (Hippocratic corpus) 32
Andromache (Euripides) 40–1
Andromeda (Euripides) 42
Anthemius of Tralles 92
Antidosis (Isocrates) 45
Antigone (Sophocles) 50, 115 n. 55
Apega 29
ps.-Apollodorus 19
Apollonius of Tyana (Philostratus) 18, 84
Apollonius Rhodius 19
archery 49, 51–5
architecture 4–5, 92–3
aristocracy 3–4, 33

Aristonicus 14
Aristonidas 83
  statue of Athamas 83
Aristophanes
  Clouds 39, 42, 57, 58, 59
  knowledge 58–9
  Lysistrata 39–40
  metatheatre 38
  mockery 58
  Peace 38, 39
  theatrical machines 38–40
  Thesmophoriazusae 35, 39, 56, 57
Aristotle 35
  Generation of Animals 73–4, 75
  hands 28
  Metaphysics 26, 66, 74
  Motion of Animals 74
  θαύματα 73
  On the Soul 73, 84
  Parts of Animals 75
  Physics 1–2, 4, 18
  Poetics 35–6
  Rhetoric 13, 36
ps.-Aristotle
  On the Cosmos 71–2
artificial generation 78
artificial speech 44–5
artificiality, as threat 50
art 75, 99 n. 9, 100 n. 10
  automated artworks 82–93
  beauty 86–7
  early Byzantine *ekphrasis* 90–3
  Gell, Alfred 81
  medium, the 111 n. 9
  superficial 87
Art, The (Hippocratic corpus) 3, 22
Art of Poetry, The (Horace) 84
artist-genius 84–5
Athenaeus
  Deipnosophists, The 70, 71
  Attic Dinner Party (Matro) 71

Attic Nights (Gellius, Aulus) 70
audiences 38, 69, 82
　perception 84–6
αὐτοδίδακτος 20–2
mechanical automata
　mobile 79, 80
　stationary 79, 80, 81
automated artworks 82–93
automatic images 40–7
automatos bios 2, 18, 59, 95

Bacchae (Euripides) 59–60, 64–6
beetles 38, 39
Bellerophon (Euripides) 39
bellows 12–13, 20, 103 n. 24
Belopoeica (Philo) 77, 78
Benjamin, Walter
　Work of Art in the Age of Mechanical
　　Reproduction, The 25
Berryman, Sylvia 24
　Mechanical Hypothesis in Ancient Greek
　　Natural Philosophy, The 16
Birth of Literary Fiction in Ancient Greece,
　The (Finkelberg, Margalit) 21
bows 49, 51–5
breathing 87–8

Callistratus 84
　automatic statues, description of 85–90
　Dionysius' statue 89
　Kairos-statue of Lysippus 86–7
　materials 87, 89
　Paean's statue 89
　Satyr's statue 88
　statue of Eros (Praxiteles) 87, 89
　statue of Narcissus 89
　statue of the Bacchante (Scopa) 87–8
　statue of the drunken Indian 87
　statue of the Youth 89
　superficial art 87
　talking statue of Memnon 88
Cassiodorus Senator 83–4
Choricius of Gaza 93
church of St Stergius 93
churches 92–3
clocks 91 / see also horologion
Clouds (Aristophanes) 39, 42, 57, 58, 59
cognitive augmentation 57
Consolation to Apollonius (ps.-Plutarch) 27

cords 77
courage 49, 51, 52
cow sculpture (Myron) 83
cowardice 51
cranes (theatrical machines) 37, 38–9
creation myths 23
Csapo, Eric 35–6
Cuomo, Serafina 3

Daedalus 14–15, 43, 88
De Groot, Jean 4
deceit 28–9, 71, 72, 86
Deipnosophists, The (Athenaeus) 70, 71
demiurge 85
democracy 44–5
Descartes, René 1
design/engineering plans 76, 79
Detienne, Marcel 66
devices 4
Dionysius 64, 66
Dionysius of Thrace 14–15
Dionysius' statue 89
Dissertationes (Tyrius, Maximus) 21
divine, the
　matter 85
divine automaton 34–5
divine intervention 16, 59–60
divine madness 34–5, 60–6
dolls 60, 108 n. 76 / see also neurospasta
double, the 25, 34
drama. See theatre
dramatic automation 31–5, 66–7
　artificiality as threat 50
　automatic images 40–7
　prosthesis 47–60
　technomimesis (on stage) 35–40

education 57, 59
eidola 7, 24, 34, 41–2
　voice 43
ekkyklema (out-roller) 37–8, 39
ekphrasis, early Byzantine 90–3
ekphrastic/descriptive animation 13–14,
　81–94
Electra (Sophocles) 42
emotion 83
Empedocles 32
Encomium of Helen (Gorgias) 47
engineers 15–16, 71–2, 76, 81, 83

Epidemics (Hippocratic corpus) 22
Eros, statue of (Praxiteles) 87, 89
Ethiopia 88
Euripides 33, 36, 40, 51
   Acharnians 39
   Alcestis 28–9, 43–4
   Andromache 40–1
   Andromeda 42
   Bacchae 59–60, 64–6
   Bellerophon 39
   as character 56
   Hecuba 45
   Helen 41–2, 43
   Heracleidai 60
   Heracles 38, 48–56, 61–3
   Hippolytus 62
   Iphigenia in Tauris 41, 44–5
   madness 61–4
   Orestes 63
   Suppliants 45
   theatrical machines 38
   Theseus 47
Eustathius of Thessalonica 17–18, 20
external force 61, 69, 73, 74, 76

feminism 24–5
Finkelberg, Margalit
   Birth of Literary Fiction in Ancient Greece, The 21
form, relationship to materials 74–5
Freud, Sigmund
   Unbehagen in der Kultur, Das 47

Galen 19, 132 n. 35
Gaza, horologion of 91
Gell, Alfred
   'Technology of Enchantment and the Enchantment of Technology, The' 81
Gellius, Aulus
   Attic Nights 70
gender 24–5
generation 74–5, 78
generation by chance 74, 75
Generation of Animals (Aristotle) 73–4, 75
glass 78–9
Gods and Robots: Myths, Machines, and Ancient Dreams of Technology (Mayor, Adrienne) 1

Gorgias 36–7
   Encomium of Helen 47
Greek Tragedy in Action (Taplin, Oliver) 60

Hagia Sophia 92–3
Halliwell, Stephen
   Aesthetics of Mimesis, The 14
hands 28
Hayles, Katherine
   How We became Posthuman: Virtual Bodies in Cybernetics, Literature, and Informatics 47
Hecuba (Euripides) 45
Helen (Euripides), 41–2, 43
Hephaestus 12–13, 14, 19, 23, 91
Heracleidai (Euripides) 60
Heracles 49–50, 51, 52–4
   madness 61–3
Heracles (Euripides) 38, 48–56, 61–3
Heraclitus 41
Hero of Alexandria 76
   Mechanics 79, 82
   On Automata Making 76–7, 79, 80, 81, 130 n. 25
   Pneumatics 76, 81, 83, 88
Herodotean wonder 91
Hesiod 11–12, 23–30
   Theogony 24, 26–7, 28
   Works and Days 24, 27, 28
Hippocratic corpus 22, 31–2
   Ancient Medicine 32
   Art, The 3, 22
   Epidemics 22
   Internal Affections 2
   On Articulations 2
   On Diet 22–3
   On Diseases 23
   Places in Man 2
   Regimen 42–3
Hippolytus (Euripides) 62
Holmes, Brooke
   Symptom and the Subject, The 2
Homer 23
   αὐτοδίδακτος 21
   gods in 16
   Iliad. See *Iliad*
   Odyssey. See *Odyssey*
hoplites 49

Horace
  Art of Poetry, The 84
Horologion of Gaza (Procopius) 12, 91
horology 91
How We became Posthuman: Virtual Bodies in Cybernetics, Literature, and Informatics (Hayles, Katherine) 47
human agents 70–2
human body 2, 40
  artificial organs 32
  enhancement 32, 33
  prosthesis 47–60
  replicas 42–4
  sense organs 56
hybrids 3

Iamblichus
  On the Mysteries 85
Ichneutae (Sophocles) 116 n. 64
Iliad (Homer) 11
  Achilles' shield 14
  αὐτόματος 17–18
  bellows 12–13, 20, 103 n. 24
  Daedalus 14–15
  handmaids 12–13, 14, 19, 23, 29
  Hephaestoteukta 12–23, 29–30
  Menelaus 18
  natural forces 17
  physis 20
  tripods 12–13, 14, 17, 18, 19
  weaponry 48–9
  wheels 17
imagination 82–3
Imagines (Philostratus) 136 n. 83
inspiration 85
instruction 57, 59
instrumentality 34
Internal Affections (Hippocratic corpus) 2
internal force 63, 73, 76
Iphigenia in Tauris (Euripides) 41, 44–5
iron 78
Isocrates
  Antidosis 45

Jentsch, Ernst
  Zur Psychologie des Unheimlichen 60–1
juggling 71, 72
justice 45–6

Kairos-statue of Lysippus 86–7
Kallippides 35–6
knowledge 56–9

Laches (Plato) 52
law, the 45–6, 53
  madness 125 n. 164
Laws (Plato) 72
Le Corbusier 4–5*f*
Life of Apollonius of Tyana (Philostratus) 18, 84
literary tropes 13–14
liveness (theatre) 43, 87, 90
  speech 44–5
Lives of the Sophists (Philostratus) 36–7
Loraux, Nicole 25
Lysistrata (Aristophanes) 39–40

machines 4
magic 13–14, 87
male anxiety 24–5
Mantissa (Alexander of Aphrodisias) 73
Marder, Elissa 35
material turn, the 84–5
materialists, the 15, 26
materials 75, 76–8, 83, 88–9
  Callistratus 87, 89–90
  divine, the 85, 89–90
  femininity 89
  form, relation to 74–5
  material turn, the 84–5
  softness/wetness 89
  Trojan Horse, the 90
Matro
  Attic Dinner Party 71
Mayor, Adrienne 23–4
  Gods and Robots: Myths, Machines, and Ancient Dreams of Technology 1
mechanical automation 2–3, 4, 11, 16, 69–70, 75–82
  automated artworks 82–93
  Berryman, Sylvia 16, 24
  Daedalus' animated statues 14–15
  Eustathius 20
  fourth century BCE 70–5
  Galen 19
  Pandora 23–4
  smallness 80
  Talos 19

Mechanical Hypothesis in Ancient Greek Natural Philosophy, The (Berryman, Sylvia) 16
Mechanics (Hero) 79, 82
medicine 3
Memnon, talking statue of 88
Menelaus 18
metal 77, 78, 83 / see magnet stones
Metaphysics (Aristotle) 26, 66, 74
metatheatre 38
mimesis 35–6, 38, 40, 84
misogyny 25
Motion of Animals (Aristotle) 74
movement 74, 90
    Bacchic movements 65–6
    perception 86
Myron 83
    cow sculpture 83

natural automation 2, 3, 11, 15, 95
    Hesiod's Pandora 11–12, 23–30
    Iliadic *Hephaestoteukta* 12–23, 29–30
natural forces 17
natural generation 74, 75
naturalism 135 n. 64
nature 4, 59, 78 see also *physis*
Neoptolemus 55
nootropics 56–60
Nussbaum, C. Martha 130 n. 25

Odyssey (Homer) 13, 14, 17, 18
    Phemius 21–2
    physis 20
    technê 20
On Articulations (Hippocratic corpus) 2
On Automata Making (Hero) 76–7, 79, 80, 81, 130 n. 25
On Buildings (Procopius of Caesarea) 93
On Diet (Hippocratic corpus) 22–3
On Diseases (Hippocratic corpus) 23
On Stones (Theophrastus) 78
On the Cosmos (ps.-Aristotle) 71–2
On the Mysteries (Iamblichus) 85
On the Soul (Aristotle) 73, 84
On the Writers of Written Speeches, or, On Sophists (Alcidamas) 46
oratory 36–7
Orestes 63

Orestes (Euripides) 63
organs, artificial 32

Paean's statue 89
Palaephatus 14–15
Pandora 23–30
Pappus 72
Parts of Animals (Aristotle) 75
Paul the Silentiary 92–3
Pausanias 53
Peace (Aristophanes) 38, 39
Pentheus 64–6
perception 84–6
perception theory 84–5
phanero-technics 4–5
phantasia 82, 83, 84–5
phantastic imitation 32–3
Phemius 21–2
Philo
    Belopoeica 77, 78
Philoctetes 54–5
Philoctetes (Sophocles) 50, 54–5
Philon 80
Philostratus
    Imagines 136 n. 83
    Life of Apollonius of Tyana 18, 84
    Lives of the Sophists 36–7
Physics (Aristotle) 1–2, 4, 18
physis see also nature
    Hippocratic corpus 22–3
    technê 20, 22
Places in Man (Hippocratic corpus) 2
Plant Explanations (Theophrastus) 78
plants 78
Plato 43, 72
    Laches 52
    Laws 72
    Sophist 32
    Statesman 1
Plutarch
    Agesilaus 36
ps.-Plutarch
    Consolation to Apollonius 27
Pneumatics (Hero) 76, 81, 83, 88
Poetics (Aristotle) 35–6
poets 37
Polybius 29
Praxiteles
    Eros, statue of 87, 89

Procopius
  Horologion of Gaza 12, 91
Procopius of Caesarea 93
  On Buildings 93
Prometheus Bound (Aeschylus) 51
prosthesis 32, 34, 47–60
  nootropics 56–60
  weaponry 48–56
ps.-Apollodorus 19
ps.-Aristotle
  On the Cosmos 71–2
ps.-Plutarch
  Consolation to Apollonius 27
puppets 70–1, 72, 73, 74 / see dolls and neurospasta
Purves, Alex 48

Quintus Smyrnaeus 90

Regimen (Hippocratic corpus) 42–3
rejuvenation 59–60
reproduction 25, 32, 73–4
Rhetoric (Aristotle) 13, 36
Ruffell, Isabel A. 70

Satyr's statue 88
Schibille, Nadine 92
Scopa
  statue of the Bacchante 87–8
Seneca
  Epistles 124 n. 153
sense organs 56
sense perception 84–6
Shelley, Mary 82
silence 117 n. 76
Simondon, Gilbert 4–5, 81
slavery 18
smallness 80
social class 33
Socrates 57, 58, 59
Sophist (Plato) 32
Sophocles 50
  Ajax 54, 61
  Antigone 50, 115 n. 55
  Electra 42
  Ichneutae 116 n. 64
  Philoctetes 50, 54–5
  Trachiniae 50, 62

soul, the 73
sound 91–2
speech 44–7
  written 46–7
spirituality 93
spontaneous generation 2, 15–16, 31, 76
  Aristotle 74, 75
  Detienne, Marcel 66
Statesman (Plato) 1
statue of Narcissus 89
statue of the Bacchante (Scopa) 87–8
statue of the drunken Indian 87
statue of the Youth 89
statues 7, 34, 40–1 / see images
  animated 14–15, 40ff., 114 n. 45, 136 n. 79
  automatic 85–90
  Callistratus' description 85–90
  cow sculpture (Myron) 83
  Dionysius' statue 89
  Eros 87, 89
  Kairos-statue of Lysippus 86–7
  Narcissus 89
  Paean's statue 89
  as replicas 44
  Satyr's statue 88
  statue of the Bacchante 87–8
  statue of the drunken Indian 87
  statue of the Youth 89
  talking statue of Memnon 88
  voice 44
Steiner, Deborah T. 34
stones 78
Strepsiades 57–8, 59
superficial art 87
Suppliant Women, The (Aeschylus) 50–1
Suppliants (Euripides) 45
Symposium (Xenophon) 71
Symptom and the Subject, The (Holmes, Brooke) 2

Taking of Ilios (Triphiodorus) 90
Talos 19
Taplin, Oliver
  Greek Tragedy in Action 60
technê 1, 2, 3, 31 / see art
  Hippocratic corpus 22–3
  Le Corbusier 5
  limits 33, 42

nature 4, 17
Pandora 30
physis 20, 22
theatre 40
technical automation 3, 15, 18–19, 31, 34–5
   fourth century BCE 70–5
   natural automation 11, 17, 18
technical wonder 81–2 / see wonder, thauma
techno-aesthetic 5
technoaesthetics 81
technology
   magic 13
'Technology of Enchantment and the Enchantment of Technology, The' (Gell, Alfred) 81
technomimesis 32–3, 35–40
thauma (wonder) 4
θαύματα 70–3
theatre
   acting/actors 35–6, 37
   audiences 38, 69, 82
   beetles 38, 39
   cranes 37, 38–9
   devices/machines 37, 38–40
   ekkyklema (out-roller) 37–8, 39
   live 44
   metatheatre 38
   tragedy 37, 39, 40
Theodorus 36
Theogony (Hesiod) 24, 26–7, 28
Theophrastus
   On Stones 78
   Plant Explanations 78
Theoroi or *Isthmiastai* (Aeschylus) 43
Theseus 53, 54
Theseus (Euripides) 47
Thesmophoriazusae (Aristophanes) 35, 39, 56, 57
theurgy 85
Thucydides 47
thymos 53
tools 76, 79
Trachiniae (Sophocles) 50, 62
tragedy 37, 39, 40
trickery. See deceit
Triphiodorus
   Taking of Ilios 90

tripods 12–13, 14, 17, 18, 19
Trojan Horse, the 90
Tyrius, Maximus
   Dissertationes 21

Unbehagen in der Kultur, Das (Freud, Sigmund) 47
uncanny, the 60–1, 110 n. 103
universe, creation of 26
unseen, the 84

Vernant, Jean-Pierre 34
visual effects 92–3
voice 43, 44
von Möllendorff, Peter 37–8

warriors 48–56
weaponry 48–56
Webb, Ruth 92
weights, moving 78
West, Martin 27–8
wheels 17
women 24–5, 26, 29
   femininity 89
   objectification 43–4
wonder trackers 86
wonder tricks 70–3, 86 see also deceit
wonder/wonderment 4, 73, 79, 91, 133 n. 47 / see also thauma
   churches 93
   explanations 91
   Herodotean wonder 91
   Procopius 91
   technical 81–2
wood 77
Work of Art in the Age of Mechanical Reproduction, The (Benjamin, Walter) 25
Works and Days (Hesiod) 24, 27, 28
Wright, Matthew E. 42
writing 46–7

Xenophon
   Symposium 71

Zeus 27–8
Zur Psychologie des Unheimlichen (Jentsch, Ernst) 60–1

www.ingramcontent.com/pod-product-compliance
Lightning Source LLC
Chambersburg PA
CBHW061833300426
44115CB00013B/2356